TK
5105.886
.T69
1998

WESTLA

Chicago Public Library

D1515434

Learn Internet Relay Chat

(2nd Edition)

Kathryn Toyer

Wordware Publishing, Inc.

Library of Congress Cataloging-in-Publication Data

Toyer, Kathryn
    Learn Internet relay chat / Kathryn Toyer. -- 2nd ed.
       p.   cm.
    Includes Index.
    ISBN 1-55622-605-5 (pbk.)
    1. Internet Relay Chat.   I. Title.
    TK5105.886.T69   1998
    005.7'1376--dc21

    98-23961
    CIP

© 1998, Wordware Publishing, Inc.
All Rights Reserved

2320 Los Rios Blvd. Suite 200
Plano, Texas 75074

No part of this book may be reproduced in any form or by any means
without permission in writing from Wordware Publishing, Inc.

Printed in the United States of America

ISBN 1-55622-605-5
10 9 8 7 6 5 4 3 2 1
9805

Other product names mentioned are used for identification purposes only and may be trademarks of their respective companies.

All inquiries for volume purchases of this book should be addressed to Wordware Publishing, Inc., at the above address. Telephone inquiries may be made by calling:

(972) 423-0090

Dedication

I would like to dedicate this book to Dr. Bill Hendricks. His continued faith in me as a writer helped me to get my writing career off the ground. He gave me much needed support and encouragement along with guidance. I owe a great deal to this very caring, giving man. Thank you for all you have done.

Contents Summary

Introduction ix

Chapter 1   **The Nets** 1

Chapter 2   **The Channels** 27

Chapter 3   **The Commands** 49

Chapter 4   **The Software** 77

Chapter 5   **mIRC Software** 89

Chapter 6   **Pirch Software** 157

Chapter 7   **Netiquette** 211

Chapter 8   **The Nitty Gritty** 221

Chapter 9   **IRC Uses** 249

Chapter 10 **Troubleshooting** 257

Chapter 11 **Summary** 263

Index 269

Contents

Introduction ix

Chapter 1   The Nets 1

   EfNet—The First Net 3

   UnderNet—The Rebels 4

   DALnet—The Game 6

   SuperChat—The Alternative 7

   Other Nets—Limitless 7

   The Servers 10

   Servers List 12

   Ports 23

   Server Terminology 24

   Summary 26

Chapter 2   The Channels 27

   Where are All the People? 27

   How Many Channels are There? 30

   How Do I Find a Channel? 31

   The Nets and Their Channels—A Composite 32

   What Can I Expect to Find in These Channels? 35

   How Do I Make My Own Channel? 43

   What are Channel Operators? 45

   Can I Join Multiple Channels? 46

   Can I Be on More Than One Net at a Time? 47

   Summary 47

Chapter 3   The Commands 49

   What are They Doing? 49

   How Do They Do Those Things? 50

   What are User Commands? 51

   What are Mode Commands? 66

   Summary 75

Contents

Chapter 4   **The Software** 77
  What is Chat Software and What's Out There? 77
  How Do I Get There From Here? 80
  Is There Other Chat Software? 82
  Summary 87

Chapter 5   **mIRC Software** 89
  What is mIRC? 90
  How Do You Custom Configure mIRC? 92
    Setup 92
    General Options 99
  What are Aliases and What Can You Do with Them? 119
  What are Popups and What Do They Do? 128
  What are Remotes and How Do They Work? 130
    Users or Friends Lists 132
    Variables 134
    Commands 134
    Events 136
    File Server 141
    Raw 142
  What Can You Do with DCC? 142
  What Other Things Do I Need to Know? 148
    System Menu 148
    Timer 149
    Smart Tools 150
    Copy and Paste 151
    Special Key Combinations 152
    Notify 152
    URL 153
    Multiple Instances 154
    Address Book 154
    mIRC Specific Commands 154
  Summary 155

Chapter 6   **Pirch Software** 157
  How Do I Connect to IRC with Pirch? 158
  What is Going on with These Channel Windows? 167
  What Do These Menu Bar Items Do? 171
    IRC and Login Menu and Toolbar Items 171

Server Menu Item 173
Channel Menu Item 174
Tools Menu Item and Corresponding Toolbar Buttons 175
Options Menu Item and Corresponding Toolbar Buttons 192
Summary 210

Chapter 7   Netiquette 211
What is Netiquette? 212
How Can I Avoid Social Faux Pas? 215
How Do I Get My Meaning Across? 216
What Do All These Acronyms Mean? 217
Summary 218

Chapter 8   The Nitty Gritty 221
Now What Do I Do? 221
What are Some Intermediate Things I Can Do? 233
What are Some of the Advanced Things I Can Do? 241
Summary 247

Chapter 9   IRC Uses 249
Why am I Here? 250
What About Me, the Business Person? What's In It for Me? 253
Summary 256

Chapter 10   Troubleshooting 257

Chapter 11   Summary 263

Index 269

Introduction

If you have picked this book up, you have done so for one of a couple of reasons. You recently got connected to the Internet, did some exploring, and found you need a little help. You are thinking about getting a connection to the Internet and you want to be prepared. Or, you have been on the chat channels for awhile and realize you do not know near enough. Good for you! This book answers most, if not all, of your questions. This book is the revised edition of *Learn Internet Relay Chat* that came out in the fall of 1996. It includes several of the new nets as well as explanations of the updated versions of mIRC and Pirch. I have also added a troubleshooting chapter to help you overcome some of the difficulties you might run up against while exploring IRC.

So, you ask yourself, what is IRC? Internet Relay Chat. Yes, that is what the acronym stands for, but what does it mean and what is all the to-do about? Internet Relay Chat has been likened to CB radio for computer users. Basically it is a lot like going to a huge party being held at a hotel. As you wander around the hotel you notice that there are many rooms. In each of these rooms you see people talking to each other. Sometimes there are only two or three people in a room. Sometimes there are dozens or more in a room.

The one thing you notice that each of these rooms has in common is the conversation. In every room people are talking to each other. They may be doing other things too, but they are all talking to each other. You may notice three or four people talking about the weather. Another three or four might be talking about their jobs. Maybe a few are huddled together telling jokes and cutting up. Then you may even notice a couple over in the corner billing and cooing at each other.

That is what IRC is—rooms, or channels as they are called, of people talking to each other using the computer. All kinds of people use IRC to chat. You can find children there. You can find college students there. You can find computer techies there. And, yes, you can even find housewives, farmers, salesmen, writers, and other people from all professions and walks of lives there. A lot of what you see at parties and social gatherings is also going on in IRC chat channels.

IRC is the only place you can go and talk to people from anywhere in the world without having to pay long-distance phone charges. Did I forget to mention the relative low cost of using IRC to communicate? That is one of the advantages to using IRC and the Internet. Usually, the only cost you have is for your Internet connection. Now you are probably wondering if there is anything else you need.

Of course, you need your phone connection. Then you need a computer, a modem, the software, and an Internet connection. The chart below outlines the standard equipment that you may already have or that you can purchase.

Required Hardware

	Minimum	*Good*	*Excellent*
PC/IBM or Compatible	386	486	Pentium
RAM	4mb	8mb	16mb+
Hard Disk	80mb	420mb	540mb
Sound	Not required	Not required	Live voice-to-voice is possible
Modem Speed	14.4 bps	19.6 bps	28.8+ bps
Phone Line	Single line Not dedicated	Single line	Multiple line dedicated
Mac	Mac II	Performa	Power Mac

As you already know, machines and information change rapidly. Use this chart as a starting point to assess your needs. As with anything else in life, of course, more is always better. However, if you have a 386 computer, you will be fine. There are a few things on the Internet that you either cannot do or that take you longer with this computer, but for chat purposes, this computer works fine. Chat is text based and therefore does not require all the extras. There are a few software applications that you will not be able to use with a 386 computer due to their size or requirements.

The next thing you need to consider is the modem. Again, for chat the modem speed doesn't make that much difference if all you are going to do is chat. However, there are other applications that come with many of these software packages that you will not be able to use without a faster modem. There are also some functions that are limited or very slow for you without a faster modem. So, again, faster is better. My suggestion is to start with a 14.4 modem. With this modem you are able to do almost anything that is offered in chat. You can purchase a 14.4 fax modem at most office supply stores for around $80.

Your phone line is your life line to the Internet and to IRC. You can get by with the one line you have running into your house. If you are using chat from your place of business, you will want to have a dedicated line for your computer. At your home you will need to disable call waiting if you have that service on your line. Call waiting disconnects you from the Internet every time a call comes in. Your local phone service gives you instructions on how to disable call waiting; usually this information is in the front of your phone book. Most of the phone companies now offer a form of call messaging. For instance, GTE offers Personal Secretary while Southwestern Bell offers Call Notes. This service automatically acts as an answering machine and takes messages for you when your line is tied up or you are not at home. The fee for this service is minimal. If you are worried about missing calls while you are on chat, this may be an option for you.

In Chapter 4 we go into detail about the software that is available for IRC. You need some kind of IRC software, or client as it's called in the Internet community. There are several good software packages available for IRC. These run from the very basic to the more elaborate. In Chapter 4, I explain two of the better and more popular software packages as well as give you places you can go to get them or any others that strike your fancy.

The last and most important thing you need to use IRC is an Internet connection. The options available to you are almost unlimited. In the past seven years since the Internet has opened up to the public, more and more companies have popped up to offer Internet connections. These are called service providers. These service providers fall into three groups: national providers, local or regional providers, and commercial online service providers.

➤ National providers are Internet service providers that offer connections all over the nation and sometimes include Canada in their scope of coverage. A couple of the more well known and popular include Netcom and Pipeline. These companies provide you with their version of software to access various services on the Internet. One of the advantages to using a national provider is they offer local phone numbers in most of the major cities in the U.S. For instance, Netcom offers 200,000 local numbers, or *POPs*—points of presence.

If you travel, a national provider allows you to check your e-mail or access the Internet almost anywhere you go for the price of a local phone call. If you are one of those people who travel, you have the added expense of a laptop. Or, you can connect to the Internet via a company computer. However, this last option requires that the company have an Internet connection and the software to access the various services on the net. Then you simply login as yourself and get your mail or log into IRC.

The fees for their services vary. Some of these national providers charge a monthly fee and include a certain number of hours' usage free. Once you exceed those free hours you are charged an hourly fee. Some found out that the competition was too tough in certain areas and converted to a strictly monthly fee with unlimited usage. One of the disadvantages of the national providers is their size. Because they are larger, their support service may not be as responsive as you would like.

➤ Local and regional providers are similar to national providers. They offer full access to the Internet. Both generally supply the software to access various services on the Internet. Unlike the national providers, local providers offer you only a local phone number to access them. Regional providers offer you local numbers in the cities they cover. Service with these two kinds of providers seems to be more personable and responsive.

➤ Three of the major commercial online services are America Online, CompuServe, and Prodigy. They are a good place to start when learning how to use the Internet. They provide exclusive services plus allow you to send and receive e-mail, and give you access to certain services on the Internet, as well as many "chat rooms," as they call them. These chat rooms are similar to the chat channels you find on the Internet.

These commercial online services generally charge you a monthly fee and give you a few hours a month free. When you exceed those free hours they charge you an hourly rate. For instance, let's say one of these services charged you a $9.95 monthly rate with five hours free. Then you use their service for 20 hours that month (which, by the way, is a very low usage rate for most people); the cost to you would be $54.20, the $9.95 plus the additional 15 hours at $2.95 per hour. You can see how those charges would add up fast.

_____

Warning:　IRC is highly addictive. You will find that time slips by rapidly when you are chatting. There are even IRC anonymous chat channels to help people with their IRC addiction.
_____

When choosing a service provider you want to shop around for the best fee. Listen to your radio, check the yellow pages of your phone book, or read the newspapers or computer papers that come out in your area to see what is offered locally. Call around and see what options you have in your area. Each of these service providers charge fees according to the service you choose from them. Some of them charge a flat rate with unlimited access. Some charge a monthly rate and include a number of hours of usage free with that monthly rate. Some have different packages for the varying needs of their clients. Shop around for the rate and usage fees that best suit your needs.

Here in the United States and Canada, you have a local connection to the Internet, a monthly service fee, and your computer. Of course there are some service providers that give you a few hours a month free, then charge you an hourly rate for any hours you go over those free hours. But many of the providers, whether local, regional, or national, normally give you unlimited access for that set monthly fee.

What does that mean for you? Well, if you have children in college, that means you can now talk to them without having to pay the long-distance charges. If you have relatives in the armed services stationed overseas, you can talk to them daily without having to pay those expensive international phone bills. If you have friends or family in other states or parts of your state, you can now talk to them as often as you want. Not to mention the thousands of new people you can meet when you go online.

Pretty impressive, isn't it? Maybe that is why so many people are jumping on the Internet and IRC. I have seen IRC grow from a few thousand users (around 3,000) back in 1993 to more than 60,000 at the end of the first quarter of 1998. This is what all the hoopla is about—the ability to talk to anyone anywhere in the world for the cost of a local phone call (and the monthly fee).

You say to yourself, fine—now how do I get on and how do I use this wonderful new communication tool? Well, that is why you bought this book. You want a tool, a guide you can use to help you learn how to use this Internet service and to help you not look like a complete idiot when you get connected.

Everything you always wanted to know about IRC but were afraid to ask is covered in this book. In Chapter 1, we look at the various networks that are available for IRC. By the time you finish this chapter you will know enough about the networks for IRC to be able to get where you want to go, rather than flounder around like a fish out of water. You will not have to rely on your service provider to dump you where it thinks you should go.

Next, in Chapter 2, you get an idea of what a channel is and what channels are available on the various networks. You are able to find the channel you want when you finish this chapter. You even learn how to create your own channel. You learn more about channels than you would ever have thought possible.

In Chapter 3, we teach you all about the commands that are available for IRC and how to use them. By the time you finish the third chapter, you will be an expert in all the commands for IRC. You will know exactly when and where to use these commands and what happens when you use them.

Chapter 4 describes a couple of the chat software packages that are offered and how to use them. Chat can be as easy or as difficult as the software you use. Learning either of the two packages we present to you gives you an advantage over those that do not have them. You will be chatting and doing things in IRC that only the expert chatters know.

Chapter 5 guides you through the steps to configure mIRC software to your preferences. Then this chapter shows you how to use this chat client in your chat sessions. It covers all the features and how to implement them.

Chapter 6 covers the chat software Pirch. In this chapter, you learn about all its features and how to configure it to your preferences and to those of each member of your family. You learn how to use all the features of this amazing software while you are using chat.

Chapter 7 discusses netiquette, the Internet's version of proper conduct and behavior. This chapter gives you the ins and outs of proper conduct on the Internet and IRC. You learn all the little tricks to help you communicate better and stay out of trouble. You find out how not to step on toes by learning what the insiders and old hands at IRC have always known.

Chapter 8 takes you step by step through the process of getting connected, logging onto IRC, finding and joining a channel, joining in the chat conversations, and using the various commands to get the most out of your adventures in IRC chat land. Everything you need to know is described in easy-to-follow steps reinforced with illustrations showing how the screens look.

In Chapter 9, we even show you how you can use IRC for your business. We show you how to use this powerful communication tool to promote your business, and keep in touch with your office and traveling employees. You learn how to take advantage of all IRC has to offer. We even show you how you can use IRC for live voice communications for teleconferencing or one-on-one conversations.

Chapter 10 gives you information on troubleshooting. You learn what various error messages mean and what you can do to resolve problems you encounter while you are on IRC and using your IRC client.

Yes, IRC is not just for idle chatter. You can use it to improve your business and even help your business grow. So, not only can you talk to people around the world or in your own town, you can use IRC to keep in touch with traveling employees, your customers, or your office.

And, when you use IRC you get a written log of your conversations. When you conduct conversations via the telephone you have to rely on your memory afterwards to document them. With IRC, you have the option to log your conversations and then print a copy of them. Other than taping conversations, IRC offers you the best means of keeping accurate records of your communications.

Wow! The advantages to IRC just keep adding up. Now, I bet you are wondering why it took you so long to find this new communication tool. And why didn't someone think of this sooner? Well, let me give you a little background information about the Internet.

The Internet has been around for over 25 years. I bet you didn't know that. Up until about seven years ago it was the exclusive domain of the military, universities, and researchers/scientists. It was originally created during the cold war as a medium for the military to communicate even if one or more cities were destroyed in war. Scary thought, isn't it? They hired a team of researchers and computer experts to design a system that would allow them to do just that. Out of those creative minds came a new computer language called Protocol which allows computers all over the world to communicate with each other, no matter what kind of computer or where it is located.

Next came the method to connect all these computers. That is where phones, satellites, radios, and fiber optics come in. The Internet is basically a massive network of networks all connected together via these mediums. Then came talk, a one-on-one method that allowed users to have real-time communication. Out of talk evolved Internet Relay Chat, shortened to IRC. IRC came into use in 1988. It is the baby of the Internet services.

A service provider taps you into the Internet through hardware and special phone lines. But I know you are not concerned with all the technical aspects of how you get there. You just want to know how to do what you want to do with your Internet connection and IRC in particular.

To get the ball rolling we will start off with the networks, or *nets* as they are called in the Internet community, and progress through until we have you ready to jump in with both feet. Then we tell you how you can use IRC to your best advantage.

## Chapter 1

The Nets

Now that we have covered all you need to know about how to get started on the Internet and you know what IRC is, you are ready to learn about all the different aspects of IRC.

> **In this chapter you learn:**
>
> ☑ What a net is and how it works
> ☑ What nets are available, their history, and what they have to offer
> ☑ What a server is and which servers you use to connect to each net
> ☑ What ports are and why they are important when choosing a server
> ☑ What some of the server terminology is and what it means

I know you are excited about learning all you can about this wonderful communication medium and all it has to offer you. So, let's begin!

Since IRC began back in 1988, it has been used in over 60 countries around the world. It gained international fame in 1991 during the Persian Gulf War. Users would gather on a single channel to hear reports from around the world. Then in 1993, users from Moscow gave live reports via IRC about the situation during the coup against Boris Yeltsin.

IRC was designed as a replacement for the BBS (Bulletin Board System) talk program. This program let computer users on the Internet talk one-on-one with each other. On the Internet, users get a split screen, one half for each of them. One user types his message and indicates the end. Then, the other user types his message and indicates the end. They do this endlessly until they tire of talking.

IRC took talk a few steps further and created a multi-user chat program. Chat users gather in channels using chat software and servers to connect to IRC nets (or networks).

Nets are the backbone of IRC. They are IRC servers linked together to form networks, or groups of servers, that allow you to chat with people. It would be similar to a mother spider. She sits on her web. The threads of her web are the servers, the computers that process information. These servers bring information to her and take information out to her babies. The babies would be us, the users. The mother is the hub, or the net. We use the web to send information back and forth to each other using these threads of the web to link us together.

These networks, or nets, are similar to the network you have at your office. However, these nets span the globe. Their servers are linked together all over the United States, Canada, Europe, Asia, Australia, Africa, and South America.

And now you ask, what are servers? And rightly so. Servers are computers that let other computers connect to them using an IRC software program, or client as it is called on the Internet. Usually these servers are at universities or at providers' places of business. They are computers that carry the programs that let you connect and talk, keep track of users and channels, and make sure all the messages that users type get to the right place.

You use your IRC software to connect to one of the many different servers that are part of the network of servers called nets. Once you connect, you are inside one of the nets. Then you simply choose your channel, join it, and start chatting.

Within the Internet there are many different nets. Some of these are furnished or sponsored by local providers, some by BBSs (Bulletin Board Systems), and some by university systems or other organizations or individuals. For the purpose of this book we are only going to talk about the four major Internet IRC nets. The four nets are the EfNet, the UnderNet, DALnet, and SuperChat (formerly SuperLink).

EfNet—The First Net

The EfNet was the first net that was formed and is the largest of the nets. It was never designed; it just happened. It has no central authority and no particular structure. If you find yourself on IRC and you are not sure what net you are on, chances are you are on EfNet.

I am not going to sugarcoat any facts here. The EfNet is very slow and unreliable. It often splits into more than one separate network when the links between servers go down. There may be times when a message you sent either does not reach its destination or does not reach it for several minutes. The EfNet is also prone to hacking and offers no protection from those hacking attempts.

The IRC operators on EfNet are often uncaring and less than helpful. You also find more nick collisions. These happen when two people try to use the same nickname. (We go into detail about nicknames in Chapter 3, The Commands.) You also often find it difficult to connect to a server.

Its size is one of the reasons for the problems with this net. At any given time of the day or night you can find almost 40,000 people connected to this net. There are more than 70 servers available for the EfNet. However, with the massive amount of people logging on or trying to log on, this is often not enough. The more users these servers have to handle and process information for, the slower they become and the more problems they experience.

This is not to say there are not advantages to using this net. For businesses, the sheer size of this net is attractive: The more people connected, the more opportunities available. There are thousands of channels to choose from. Another advantage is the number of computer guru channels. So if you have a computer problem, this is the net you would use to find an expert to help you.

And, of course, each of these nets has its own unique society of people. This net may be the one where you find your long-lost friend from high school or even make a new friend you would not have met anywhere else.

UnderNet—The Rebels

The UnderNet evolved out of the EfNet. It began its existence on the Internet in 1992. It was formed when a group of *netizens* (net citizens) decided to form a new net after they grew discontented with what they perceived as privacy breaches and lack of *bandwidth,* which is the data capacity of a data line. They formed their own net of a smaller and more tight-knit group of users. Since it began, it has grown from 1,000 users in February of 1995 to over 25,000 users at the end of the first quarter of 1998. By the time you read this book, that number may be closer to 30,000 or more users.

This group of rebels set about to make this new net more organized. The UnderNet operators agreed to cooperate with each other to get the best links to servers and to make your time on their net more pleasant. These operators began with the goal of keeping the Under-Net a friendly place and helping users with any problem. However, because it has grown at such an unforeseen rate, they have not been able to keep up with the demands put on them. The UnderNet has grown to almost match the size and scope of the EfNet and is experiencing many of the same problems that caused its founders to create it. It now experiences the same problems with hackers, netsplits, lags, and takeovers that the EfNet experienced before the UnderNet was formed.

In 1997 a teenager from Romania was successful in kidnapping the UnderNet and holding it hostage for several minutes. He hacked into a provider in South Carolina, took power away from the IRCops so that they could not present an obstacle to him, and then denied them access to the UnderNet. Once he had removed all his obstacles, he announced to all the users online at the time (fortunately this occurred during the wee hours of the morning U.S. time) that he had taken over the UnderNet and tried to flood everyone off the net. The IRCops were able to regain control within a few minutes, restored order to the UnderNet, and had the offending teenager's service cut off by his provider. This is just an example of the kinds of problems that IRCops are responsible for preventing or handling on a regular basis.

When the UnderNet was formed, the founders made some changes over the tried-and-true EfNet way of doing things. One of the changes was adding features to the servers that assist operators and users.

Routing for servers is another area where the UnderNet differs from EfNet. The UnderNet strives to get the best route to its servers. Routing servers is very much like what the telephone company does with your telephone lines. If the direct route between a server in, say, Texas and one in New York is busy, the route is redirected to go through Kansas City and then through Chicago or wherever necessary to get the fastest connection between servers.

They also established a Channel Service to help make the UnderNet a happier place to be. This service functions to help preserve channels, prevent hostile takeovers, and register channels. We talk more about this in Chapter 2, The Channels.

The UnderNet has also formed several committees to assist users. These committees also have mailing lists you can subscribe to so you can keep up to date on the latest UnderNet happenings. They include the following:

Wastelanders—the main mailing list for the UnderNet and its operators—subscribe to wastelanders

User Committee—gives users a say in changes and organization of the UnderNet. There is a set of guidelines to follow outlining what this committee gets involved in and what it won't get involved in—subscribe to user-com

Documentation—provides standardized and helpful documents to users—subscribe to doco-com

Public Relations Committee—in the setup phase but has established a set of guidelines—subscribe to pr-com

Coder Committee—for coders of the UnderNet's protocol (language that lets computers talk to each other)—subscribe to coder-com

Routing Committee—handles the routing of servers and new link applications—subscribe to routing-com

UnderNet Announcements—a moderated list; its primary purpose is to provide a quality list for announcements—subscribe to undernet-announce

If you would like to subscribe to any of these lists, simply send an e-mail to majordomo@undernet.org. In the body of the message type **subscribe** followed by the name of the list you want to subscribe to. Be sure to place a space between subscribe and the name of the list.

The UnderNet also gives its users news and newsletters with information to help users and keep them up to date on happenings on the net. The newsletter is touted as a fun yet informative publication of the UnderNet Public Relations Committee. This newsletter helps users keep abreast of the latest UnderNet happenings and current issues affecting the UnderNet. For a peek, go to the web at this site location: http://www.pr-com.undernet.org/.

The UnderNet News is about the UnderNet in the news. It gives links to news stories and articles found on the Internet about the UnderNet. It includes the bad along with the good. You can view this site and these links at http://www.undernet.org/news.html.

The UnderNet has its own site on the web which has a lot of very useful information and links to other sites with information that is of benefit to you. The site welcome page is at http://www.undernet.org/.

So, if you need more organization, this net is for you. You find many of the same channel names here as you find on the EfNet. You may even see some of the same characters from time to time on both nets. You may notice these people on both nets at the same time. I explain how to do this later in this book.

DALnet—The Game

One of the smaller nets of the Big Four is DALnet. This net started as a role-playing-game alternative network. It started off with a rather cultish group of users. Originally, you could find an average of 130 users on this net. However, with the recent growth of the Internet and IRC usage, this net has grown to over 20,000 users during peak hours.

DALnet prides itself as being the friendliest IRC network. It recognizes the fact that without its users, IRC would be nothing. DALnet's policy is to be as friendly and open to its users as possible. It, too, has made changes to its servers, making them as user friendly as possible. Its servers are also designed to minimize your harassment from other users.

DALnet allows users to have longer nicknames and to register those nicknames. It is the only one of the Big Four nets that lets you register a nickname. At one time you were able to register a nickname on the EfNet; however, that service was discontinued in 1994 and will not be renewed. There are just too many users on the other two nets for nickname registration to be feasible.

If you are looking for a quieter place to go, try DALnet. If you need to carry on an intense conversation with someone without worrying about being interrupted, this net is the ideal spot.

SuperChat—The Alternative

The last and smallest of the major four nets is SuperChat. SuperChat, also the youngest of the nets, formed in early 1995. Originally it was called SuperLink net. It began as a very elite net. Since changing over to SuperChat it has opened its doors and allows as many people on as can get a connection. At any given time you will see no more than 500 users. As the Internet continues to grow and more and more people go online, the number of users on each net grows proportionately.

SuperChat's organization is very similar to the UnderNet's. It allows you to register channels. It also strives to keep the servers functioning at optimal levels. Its community is growing. As the other three bigger nets become overcrowded, you will see more and more users switching over to this net. So, if you like the idea of being part of a much smaller group that is growing, this net is the one for you.

Other Nets—Limitless

There are a dozen or more other nets out there on the Internet. New nets are being added constantly. As more and more people get connected to the Internet, the older nets will not be able to handle all the traffic.

Already, the UnderNet is undergoing many of the same problems that drove its founders to establish it. As more and more people get frustrated, the demand creates the supply.

In my travels on the Internet and IRC, I have heard tell of or found a few of the other new nets for you. Here are several I have found:

IRCnet—a fairly new net that grew very fast. It formed in July of 1996 when several of the EfNet servers broke off to form their own net. It boasts over 130 servers and approximately 25,000 users.

StarLink—a fairly small net that has 14 servers and has approximately 1,000 users. It was created around July of 1996. Sex and warez (hacker) channels are not allowed on this net.

WarpedNet—was created in December of 1996. This net has 14 servers and approximately 150 users online. It does not allow bots. (For an explanation of bots, see Server Terminology at the end of this chapter.) I did not notice any sex or warez channels, but I also did not note any overt denial of these kinds of channels from any of the IRCops or administrators.

ChatNet—has grown since the first edition of this book and since its inception in March of 1996. Administrators claim it was born out of the ashes of an older network (SuperChat, formerly Super-Link). This network, like the UnderNet, also offers channel bots and registration. It is a midsized network with a loyal user base and friendly hosts. This network does not allow sex or warez channels. It has 17 servers you can use to access its net. It averages around 1,500 or more users during peak periods.

GalaxyNet—began in April of 1996. It offers a net bot that lets you register your nickname and your channel. This is very similar to what DALnet uses. It has 33 servers and averages around 3,500 users. This net does allow sex and warez channels, and I noticed several of these.

StarLink-IRC—came online in January of 1997. It refuses to host sex or hacker channels. It has eight servers and approximately 350 users on at any given time.

AUSTnet—a new net which began in early 1996. It is a medium-sized net that averages around 1,800 users. It has 20 servers.

NewNet—came online in April of 1996. It was originally formed by the irc.eskimo.com server after being forced off EfNet. It soon grew from a small network into one of medium size. It has 30 to 35 servers and around 2,300 users online. This net does allow sex and warez channels.

AnotherNet—an older net that was founded in 1995 but still remains fairly small. It has six servers and approximately 1,300 users.

Xworldnet—formed in September of 1996. It is a small net with 16 servers and over 400 users.

MultiNET—another small net. It has ten servers and averages around 100 users.

AlterNet—a small net with eight servers and less than 200 users.

SorceryNet—formed in January of 1997. It was created as a new network running on guidelines similar to DALnet, and is managed by experienced administrators of former DALnet servers. It has eight servers and over 100 users.

FEFnet—another small net. It boasts strict abuse control as one of its pros. However, unlike most others of this kind, channel subjects are not restricted. It has 10 servers and over 200 users.

AfterNET—this net formed in September of 1996 and is still a rather small net. It has 12 servers and over 100 users.

FireStar—a fairly new net formed in August of 1997. It is a small net with four servers and less than 100 users.

StarChat—formed in June of 1997. It has around 18 servers and over 650 users.

SandNET—is a small net formed in December of 1996. It has ten servers and over 180 users.

CastleNet—formed in May of 1997. It has ten servers and less than 100 users.

Earth International Chat Network—a new net that has six servers and approximately 150 users.

ValhallNet—one of the newer nets formed in May of 1997. It has 13 servers and over 100 users.

MicrosoftNet—the comic chat network. You can use the Comic Chat software you read about in Chapter 4 on this net. It averages around 1,500 to 2,000 users on three servers. This net allows any type of channels, so you can find sex and warez channels here.

LinuxNet—devoted to Linux and help with Linux software and all computer system users. It has 14 servers and approximately 200 users.

Kidlink—is a private net for participants in KIDLINK: Global Networking for Youth 10-15. Registration is required to use this net.

ScoutLink—this server was set up so that Scouts in various parts of the world could have meetings in various languages. There is also a link from within this network to Scouting channels all over IRC. It has 11 servers and 100 or more users.

ZAnet/South African IRC—has all its servers in South Africa. Three or four servers let anyone on. During the day you can find 250 or more people on this net.

Australian IRC—also known as Ozorg. One of the world's largest IRC networks. It's made up of servers that used to be the Australian part of the UnderNet. It has seven servers and over 3,000 users.

WorldWide Free-Net—a chain of Free-Nets linked around the world. Free-Nets are exactly as they sound. They are free to their users, but do ask for donations of time or money to offset expenses. These Free-Nets are linked by their own servers. They allow no pornography and provide a clean, enjoyable place to exchange cultures and ideas from around the world. This net includes the following Free-Nets: Alachua Free-Net, Prairienet Free-Net, LA Free-Net, FEN Free-Net, Omnifest Free-Net, Greater Detroit Free-Net, Grand Rapids Free-Net, and Chester Community Interlink.

There are probably more nets than this, but this list gives you an idea of what is out there. There are also several more local nets for various countries. Visit the ones listed here and see what they have to offer. They may become the new alternatives to the other four mentioned previously. The Internet is growing so fast, anything is possible.

A few of the nets that were highlighted in the first edition of this book are now defunct. Some of them have disappeared completely and some have divided and evolved into other nets. The ones that are no longer nets that were mentioned in the first edition are Innernet and Iaonet.

The Servers

As I mentioned before, the nets are networks of servers. Servers are what you use to connect to these nets. Each net has its own group of servers to let you connect to it. Servers are very important, because without them, IRC is useless to you. In the next section I give you a list of servers for each net.

First, you need to get an understanding of how servers work and about addresses on the Internet. Everything you do on the Internet requires an address. When you subscribe to a provider, you are given an address. That address is your e-mail address. Your e-mail address is your identification no matter where you go on the Internet.

Servers have their own address. This address consists of where the server is located and the net it accesses. For instance, to access the UnderNet, you need a server that belongs to the UnderNet. Every server for the UnderNet ends its address with undernet.org. This stands for undernet organization. America Online (AOL) has its own UnderNet server. This server is located in Washington, D.C. Therefore, the address for the server is washington.dc.us.undernet.org. Notice the address contains where the server is located, washington.dc.us. There are servers all over the world, therefore, the address also contains the country where the server is located. Since this is an UnderNet server, it ends in undernet.org.

Also note the periods that separate the address. In Internet terminology these are not called periods; they are called dots. So the address for AOL would be pronounced and read washington-dot-dc-dot-us-dot-undernet-dot-org. Generally, anytime you see an address you see dots separating areas of that address. These are always pronounced and read as dots, not periods.

As I mentioned before, each net has its own group of servers, and these servers each have their own address. For instance, the EfNet has over 70 servers, the UnderNet has over 40 servers, DALnet has over 30 servers, and SuperChat has about ten. I give you a fair number of servers for each net; by the time you finish this book, you will be able to recognize what servers are and where to find them on your own.

Note: Both the EfNet and the UnderNet ask that you try to connect to the server that is geographically closer to you.

You can choose any server from the list to connect to the net of your choice. However, you may not always be allowed to connect to every server. For instance, several of the European servers do not look too kindly on U.S. users trying to connect to their servers. I explain more about this later in this chapter, after the servers list.

Servers List

Following is a list of servers for most of the nets we have talked about in this chapter. Add any or all of these to your server lists in your chat software. Explore the different nets to see which one feels right for you. Remember that the Internet is growing by leaps and bounds. It grows so fast that it evolves faster than most people can keep up with it. These lists should give you a starting point for your IRC exploring.

EfNet Servers

Address	Location
irc.magic.ca	Canada
irc.colorado.edu	Colorado
irc.c-com.net	Texas
irc.blackened.com	Arizona
irc.stanford.edu	California
irc-e.primenet.com	D.C.
irc.emory.edu	Georgia
irc.mcs.net	Illinois
irc.umich.edu	Michigan
anarchy.tamu.edu	Texas
irc.umn.edu	Minnesota
irc.mo.net	Missouri
irc.idt.net	New Jersey
irc.psinet.com	New York
irc.choice.net	Ohio

This is by no means a comprehensive list. It does, however, give you a good start. Refer back to this every time you try to connect to IRC via the EfNet.

UnderNet Servers

Address	Location
ann-arbor.mi.us.undernet.org	Michigan
austin.tx.us.undernet.org	Texas
blacksburg.va.us.undernet.org	Virginia
chicago.il.us.undernet.org	Illinois
davis.ca.us.undernet.org	California
newbrunswick.nj.us.undernet.org	New Jersey
manhattan.ks.us.undernet.org	Kansas
norman.ok.us.undernet.org	Oklahoma

Address	Location
okc.ok.us.undernet.org	Oklahoma
phoenix.az.us.undernet.org	Arizona
pittsburgh.pa.us.undernet.org	Pennsylvania
sanjose.ca.us.undernet.org	California
washington.dc.us.undernet.org	Washington, D.C.
us.undernet.org	United States
ca.undernet.org	Canada
eu.undernet.org	Europe
uk.undernet.org	United Kingdom

The last four servers listed in this UnderNet servers list are server routers. These servers connect you to the first available server they find. They function similar to multiple phone lines at a business, rolling over to the next available server when they receive a busy or, in this case, "no more connections" notice. There are many more servers: European, Canadian, or otherwise. But this list gives you a good start on getting connected.

DALnet Servers

Address	Location
irc.dal.net	server pool
irc.services.dal.net	server pool
glass.oh.us.dal.net	Ohio
groucho.ca.us.dal.net	California
cin.dal.net	Ohio
datashopper.dal.net	Denmark
davis.dal.net	California
dragon.dal.net	unknown
igc.dal.net	unknown
liberator.dal.net	unknown
phoenix.dal.net	Arizona
toronto.dal.net	Canada

The DALnet has grown a lot since the first edition of this book. It now has over 30 servers. The ones listed here are the original servers and are still in effect. You should have no trouble connecting to any of these servers.

SuperChat Servers

Address	Location
irc.superlink.net	server pool
houston.TX.US.SuperChat.Org	Houston
server.superchat.org	server pool
los-angeles.ca.us.superchat.org	California
normal.il.us.superchat.org	Illinois
neworleans.la.us.superchat.org	Louisiana
Server.SuperChat.Org	server pool
kentville.ns.ca.superchat.org	Canada
sanantonio.tx.us.superchat.org	Texas
okc.ok.us.superchat.org	Oklahoma

This net was formerly known as SuperLink net but has changed to SuperChat. With the change, it has more servers and invites any and all users. These are most of SuperChat's servers.

IRCnet Servers

Address	Location
irc.ncal.verio.net	California
ircnet.irc.aol.com	D.C.
irc.anet.com	Illinois
irc.cifnet.com	Illinois
irc.webbernet.net	Michigan
ircd.webbernet.net	Michigan
irc.stealth.net	New York
ircd.stealth.net	New York
ircnet.sprynet.com	Washington
yoyo.cc.monash.edu.au	Australia
irc.usyd.edu.au	Australia
chat.btinternet.com	UK
eris.bt.net	UK
irc.warwick.ac.uk	UK

This fairly new net grew quickly and sports over 130 servers, of which this is only a partial list. Many of the servers are in European countries.

StarLink Servers

Address	Location
San-Francisco.CA.US.StarLink.Org	California
Aspen.CO.US.StarLink.Org	Colorado
Denver.CO.US.StarLink.Org	Colorado
Durham.NC.US.StarLink.Org	North Carolina
NewYork.NY.US.StarLink.Org	New York
Pittsburgh.PA.US.StarLink.Org	Pennsylvania
RockHill.SC.US.StarLink.Org	South Carolina
WichitaFalls.TX.US.StarLink.Org	Texas
Seattle.WA.US.StarLink.Org	Washington
Richmond.VA.US.StarLink.Org	Virginia

This small net has the above servers and very few users online at any given time.

WarpedNet Servers

Address	Location
irc.mit.edu	MIT
irc.warped.net	server pool
elite.warped.net	unknown
tawa.math.orst.edu	unknown
osu.us.warped.net	Oklahoma
irc.mentasm.com	unknown
beorn.ca.warped.net	Canada
domino.UK.warped.net	UK
bottom.uk.warped.net	UK

This is another of the smaller nets.

ChatNet Servers

Address	Location
Portland.OR.US.Chatnet.Org	Oregon
SF.CA.US.Chatnet.Org	California
WalnutCreek.CA.US.Chatnet.Org	California
LosAngeles.CA.US.Chatnet.Org	California
Pensacola.FL.US.Chatnet.Org	Florida
Tupelo.MS.US.Chatnet.Org	Mississippi
RockHill.SC.US.Chatnet.Org	South Carolina
Louisville.KY.US.Chatnet.Org	Kentucky

This is one of the midsized nets. It has grown since the first edition of this book and has added several new servers and generated a loyal user base.

GalaxyNet Servers

Address	Location
Albany.NY.US.GalaxyNet.Org	New York
Atlanta.GA.US.GalaxyNet.Org	Georgia
Austin.TX.US.GalaxyNet.Org	Texas
Bristol.UK.GalaxyNet.Org	UK
Charlotte.NC.US.GalaxyNet.Org	North Carolina
Gainesville.FL.US.GalaxyNet.Org	Florida
Honolulu.HI.US.GalaxyNet.Org	Hawaii
Macon.GA.US.GalaxyNet.Org	Georgia
Marshall.MN.US.GalaxyNet.Org	Minnesota
SaltLake.UT.US.GalaxyNet.Org	Utah
Sedona.AZ.US.GalaxyNet.Org	Arizona

This is another of the midsized nets with about 33 servers. You find sex and warez channels on this net. This is only a representation of the servers you can find for GalaxyNet.

StarLink-IRC Servers

Address	Location
ROCHESTER.MI.US.StarLink-IRC.Org	Michigan
HOUSTON.TX.US.StarLink-IRC.Org	Texas
ATLANTA.GA.US.StarLink-IRC.Org	Georgia
WILLIAMSLAKE.BC.CA.StarLink-IRC.Org	Canada
GRANDFORKS.ND.US.StarLink-IRC.Org	North Dakota
GOTHENBURG.SE.EU.StarLink-IRC.Org	Europe
AMSTERDAM.NL.EU.StarLink-IRC.Org	Europe
SUSSEX.WI.US.StarLink-IRC.Org	Wisconsin

This is another of the smaller, newer nets. These are the eight servers for this net. It strives to be as friendly as possible and open to suggestions.

AUSTnet Servers

Address	Location
cyberverse.ca.us.austnet.org	California
explorer.ca.us.austnet.org	California
olympic.ca.us.austnet.org	California
webmaster.ca.us.austnet.org	California
sound.mo.us.austnet.org	Missouri
atlas.oh.us.austnet.org	Ohio
tavern.oh.us.austnet.org	Ohio

This is one of the newer nets and is still quite small. There are very few users and several servers for this net at this time. These are only a few of its servers.

NewNet Servers

Address	Location
irc.tyme.net	Michigan
irc.lcia.com	Florida
irc.salamander.com	Iowa
irc.intergate.bc.ca	Canada
irc.klis.com	Canada
irc.dragondata.com	Illinois
irc.aye.net	Indiana
irc.terraworld.net	Kansas
irc.yoc.com	Utah
irc.bluegrass.net	Kentucky
irc.lstnet.com	Louisiana
irc.busprod.com	Oklahoma
irc.netreach.com	Pennsylvania
irc.eskimo.com	Washington

This midsized net has approximately 30 to 35 servers and averages 2,300 users online. You find sex and warez channels on NewNet. This list includes a random sampling of NewNet's servers.

AnotherNet Servers

Address	Location
irc.another.net	server pool
neato.ca.us.another.net	California
neato-2.ca.us.another.net	California
together-2.vt.au.another.net	Australia
together.vt.us.another.net	unknown
hacker.another.net	unknown

This is a medium-sized net with six servers and an average of 1,300 users. There have been rumors among the net's system administrators of charging a fee to join this net and to exclude Mac users.

Xworldnet Servers

Address	Location
buffalo.ny.us.xworld.org	New York
california.md.us.xworld.org	Maryland
kansas-city.ks.us.xworld.org	Kansas
marietta.oh.us.xworld.org	Ohio
maui.hi.us.xworld.org	Hawaii
meadville.pa.us.xworld.org	Pennsylvania
cosmos.lod.com	Florida
rio-de-janeiro.br.sa.xworld.org	Brazil
rockhill.sc.us.xworld.org	South Carolina
telford.uk.eu.xworld.org	UK
valencia.ca.us.xworld.org	California
wesel.de.eu.xworld.org	Germany
winnipeg.mb.ca.xworld.org	Canada

This is a relatively small net with 16 servers. This chart represents several of the servers for this net.

MultiNET Servers

Address	Location
irc.bse.bg	Bulgaria
ircd.vabo.cz	Czech Republic
irc.horizon.nl	Netherlands
rood.sci.kun.nl	Netherlands
studs.sci.kun.nl	Netherlands
irc.vltmedia.se	Sweden
irc.dunimas.com	U.S.

This is one of the smaller nets with only seven servers. Most of the servers for this net are European servers.

AlterNet Servers

Address	Location
alternet.luc.ac.be	Belgium
alternet.one.se	Sweden
alternet.sonn.com	California
irc.3sheep.com	Massachusetts
alternet.sru.edu	Pennsylvania
alternet.tamu.edu	Texas
irc.dunk-admins.com	Texas

Another small net with only a few servers.

SorceryNet Servers

Address	Location
voyager.sorcery.net	California
nexus.sorcery.net	Sweden
kechara.sorcery.net	Massachusetts
mordor.sorcery.net	Texas
zanzibar.sorcery.net	Utah
irc.sorcery.net	server pool

Small net with a few servers. SorceryNet is run similar to DALnet.

FEFnet Servers

Address	Location
vendetta.fef.net	California
liii.fef.net	New York
medina.fef.net	Virginia
wolfen.fef.net	Washington
tower.fef.net	Texas
villagenet.fef.net	New York
sysfail.fef.net	Oregon
stf.fef.net	Arizona
quantum.uk.fef.net	UK
unseen.hub.uk.fef.net	UK

Small net with no channel controls and ten servers.

AfterNET Servers

Address	Location
irc.afternet.org	server pool
infinet.afternet.org	Canada
digitald.uk.afternet.org	UK
merconline.afternet.org	California
storm.afternet.org	California
defiant.afternet.org	Indiana
scorpion.latech.edu	Louisiana
twolf.afternet.org	Missouri
happy.afternet.org	New Mexico
schumana.rhn.orst.edu	Oregon
agora.afternet.org	Oregon
asp.afternet.org	Wisconsin

Small net with several servers but few users.

FireStar Servers

Address	Location
irc.firestar.org	server pool
orion.fl.us.firestar.org	Florida
saturn.oh.us.firestar.org	Ohio
firechild.ok.us.firestar.org	Oklahoma

Another small net that has many of the same features of DALnet.

StarChat Servers

Address	Location
avenger.starchat.net	Maryland
beavis.starchat.net	Florida
beer.starchat.net	Virginia
centurion.starchat.net	Massachusetts
constellation.starchat.net	New Hampshire
darkness.starchat.net	California
eclipse.starchat.net	Colorado
milkyway.starchat.net	Oregon
millennium.starchat.net	Michigan
oceana.starchat.net	Georgia
polaris.starchat.net	Washington
severious.starchat.net	Massachusetts
spooky.starchat.net	Texas

A medium-sized net with several servers and many of the same features of DALnet.

SandNET Servers

Address	Location
tombstone-az.sandnet.net	Arizona
stlouis-mo.sandnet.net	Missouri
rolla-mo.sandnet.net	Missouri
laredo-tx.sandnet.net	Texas
miami-fl.sandnet.net	Florida
hattiesburg-ms.sandnet.net	Mississippi
normal-il.sandnet.net	Illinois
tulsa-ok.sandnet.net	Oklahoma
jackson-ms.sandnet.net	Mississippi
vancouver-bc.sandnet.net	Canada

Another small net with a few servers that functions similar to DALnet.

CastleNet Servers

Address	Location
cumulus.co.castlenet.org	Colorado
matnet.ak.castlenet.org	Alaska
datapro.id.castlenet.org	Idaho
roanoke.va.castlenet.org	Virginia
heaven.nh.castlenet.org	New Hampshire
horsetooth.co.castlenet.org	Colorado
monroe.mi.castlenet.org	Michigan
bakersfield.ca.castlenet.org	California
whiteknight.in.castlenet.org	Indiana
springfield.ma.castlenet.org	Massachusetts

Another smaller net with several servers.

EarthInternational Servers

Address	Location
atlanta-r.ga.us.earthint.net	Georgia
combase-2.fl.us.earthint.net	Florida
shadow.fl.us.earthint.net	Florida
atlanta.ga.us.earthint.net	Georgia
burghcom.pa.us.earthint.net	Pennsylvania
chicago.il.us.earthint.net	Illinois

Small net with a few servers.

ValhallNet Servers

Address	Location
abyss.co.us.valhall.net	Colorado
casino.az.us.valhall.net	Arizona
fizzx.mn.us.valhall.net	Minnesota
vinland.ri.us.valhall.net	Rhode Island

Small net founded on the Nordic myth and Atari game symbols. Has several servers, many European.

MicrosoftNet Servers

Address	Location
MIC1.microsoft.com	unknown
comicserv1.microsoft.com	unknown
comicserv2.microsoft.com	unknown

MicrosoftNet is your gateway to the comic channels. These are channels that let you use comic strip-like characters in comic strip-like settings in your chat sessions. This net has three servers and is a midsized net averaging around 1,500 to 2,000 users.

LinuxNet Servers

Address	Location
linux.mit.edu	unknown
accessus.net	unknown
curio.cabi.net	unknown
irc.wisp.net	unknown
irc.lame.org	unknown

A small net catering to the needs of Linux users. These are but a few of the servers for this net.

ScoutLink Servers

Address	Location
on.ca.scoutlink.org	Canada
utah.us.scoutlink.org	Utah
ut.us.scoutlink.org	Utah

Specialized net for Scouts to connect and conduct meetings. These are just a few of the servers for this net.

Ozorg Servers

Address	Location
mpx.sydney.oz.org	Australia
aussie.sydney.oz.org	Australia
omen.perth.oz.org	Australia
tig.melbourne.oz.org	Australia
wollongong.oz.org	Australia
rockhampton.oz.org	Australia
davis.oz.org	Australia

This chart includes all the servers for this Australian net. It boasts around 3,000 users.

WWFINnet Servers

Address	Location
irc.freenet.victoria.bc.ca	Canada
fen.wwfin.net	Germany
lafn.org	California
irc.afn.org	Florida
prairienet.wwfin.net	Illinois
macatawa.wwfin.net	Michigan

This chart includes several of the servers for some of the Free-Nets.

While these lists are far from complete, they give you a base on which to start your travels in IRC land. I cannot guarantee that you will be able to connect to all of these servers. A lot depends on the time you choose to connect and the various servers. If one fails to let you on, keep trying other servers until you find one that will let you connect. You will find as you use IRC more and more that you'll get proficient at learning which are the best servers for you and your area.

Ports

When you are trying to connect to servers you are often asked which port you wish to connect to. A port is like a line into the server. Ports come in numbers. Almost all of the servers let you connect to the universal port of 6667.

Most of the EfNet servers have additional ports you can use. If you are having a hard time getting connected to a server on the 6667 port, then try one of the alternate ports. For the EfNet servers, the ports range from 6660 to 6670.

The UnderNet servers also use the universal or default port of 6667. However, you may be able to get a better or faster connection by using one of the alternate ports of 6660 through 6669.

Since the other nets are much smaller than the other two, the default port of 6667 is probably all you need. However, as these nets grow, you may need to try different ports. These ports should be consistent with the other nets, so try using one in the range of 6660 through 6669.

Server Terminology

This next section gives you some of the terminology that you see bandied about on IRC in reference to servers. Defining these terms for you here helps you be more knowledgeable when you do get connected. Then you can sit back and chuckle at the newbies who were not smart enough to buy this book and learn before they leapt into the cold and often murky waters of IRC.

One of the first things you might see when you do try to connect to a server is something called a *site ban* or *K-lined*. A site ban or K-line by a server means that it has banned your provider's address. Usually you find this kind of ban on the European servers. Like I said earlier, these servers get a little testy when users from other countries try to use their servers. They are trying to reserve space for people in their own countries. So, do not be offended. Just pick another server and try again.

Another phrase you might run across when you try to connect is **No Clone Bots** or **K-lined No Clone Bots**. Let me explain what bots are first. Bots are self running programs—like a robot, therefore, bot for short. These are usually programs that greet people and perform other mundane tasks for their users. Clone bots are programs that can replicate users' addresses. Again, do not be offended if you get this message. Just try another server. However, if you are concerned, call your provider and report the problem to them. Often, it is just a misunderstanding that they can resolve with the server administrators. Other times it may be a problem with one or more users that they need to be aware of.

Another message you might run across when you are trying to connect to a server is **Ghosts are not allowed on IRC**. This means you or your site have been banned from that server. This could be for the same reasons you get the No Clone Bots message from another server. Your only recourse is to try another server.

Once you are connected and participating in a channel, you will see two terms come up quite often, especially if you are on either the EfNet or the UnderNet. These two terms are *netsplits* and *lags*. A netsplit is when one or more servers splits off from the net. Usually this is caused by an overload of users. This server and all the users still think they are part of the whole network. They are still able to communicate; however, the users are only able to talk to or chat with other users on that server or with the other servers that split.

Let me use the spider and web analogy again to explain how lags and splits work. The threads of the web are your servers. When a split happens it is as though someone swept away or disconnected a part of the web. Then the spider quickly goes to that damaged area and brings the thread back together, repairing the damage. The users hanging onto those threads that were disconnected are still connected to each other via their threads, but until mother spider brings them back to the rest of the web, they cannot communicate with the whole web.

You recognize a netsplit when you see a group of people leave your channel all at once. It appears as though they have all signed off at the same time. You also notice that they all have a common server name. Have no fear—netsplits do not last very long. Eventually, the servers repair themselves and rejoin the rest of the network. Just be patient. However, if you notice that your server seems to be splitting a lot in one given session, you may want to change servers.

Sometimes associated with netsplits are what are called lags. Lag is the time it takes for your message to travel from your server to the network. Many times before a split, you notice the lag is very long. This is usually an indication that the servers are overloaded and experiencing problems. Sometimes this lag only affects one or two servers, and sometimes it affects many servers. Your best bet is to try to ride out the storm. But if your lag is so bad you are unable to keep up or see anything anyone else might be saying in the channel, you can change servers. This is often the best solution to this problem. The only drawback to this is finding a server that is not lagged. There are ways to do this and I explain them further in Chapter 3, The Commands. If your screen of messages is moving slowly, you could ask the others there which servers are not lagging and then try one of those.

Summary

After reading this chapter you should have a very good understanding of what a net is. You can see how IRC began and how it has evolved into this monstrous communications medium that lets you talk to people all over the world.

Using any one of the numerous nets that are available to you and the servers listed for those nets, you are able to keep up with late-breaking news when there is a crisis at hand. You are able to talk to friends and family without having to take out a second mortgage on your home just to pay your phone bills, and can make new friends all over the world.

These nets are your doorway to a vast resource of friends, family, and many other opportunities. Each net has its own set of servers to let you access them and enjoy the full potential of what they have to offer.

With the server terminology you learned you are able to detect when you are lagged and when there is a netsplit. Having this information handy makes you look like one of the old pros of IRC rather than a newbie.

Now let's take what you have learned here and add it to what you learn in the next chapter about channels, or rooms if you prefer, on IRC.

Chapter 2

The Channels

You have learned all about the nets and how they work. Now let's take a look at channels and see what you need to learn about them for you to navigate through IRC with ease and comfort.

In this chapter you learn:
☑ How many channels there are for each net
☑ How you can find a channel you want to participate in
☑ What you can expect to find when you join any of these channels
☑ What channel operators are and what they do
☑ How you can be on more than one channel or net at a time

Everything you need to know about channels is covered in this chapter. Read on and find out the lowdown on what is available to you before you jump in and get your feet wet.

Where are All the People?

There are millions of people connected to the Internet. Out of all those people there are thousands who find their way to one of the various nets each morning, afternoon, evening, and night.

So, where do all those people go? They go to what are called channels in IRC. Channels are like rooms where people or users gather to chat. You can find channels with people in them in your own age group. You more than likely can find channels that were formed to talk about a particular hobby. You can also find channels set up for professional discussions or technical talk. And, yes, as you have heard on the news, you can find many channels that were created to talk about sex.

There are as many different channels on any one of the nets as there are different ideas, tastes, and interests. Later in this chapter we discuss the different kinds of channels and what you can expect when you go to them.

So, what is this going to look like when you get into IRC? If you log onto IRC using a Windows-based program as most of you are, you get a window just like you do for your other applications. When you select the channel you want to join, you get a window inside your window. This is your channel window; it is where you carry on your chat conversations.

Sounds pretty simple, doesn't it? It is. The hardest part is learning all the IRC commands. But I help you with all those in the next chapter. These channel windows are pretty similar to any other windows you open. You can do many of the same things with them that you would do with other Windows applications, like resize them, hide them, etc. So, it should not be that hard for you to adapt to using these windows for chatting.

What you see once you join a channel depends on the channel you join. Sometimes when you join a channel you are the only one there. Some channels have two or three others in them. Then there are many channels that have dozens or more people in them.

 Tip: When you join some of these larger channels, it may be hard for you to keep up with what is going on at first. The conversation on the channel goes by rather quickly; this is called *scroll* in IRC.

If you join a channel where you are the only one there, you won't see anything until you start typing. This might be a good place for you to try experimenting with things you learn in this book.

When you join a channel that has other people in it, you almost immediately see conversations rolling by. Some of these messages may even be directed at you. IRC users tend to be a friendly group. They often greet newcomers to their channel. They may even ask you questions to draw you into the conversation or to make you feel welcome. If not, sit back and watch the conversation for a few minutes to get a feel for the group. Then jump right in when you feel comfortable.

Be cautious about how long you sit back and observe, though. The IRC community is leery of people who do not participate. Sitting back and just observing is called *lurking* on the Internet. Lurking too long could raise suspicions with the rest of the group on the channel. There is really no need to be shy, so join in the conversation.

Most of these channels are small communities or societies of people. They are an accepting group. As long as you treat them with respect and courtesy, they return the same to you. It is similar to going to a party. If you sit on the couch and do not talk to anyone, one or two people may come over and try to draw you out. However, if you keep sitting on that couch, keeping to yourself, sooner or later they start ignoring you.

If you jump right in, you find that these people are very much like the people in a small town or that you work with. They want to get to know you and for you to get to know them. They usually are on the channel to relax after work or just to sit and talk to friends, be those friends in their own town, in their state, across the country, or even around the world.

Whatever you do, do not be afraid to ask questions. These people will try to help you if they can. At the worst they will tell you where to go to find your answers. If, for instance, you were to ask them a question about how to do something in IRC, they may direct you to one of the *newbie* channels. A newbie on IRC is someone who is new to it.

Jump right in and join in on the fun and frivolity of the channels you select. If you choose one of the professional, technical, or hobby channels, observe for a few moments what the topic of discussion is before you jump in. If you have a question to ask, wait for a lull in the conversation or, if there does not seem to be one, when you feel comfortable.

If you use common sense and good manners when you join channels, you should do fine. However, remember that these people do not take kindly to rudeness. And they have the power to do something about it.

If they do not like something you said or the way you said it, they can kick you out of their channel and fix it so you cannot get back in.

Play nice and others will want to keep playing with you. Just remember there are humans behind those keyboards. Treat them as you want to be treated and you will find more friends and associates than you could ever hope for.

How Many Channels are There?

Each net has its own set of channels. The number of channels for each of them vary according to the time of day or night you log on. For the larger nets, EfNet and UnderNet, there are thousands of channels. For the smaller nets, that number can range from ten channels to hundreds during peak hours.

The EfNet, for instance, has around 7,000 channels during the day and more than 8,000 in the evening hours. The UnderNet might have close to 5,000 channels available at any time. DALnet averages between 2,300 and 3,000 channels. ChatNet, one of the smaller nets, averages between 250 and 300 channels no matter what time of the day or night you join.

The names for these channels can range from #AA (yes, there is an online Alcoholics Anonymous chat channel) to numerous sex channels. There are channels set up for socializing, like #teenchat or #teenland for teenagers and #letstalk or #friends for adults. There are channels set up for professionals, such as #writers or #realestate. There are channels set up for technical help, like #techtalk or #WindowsNT. And, of course, there are help channels, like #newbies, #mirc, and #wastelands. Channels like #coins or #crafts are for collectors and crafters. There are numerous state and city channels set up to attract people from those areas, like #michigan or #minnesota. Then of course there are several sports channels for sports enthusiasts to come and talk sports. Almost every subject imaginable—and some you would rather not imagine—has a channel on IRC.

Tip: You probably noticed the number symbol (#) in front of the channel names. This symbol is very important. You need to include this for every channel you want to join. This symbol is part of the computer program for IRC. It tells the computer that you are giving it a command or requesting information about a channel.

The number of channels you find on each net is in direct proportion to the number of people logged on. As more people are logged onto IRC, many of the channels have dozens of people on them chatting.

At any give time you can find from 30,000 to over 40,000 users on the EfNet. On the UnderNet you may find between 20,000 and 30,000 users. The DALnet is a little small; you may only find between 15,000 to 20,000 users on at any time. The smaller nets, like ChatNet, have any-where from 1,300 to 2,000 users on during peak hours.

As you can see by the number of users for each net, this affects the number of channels a net has. It also affects the number of people you find in certain channels.

How Do I Find a Channel?

With so many channels out there, you are probably wondering how to find a channel you want to join. You might even be asking, "How do I know what channels are available on IRC?" Well, IRC has thought of that. It has a command you can use to pull up a list of all the channels on the net you are on.

When you use the command to get a list of channels on the net you are on, you get an alphabetized list of every channel. This list gives you the name of the channel, the number of people that are in that channel at that time, and the topic that was set for the channel, if there is one.

 Warning: With the larger nets, pulling up a channels list can disconnect you from your server. These lists are so long some servers see them as *floods*. Floods are excessive lines of text being generated by one user.

Some of these lists can be quite long and it may even take several minutes for your program to load all the names. It may take you awhile to read through all the channels to find the one you would like to join. But, until you find a home, this is the best way to find out what is being offered on any net.

 Warning: This list includes every channel that is on that net. Therefore, if you have children, you do not want to run this list while they are present. You may also want to run the list and write down the names of the channels that would be appropriate for them to visit and instruct them which channels they may visit. There are sometimes upwards of 50 or more sex channels formed on at least two of the major nets.

The Nets and Their Channels—A Composite

Following is a composite list of the nets and the channels you can find in those nets. This is only a partial listing. By the time you buy this book and get on IRC, I'm sure the lists will have grown considerably. These lists give you an idea of what is available on each of the nets.

What is to follow are screenshot samplings of a channels list I ran for several of the nets. I am not going to include every channel that appeared on those lists; you could almost fill a whole book with them. However, these are samplings from several nets, including DALnet, UnderNet, EfNet, and ChatNet. These give you an idea of what kind of channels are being offered as well as what a list looks like. One thing you notice about these lists is that they are alphabetized. This makes it easier for you in the long run to find the channel you would like to join.

I have included a screenshot of the list showing some of the numerous sex channels. I do this to give you an example of what you can expect to see when you do a channels list (see Figures 2-1, 2-2, 2-3, 2-4, and 2-5).

```
#!center          1     ■■■■ iCENTER.net Admin Channel ■■■■
#30plus           2
#40plus           2
#50+Central       1     ■■■■■■■■■■ Welcome..Clean, Light, Chat :} ■■■■■■■■■■
#ad&d             1
#admin            1
#antillies        1     antilies is only a memory, everyone is on #IrishPub
#Banzai           2
#beginner         1     Beginner Help/Chat Channel---*All Are Welcome Here*!
#bridge           2
#bt               4
#castlegarden     3     the Roses are Blooming ... must be Spring!
#chat             2
#Christians       2     -= #Christians =- <><> Welcome ■ Fellowship/Discussi
#delphi           1
#hardradio        1
#havenet          2
#hey_you          1
#html             1
#IMUG             1
#intp             1
#irchelp          2
#lastwlkabout     2
#macintosh        3
#Magic-Oracle     1
#MaximumExposure  1
#MLsPlace         2     Where the gift of submission is the greatest gift of
```

Figure 2-1

```
#■■■■■■■sexpix         1
#■■■■■■■■■■■■          1
#!!!!!!!!!!!!!!!ANIMATED          1
#!!!!!!!!!!!!xxx-site   7
#!!!!!!!!!OralCopulation          1
#!!!!!!!!torch10        2
#!!!!!!!amateur_wife_pics          1
#!!!!!!amature_wife_pics           3
#!!!!!BigTitTrade 3
#!!!!!ohioboy      1
#!!!!ADULT_CLIPART      1
#!!!!Bro_Sis_Sex 1
#!!!!Flirt        10
#!!!!FreeEroticaPics    3
#!!!!sexpics       3
#!!!adultpictrading!!! 2
#!!!amateur_wife_pics 1
#!!!FLIRT          2
#!!!Northern_Virginians          1
#!!!yngteensexpics      4
#!!!younggirlsex 2
#!!businesswebadvertising         1
#!!Married&Playing      12
#!!SexPicNet      1
#!!teensex        1
#!COOL!           1
#!DIP-CREW!       2
```

Figure 2-2

```
#Jesus             1    Come and talk about Jesus!
#JESUS!            1    ■JESUS! the Ministry Channel on EF-Net - http://www.an
#Jesus-Loves-U     8    Jesus is King of Kings, and wants Relationship with yo
#JesusCafe         1    "Jesus"  God's Antidote to sin!
#jet               1    goto #NASCAR_WINSTON_CUP
#jo'sroom          1    welcome......friendly chat only
#juggling-group    1    Not just about juggling..........Chat about anything!
#k`ilaj-ta         1
#KansasCity        2    Big Blue Kansas Sky.... not, brrrrrrrr!
#karmacafe         6    Congratulations Corwyn, and Kristinia too!!!
#KCbi              1
#Kelekona          1    A home away from home for thoughtful dragons. See also
#KellKatChat       1    Come on in and talk to the GREAT KELLKATT!!!!
#Kentucky2         1    Kentucky Chat
#kewl_chat         1    SHIT!! I'M ADDICTED!!!! I DIDNT EVEN GO TO CLASS!!!
#Kewlcafe          3
#kimiesplace       1
#KineticMadness    2
#kku               1    ■■Hello Khon Kaen■■
#koolsk8ers        1    I   JUST DYED MY HAIR! WOOHOO
#kricket's_korner  2    RollingOnLaughingFloor
#kryptoks_kabin    5    Ok, it wasn't never, it was 2 hours late.
#kugkai            1    ■■How deep of Your Love■■
#Lady-in-Red's_Place 2       COME IN AND PULL UP A CHAIR
#lake              2
#lchat             3    A friendly chat channel for ladies (no men)
```

Figure 2-3

```
#mellon            1
#mellow_gold       2
#melonpatch        2
#Melrose_Place     1
#melvin            1
#men               1    ladies looking for men...
#mentos            2
#Menzoberranzan    1    The City Of The UnderDark.
#MERP              1
#MESSIAH           1
#metalchat         1
#mexicanos         1
#mexico2           1
#miccey            1
#Michigan          17   Welcome to Michigan
#michiganchat      6    -==</>==<|>==</>==- THE Michigan CHAT Zone -==</>==<|>
#michiganfreinds   1
#michiganfriends   2
#mid               1    Kansas and Mid America
#MIKKL             1
#military          3    welcome  military  vets friends and families
#military2         8    Welcome Military, Vets, Families & Friends...Come in a
#MilujemTa         2    Je t'aime
#mine4             1    out of room ... play song
#ministry          3    The Christian MINISTRY Channel ----->Homepage http://w
#minnesota         1
```

Figure 2-4

```
#sanctuary        1
#sand-bar         14    Where the ACTION is: come to the bar and meet people!
#sandbach         1
#sandman'sXXX     2
#saodem           3
#saplings         1     Pagan youth channel: Homepage at http://www.cruzio.com
#sarah            1
#Saskatoon        1
#satan            8     Satanism discussions. For information about satanism,
#satanspit        1
#Saudi            1
#sca              3
#scahs            9
#scandinavia      1     Här är jag!Mr Sweden!
#Sci-Fi           2
#scotland         5
#scouts           2     scOUTing all over the place!!!
#screenwriters    1
#scuba            4     " The Diving Channel "
#scumm_bar        1
#secrets          1
#semmm            1
#Sensual          1
#seoul            4
#sepultura        6
#serbian          2
```

Figure 2-5

What Can I Expect to Find in These Channels?

When you look at the list you just requested, you probably wonder how you know which channel to choose. You look at that list and wish you knew how to pick the right channel out of all those channels.

Let me give you an idea of what you can expect to see from some of these channels. I give you a description of some of these channels, then I give you a view into one or two of them.

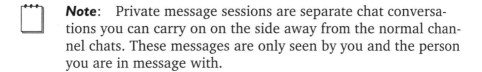

Note: Private message sessions are separate chat conversations you can carry on on the side away from the normal channel chats. These messages are only seen by you and the person you are in message with.

First, let us get the sex channels out of the way. Depending on which one of the sex channels you select, you may or may not see sex being chatted about. Several of these channels have normal chat conversations going on on the surface. Under the surface, in private chat sessions, may be a whole different story. Some of the tamer sex channels include: #netsex, #swingers, #hotsex, and #cybersex. However, when you join one of these sex channels be prepared to receive private messages from people in the channel.

> **Tip:** These private chat sessions, which vary from intense flirting to actual sexual banter, are called *hot chats*.

If you select one of the state or city channels, you are likely to find most of the people there are from that area. These people are either living there now or living elsewhere and are homesick for contact with others from their state or city. These people gather together because they have a common interest, their state or city. The conversation can range from the inane to serious discussions about anything one of the group has on their minds. Some examples of state channels you can find are: #texas, #arkansas, and #florida (see Figure 2-6).

state
channels

Figure 2-6

When you join any of the numbered channels like #30plus, #40plus, or #webe30+, you find people in there within that age group. Some of them are married and just enjoy chatting with others their own age. Some of them are single. Out of these single people you find some who are looking for their soul mate. Many a relationship has started on IRC and progressed to the church (see Figure 2-7).

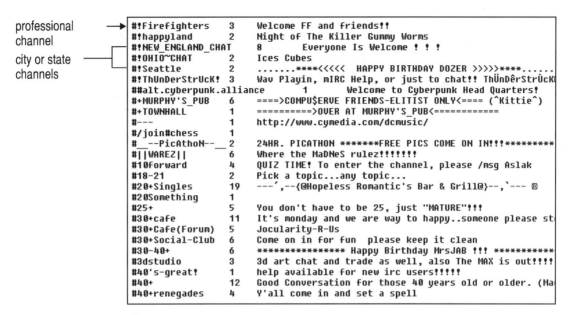

professional channel →

city or state channels

```
#!Firefighters         3    Welcome FF and friends!!
#!happyland            2    Night of The Killer Gummy Worms
#!NEW_ENGLAND_CHAT     8         Everyone Is Welcome ! ! !
#!OHIO~CHAT            2    Ices Cubes
#!Seattle             2    .......****<<<<<  HAPPY BIRTHDAY DOZER >>>>>****......
#!ThUnDerStrUcK!      3    Wav Playin, mIRC Help, or just to chat!! ThÜnDêrStrÙcK(
##alt.cyberpunk.alliance     1        Welcome to Cyberpunk Head Quarters!
#+MURPHY'S_PUB        6    ====>COMPU$ERVE FRIENDS-ELITIST ONLY<==== (^Kittie^)
#+TOWNHALL            1    =========>OVER AT MURPHY'S_PUB<============
#---                  1    http://www.cymedia.com/dcmusic/
#/join#chess          1
#__--PicAthoN--__     2    24HR. PICATHON *******FREE PICS COME ON IN!!!*********
#||WAREZ||            6    Where the MaDNeS rulez!!!!!!!
#10Forward            4    QUIZ TIME! To enter the channel, please /msg Aslak
#18-21                2    Pick a topic...any topic...
#20+Singles          19    ---´,--{@Hopeless Romantic's Bar & Grill@}--,`--- ®
#20Something          1
#25+                  5    You don't have to be 25, just "MATURE"!!!
#30+cafe            11    It's monday and we are way to happy..someone please st
#30+Cafe(Forum)     5    Jocularity-R-Us
#30+Social-Club      6    Come on in for fun  please keep it clean
#30-40+              6    *************** Happy Birthday MrsJAB !!! **********
#3dstudio            3    3d art chat and trade as well, also The MAX is out!!!!
#40's-great!         1    help available for new irc users!!!!!
#40+                12    Good Conversation for those 40 years old or older. (Ma
#40+renegades        4    Y'all come in and set a spell
```

Figure 2-7

Most of the people on these channels are looking for a place to come and unwind after a long day at work. You see a lot of silly antics going on as these people relax and let the stresses of the day float away. You also see them come to the aid and support of any of their group in need. These channels are tight-knit little communities of people. They are almost like an extended family.

Then, of course, you have the dozens of teen channels, like #teen13, #teen15, #teendate, and #teenshack. Teens have their own channels so that they can have a place to chat with others their own age about clothes, school, sports, boys, and girls. They come to these channels to meet friends and to relax after a day's pressures from school, parents, and their peers (see Figure 2-8).

```
#Takeover         1
#talk1            1
#tamil            2
#tampa            2
#Tattoo_You       2
#tcg              1
#Teachher         1
#teapot           2
#Techno/House     1
#teen_Bible       1
#teen13           1
#TEEN15           3
#Teen2            1
#teenbar          2
#teenchat2        1
#teenchats        1
#teencool         1
#TeenCUseeme      1
#teendate         1
#teenland         1
#teenmamak        2
#Teenpics         1
#teenragerz       1
#teensexpics      3
#teenshack        1
#teensysop        9
#tehotarik        1
```

Figure 2-8

In the few professional channels you find people within that profession. For instance, in the #writers channel you find writers from all genres, some published and some who are trying to get published. You also find publishers and editors there. Generally, the discussion runs along the lines of whatever the channel name is, professional discussion. When you visit the #writers channel, you find the people talking about writing. They are either getting updates from each other about how their writing is progressing or they are chatting about the various technical or mechanical aspects of writing. Some other professional channels you find include: #artists, #pianists, and #aviation (see Figures 2-9 and 2-10). If you do not find a professional channel that fits your needs, you can certainly create your own. I explain how to do that later in this chapter.

professional or support channels

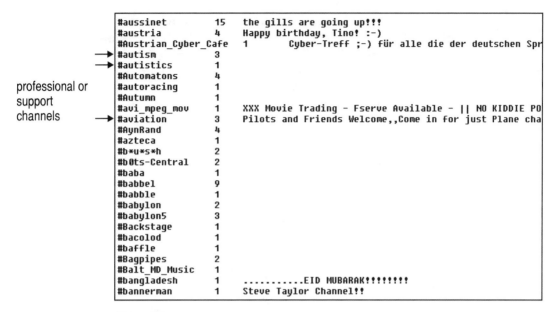

```
#aussinet              15     the gills are going up!!!
#austria                4     Happy birthday, Tino! :-)
#Austrian_Cyber_Cafe    1         Cyber-Treff ;-) für alle die der deutschen Spr
#autism                 3
#autistics              1
#Automatons             4
#autoracing             1
#Autumn                 1
#avi_mpeg_mov           1     XXX Movie Trading - Fserve Available - || NO KIDDIE PO
#aviation               3     Pilots and Friends Welcome,,Come in for just Plane cha
#AynRand                4
#azteca                 1
#b*u*s*h                2
#b0ts-Central           2
#baba                   1
#babbel                 9
#babble                 1
#babylon                2
#babylon5               3
#Backstage              1
#bacolod                1
#baffle                 1
#Bagpipes               2
#Balt_MD_Music          1
#bangladesh             1     ...........EID MUBARAK!!!!!!!!
#bannerman              1     Steve Taylor Channel!!
```

Figure 2-9

professional channel

```
#argh                   1
#arkansas               1     lynn's here now...  :)
#Armenia                1     Welcome to Armenia !!!
#arsenal                1     Arsenal FC: http://zeus.bris.ac.uk/~bzims/irc.html
#Art_Bell               1
#artis                  1
#artists                1
#arvika                 1     test
#Ascension_Jr           1
#asd                   13     lagg monster attacking
#ashesburning           1     Now Serving: Green Eggs and Ham
#ashok                  1
#asia                   1
#asians                 2
#Astrology              1
#astronomy              1
#ASTURIAS               5     Cena con sidra el día 10 a las 11 en Avilés
#asylum                 2     I'm the master of the world and I have no fear of man.
#Athas                  1
#atheism                2     Why is life so much more wonderful after Panty lays an
#athletic               1     Cercata está dormido
#atlanta2               1
#atlantic.canada        1
#atomic                 1
#auco                   1
#AuQuebec               1
```

Figure 2-10

There are several channels that you can go to for technical help. Some of these channels are set up to help you with IRC questions, like #irchelp, #ircnewbies, and #wastelands. Some of these are set up to help you with IRC software, such as #mirc or #helpcastle. And still others are set up to help you with other parts of the Internet like #webmaster, #html, or #linpeople. These are help channels so you do not see a lot of idle chatter going on here (see Figure 2-11). You have knowledgeable and helpful experts answering questions from visitors. So, do not be afraid to come to any of these channels if you need help.

```
→  #helpcastle        1    Mirc <----------------- neubie help & chat ----------
   #hispanos_amigos  1    ¡LATINOS! ¡ESPAÑOLES! ¡HISPANOABLANTES EN EL MUNDO! ¡U|
   #Hole-in-the-Wall 1    Put your own hole in......
   #HomeSchoolers     1    Lunch Break(SixMEs4U)
   #hornylonleygirl  1    Ladies come in and relex yourselves. Only 18+ and Over|
   #horses            2    Welcome to the CyberBarn
   #Horsin            2
   #hot_sex          15     !!!!! 18+  leave your clothes at the door and let's h|
   #hot_tub          12    Kitty says Congratulations tbolt...kisses....
   #house_of_Art      1    A Gorean Tavern where the slaves are hot and the paga |
   #Humblepie         1    Leila's throne room
   #Imsco             1
   #IndecentProPosals      3        Reward-> for anyone with a clue
   #Indigo-girls      1    it's a long, long way to tipperary...
   #INNMates          1
   #insurance         1    Yeah right
   #inutopia          4    The Best Little Chat Channel on DAL
   #ircbar           15    Self-Serve Bar.... Make Your Own Party !!!!
→  #irchelp           5    Welcome to the IRC Help Channel.  If you have any ques|
   #irclub           12    Chass's House of horror...
   #ircnewbies       16    IRC / mIRC Questions Answered If We Feel Like iT! :-P
   #Iron_Earnie       1    are we having fun on 4.1?
   #Iroquois~TeePee   1    Sit In the babbling brook and babble while your buns g|
   #israel            1    The Falafel bootke
   #jamestown         2    Bullwink was here..where were you???
   #jellybeanz        9    k so like its monday!!!!! cheer up people.....we got t|
```

help channels

Figure 2-11

These are just some examples of what you can expect to find out there on IRC. It is a sampling of some of the channels that are available for you to try. Each channel has its own separate group of people. These people all have their own personalities, as does the channel. You need to test the waters until you find the niche that feels right for you.

You find as you wander around, or surf as the Internet community calls it, that these channels are like having a group of friends all meet at someone's house for a picnic or a little party. As these groups form you find the same things going on here that you find in real life. You have some who are the leaders, the ones others look to for guidance or direction. You find moderators here. These are the ones who step in and become referees whenever there is trouble or strife.

Yes, you see that happen here, too. Although you are communicating over the computer and across miles using a modem, these are still people out there with their varying personalities and opinions. Just as you have little arguments and disagreements occur in real life, you have them here. Sometimes these arguments escalate into full-blown battles. When that happens, some of the group takes off and forms a new channel.

Just as arguments and battles can and do happen in channels, so do tight bonds form. As I mentioned before, many people have met on IRC and later gotten married. The same kind of close relationship also forms between the other members of these channels. These groups of people become almost like an extended family. When one member is going through a tough time, either financially or emotionally, the other members rally around that member and offer their support and advice or just lend a shoulder to cry on. They also come to the defense of any of their members if a stranger comes in attacking someone.

Such close bonds are formed in these channels that many of these channels plan and hold parties. People from these channels drive or fly thousands of miles to attend one of these parties. They have talked to these people online for months or even years and want to meet them face-to-face. These IRC parties are being held all over the country almost all the time.

One of the reasons many of the people on IRC believe these close ties are formed is due to the very nature of IRC. It lets you get to know the person before your eyes let you form opinions about them. What you get on IRC is pure and simple personalities. There are no races, no color on IRC. If you want to get technical about it, everyone is black and white—the black and white of the words on the screen. Everyone is equal. Depending on the nickname you give yourself, you can even be genderless.

Granted, there are some people on IRC, just as there are in real life, who pretend to be other than they are. There are some who come to IRC to act out a fantasy. And, yes, since no one can see you, you can be whoever or whatever you like. However, eventually the true person does come out. Your personality does eventually come shining through. And, I would add, a good majority of the people on IRC can see through subterfuge.

Warning: If you are female and choose a feminine-sounding nickname for yourself, you can expect to get private messages from strangers. These messages often are sexual in content. Therefore, if you wish to avoid these, choose an androgynous nickname or a more masculine one. If you choose to stay with a feminine nickname, you have to learn how to handle these kinds of messages.

I know that many of you parents out there are concerned about your children being on IRC. You have heard the stories on the news about pedophiles who stalk children, often luring them into their webs. You should be concerned. It certainly does happen. This is where your parenting skills are put to the test. My advice to you is to counsel your children about this kind of thing happening. Advise them to call for you to come help them if one of these people starts sending them messages that make them uncomfortable.

I have met several children whose parents sit beside them when they are on IRC. These parents choose the channels their children are allowed to go to. They are there to offer their support if the child needs it. This may not be an option for you depending on the age of your child. We all know how much teenagers value their privacy. However, it would be a good idea to let your child be aware of what can happen out there in IRC land and let them know you are there to help them or to come to their rescue if they need you.

One more note for your reference: The IRC community is a self-governing community. You find that these people are quite good at policing themselves. If someone is acting out of turn or in an abusive way to other members of the group, one or more of the members takes over and takes care of that person. The same holds true with children on IRC. If a child lets another adult know that someone is messaging them with lewd messages or trying to send them smutty pictures, the adult takes care of the offender. I myself have done this.

The majority of the IRC community is just like your friends and neighbors. They are on IRC to have a good time, to meet friends, and to relax. They form tight bonds and do not allow anyone to abuse their members or their sanctities, their channels. This may be one of the reasons that IRC is so popular and so addictive, the relationships you form here. Go into it with your eyes open and do not keep looking at that clock. Time slips away from you very quickly while you are chatting. Just enjoy, make friends, and be yourself.

How Do I Make My Own Channel?

You have brought up a list and you cannot seem to find any channel that you want to join. Or, you have joined some of the channels, made a few friends, and now want to create your own channel. How do you do create your own channel? you ask.

There are a couple of ways to create your own channel. The first and easiest way is to just pick a channel name that is not already in use and simply join that channel. Then you would just invite your friends to join you on your new channel.

 Tip: To join a channel, you type forward slash join #channel name. It would look like this: **/join #<channel name>**. Within the brackets you would type the name of the channel. Notice there is no space between the slash and join but there is between join and the # symbol. Also note that you do not include the brackets when typing a channel name.

With a couple of the nets you can register a channel. What registering a channel does for you is make it permanent. In other words, the channel is there even when you cannot be. When you simply join a channel that you create, the channel disappears when the last person leaves that channel.

When you register a channel with the nets that allow you to do that, the administrators of that net put what is called a *bot* on your channel. A bot is a self-running program. The bot belongs to the net organization and its only purpose is to keep your channel open and protect it.

Of course, you may put your own personal bot on your newly created channel. It keeps your channel open for you. However, this means leaving your computer on and connected to your Internet account and IRC 24 hours a day. For many this is just not a feasible option. I go into bots more later in this book.

With the UnderNet and ChatNet, you can register your channel with their organization committees. They have a form for you to fill out. The information they request is pretty much standard between these two nets. Following is an example of the information these two nets request. This one is from the UnderNet (see Figure 2-12). The Under-Net registration form can be found at: http://irc.direct.ca:7357/.

```
################################################################
#                    Undernet Channel Service                  #
#                      Registration Form                       #
################################################################
# Instructions:                                                #
#  o Read the Channel Service Committee Guidelines             #
#     This document can be obtained from:                      #
#       ftp://ftp.undernet.org/pub/irc/docs/X/CSC-guidelines   #
#       /msg helpbot get CSC-guidelines                        #
#  o Fill out this registration form completely                #
#     If you need help, ask in #cservice.                      #
#  o Email completed form to cservice@undernet.org             #
#     Please be sure to include this form in the               #
#     BODY of your email, NOT as an attachment.                #
#  o If you do not receive acknowledgement of receipt of       #
#     this form within 2 weeks, please email it again,         #
#     stating that it is a second attempt.                     #
#  o If your channel is not registered within 4 weeks,         #
#     you may email cservice@undernet.org to find out why      #
################################################################


-----------------------------------------------------------------
NOTE:  Channel registration is not meant as a means to start a new
       channel. It is meant for previously established channels
       to have an opportunity to have some stability. If you are
       first starting a new channel, then just start it, give it
       some time to make sure you have a decent userbase, and then
       consider registration. Thanks.
-----------------------------------------------------------------


A) Your Real Name :
B) The usual nick you use :
C) Your E-mail address :
D) The user@host that you use on irc :
   {the address in your /whois on IRC}
   {please try to include asterisks (*) wherever necessary}
E) Channel Name :
F) Purpose of channel :
   {brief description}
G) Supporter's list :
      This is a list of people who support you as channel
   manager of this channel and who will frequent the channel.
   You may want to CC them a copy of your application.
   -Please do NOT include yourself as a supporter.
   -Please do NOT use 2 (or more) different email addresses
   of a user as being 2 (or more) different supporters.
   Each entry in this list must be a different user.
```

```
--------------------------------------------------------------------
         Nickname        |        E-mail address
--------------------------------------------------------------------
  1:
  2:
  3:
  4:
  5:
  6:
  7:
  8:
  9:
 10:
--------------------------------------------------------------------
PLEASE NOTE -- You must have at least 10 supporters to register
          a channel. You also may only register 1 channel.
--------------------------------------------------------------------
```

Figure 2-12   UnderNet channel registration form

It takes anywhere from one to three weeks for you to get a response back on your request to register your channel. Once your application has been approved by the net's committee, it issues you a bot. It sends you an e-mail notifying you of its acceptance of your registration and informing you of your bot status. You also receive instructions on how to program and use the bot on your channel.

Then you simply invite the bot onto your channel and program him. Yes, the bots have a gender—they are male. Now your channel remains open and listed on the channels list 24 hours a day. You have control of your bot and only you can determine if you wish to allow others to have equal access to your bot. A word of advice here: Only let someone you would trust with your life have access to your channel bot. Remember, this bot belongs to the net, not you. Anything someone else does to that bot reflects on you. You are responsible for the bot and if someone abuses it, you are the one the net administrators come to.

What are Channel Operators?

Now you have created your own channel or have registered your channel. What happens next? When you join to create your own channel, you notice that there is a little symbol beside your name. This symbol is the @ sign. This signifies that you are the channel operator. When you get your bot, he has that symbol beside his name.

A channel operator is the person who is the channel manager or the person in charge. The @ symbol gives you certain powers. With the channel operator's status, you have the power to create a topic, give others operator's status, kick people off your channel, and, if you want, keep those pesky people from coming back. You also have the power to set the modes for your channel. I go into more detail about all these commands and modes in the next chapter.

With a registered channel the bot has the power. As administrator for that bot, you have access to it and can request that the bot appoint you a channel manager too. Then, because you are the administrator of the bot, you can request from him that others be made channel operators and you can also use him to do all the things you can do as a channel manager. Or you can do them yourself. The advantage to using the channel bot to do these things is that the others in the channel do not know who is bestowing favors on them or who is kicking them from the channel. Another advantage is that some of the commands you use through the bot are more permanent.

Can I Join Multiple Channels?

After you have requested your list, you may find that there are a couple of channels that you would like to join at the same time. Can you do that? Of course you can. It is like having two files open in a windows package. You have a window for each channel you join.

As with your other windows applications, you can tile or cascade these windows. You can resize them and rearrange them any way that is to your liking. This is, of course, assuming you are using a Windows-based chat software program. Later in this book I detail two of the more popular Windows-based chat software programs for you.

Once you have joined the channels you want, simply toggle between the channel windows and carry on or observe the conversations in both channels. I have witnessed some people on IRC joined in up to ten channels at a time. I personally would not advise this. It is very hard to keep up with the conversations going on in one busy channel sometimes. Ten channels could not only tax you but your computer. It does not break it by any means. However, you could get dumped from IRC rather quickly because your machine cannot keep up with all the activity.

Can I Be on More Than One Net at a Time?

As you become more comfortable and proficient in your IRCing, you may want to try your hand at joining channels in more than one net. Can you do that? Of course you can. However, you have to have the software to be able to do it.

To be in more than one net at a time, you either need to have a second copy of your chat software or you have to have one particular piece of chat software that has been designed to let you be on more than one net at a time. But it can be done.

To be in two or more nets at one time, you open one of your chat software programs and select the server to connect you to the first net. Then you join the channel or channels you wish to be on. To get to the second net, you open the second chat software program, and select the server for the second net. You just repeat this process for each of the nets you wish to be on.

With the special software, you simply log onto each of the servers for the nets you wish to be on. With this software, each server and each channel gives you a window within your window. Then you simply toggle between the windows. With the two chat programs, you have to minimize the application windows and tile them. Then you toggle between the two or more application windows and chat windows.

Summary

With the information you have received in this chapter, you should feel pretty comfortable joining just about any channel you choose once you get connected to any one of the dozens of nets out there. You now have a pretty accurate idea of what to expect out of the behavior and activities that go on in these channels.

You can now call up a list of channels and confidently pick a channel that you enjoy being a part of. You are able to determine what kind of people you find there and what they are talking about, in general terms of course.

You know the kinds of channels that each net has to offer. You also know which channels you should avoid if that's not your cup of tea. You know where to go if you are looking for professionals to help you or in your field of expertise. If you have children, you know where to send them and where to steer them clear of.

Once you learn how to use all the commands that are covered in the next chapter and choose the software that suits your needs, you are able to join more than one net at a time. You may even want to take what you have learned in this chapter and get yourself involved in more than one channel in each chat session you participate in.

Let's move on to Chapter 3 and learn about IRC commands.

Chapter 3

The Commands

Now you have learned how to select a channel and how to join it. You have probably even been sitting back and watching the conversations rolling by and maybe you have even joined in on some of those conversations.

> ### *In this chapter you learn:*
> - ☑ What those strange-looking characters and phrases mean that appear on channels
> - ☑ What the difference is between user commands and mode commands
> - ☑ What all the IRC commands are, how to type them, and what they do to the channel, to you, or to other users

Commands are the foundation upon which all your IRC adventures and conversations are based. Let's see what commands can do for you or to you.

What are They Doing?

You are feeling a little more comfortable with your IRC experience and you begin to notice things going on within the channel that you do not understand. You ask, What are they doing?

You see things like people making action statements that look something like this: ***katy welcomes joe to the channel**. Sometimes you see certain messages appear in color. This depends on which IRC software program you are using. You wonder how they do those things.

There may even be times when you notice messages appear on the screen that are not part of the conversation. These are channel mode messages. They look something like this: **katy changes channel mode to +nt** or **katy changes channel mode to +o joe**. You want to know how you can do these things too.

You see all these strange things popping up on your screen. Some of these things look like they change something within the channel or affect people in the channel. Some of them even change the appearance of the messages in the channel. You wonder what they are, what these things mean, and how they are done.

These things are called commands. There are several different kinds of commands you can use to make these changes happen. Some of them you can do no matter what your status is on the channel. For others, you have to be a channel operator in order to perform.

It is very important for you to understand and learn all the various commands. Most of them work with almost all of the IRC software programs that are available. These commands were designed to work with the IRC servers. (Remember, IRC servers are the computers that make all of IRC possible.) You need to learn all the commands to be able to do all the things that can be done in IRC.

To make learning commands easier for you I am going to break them down into two categories, user commands and mode commands. *User commands* are those that you, the user, type to create changes for yourself or that affect only you or one other person. *Mode commands* are those that create changes within the channel or that affect other users.

How Do They Do Those Things?

This is all fine and dandy, you say to yourself. But how do those people do all those things and how can I learn to do them? The first and most important thing for you to know is that all commands on IRC are preceded with a forward slash. In the last chapter I gave you the command for joining a channel—**/join #<channel name>**. This is an example of an IRC command.

The forward slash tells the server that processes all these conversations and makes sure messages get to where they are intended that there is a command coming its way. The servers use a special language called a protocol to communicate with each other. These forward slashes are part of that language. They tell the servers that they should sit up and listen, and follow instructions.

If you always remember to type a forward slash before you type any command you'll save yourself a lot of time and, most important, a lot of embarrassment. Many a user has forgotten that forward slash and sent a private message to the channel or sat there and watched as the command they were trying to execute appears on the screen as a part of the conversation. Then they have to retype the command again, remembering to type in that little slash to make the command work the next time. Not only that, they get to be the brunt of ribs from the others on the channel at their faux pas.

What are User Commands?

You are sitting at your computer watching the conversation on your favorite channel roll by when you notice someone change their nickname. A little bit later you notice someone type a message that is different from the others, like they are actually doing something rather than being a passive chatter. You sit up in your chair and ask, What is going on here?

What you are seeing are called user commands. User commands are those that you type to get information, whether that be information about yourself or others, or helpful information like help files or lists of channels or people on channels. These commands can also be used to send messages privately to others or to send them information you have in your files.

You can also use some of these commands to change the way your message appears on the channel or even to change your nickname. Usually these user commands only affect you and at the most one other person. Following is a list of the various user commands and what these commands do.

Note: In the following list of commands you notice instructions inside brackets, like /command <instruction>. When typing these commands, do not use the brackets and replace the instruction with the appropriate name.

/nick <nickname>—this command will allow you to give yourself a nickname. At any time you can change your nickname simply by typing this command. For instance, if you wanted to give yourself the nickname of betyboop, you could do so by typing **/nick betyboop**.

Note: When you log onto IRC you want to give yourself a nickname. This is part of the IRC culture—using nicknames. Beware, women, using a feminine nickname attracts advances from the males and IRC equivalents of mashers or Don Juans. So select your nickname carefully.

/join #<channel name>—this command lets you join a channel. Whenever you wish to join a channel, type this command along with the channel name. For example, if you wanted to join the channel #cartoons, you type **/join #cartoons**.

 Warning: Other than on DALnet, there is no way to protect your nickname from being used by someone else. If you do log on and someone else is using your favorite nickname, either select another one or add a number, a dash, or an underline to the end of your nick.

/topic #<channel name>—gives you the topic that has been set for the channel you indicated (see Figure 3-1).

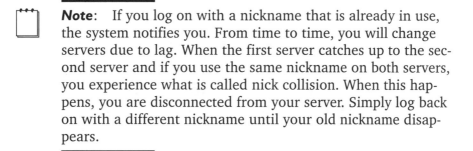

The topic
appears here in
the status window
when you type
the /topic
#<channel name>
command. ——→

Figure 3-1   /topic #<channel name> command

Note: If you log on with a nickname that is already in use,
the system notifies you. From time to time, you will change
servers due to lag. When the first server catches up to the second server and if you use the same nickname on both servers,
you experience what is called nick collision. When this happens, you are disconnected from your server. Simply log back
on with a different nickname until your old nickname disappears.

/list—gives you a list of all the channels on the net you are connected
to. When you connect to a server you can type this command in
the prompt line of your window to get a listing of channels. This
more than likely takes several minutes depending on which net
you are on and the number of channels that are available.

/list <parameters>—this command lets you set parameters for the
list. This lets you tell the command to limit the list to a certain
number. For instance, if you would only like to see a list of channels with at least five users and no more than ten users, you can
set those parameters in your command. It would look like this:
/list -min 5 -max 10. Then you only get a list of channels that
have a minimum of five people on them and a maximum of ten.
Of course you may use either the minimum -min or the maximum
-max parameter settings by themselves as well: **/list -min 5** or
/list -max 10.

/names—does the same as the /list command but it gives you a list of nicks that are in each channel.

/server <server address>—connects you to a server. For example, if you wanted to connect to ChatNet, you can type **/server irc.superlink.net**. Then you are logged onto that server and can type the **/join #<channel name>** command or the **/list** command.

/links—gives you a list of all the servers that have links to the server you log onto. The use for this command would be to tell you which servers would split off with yours in the event of a netsplit. (Remember we talked about netsplits in Chapter 1.)

/time—gives you the time for the server you are connected to.

/time <nickname>—gives you the time for the server of the nick you typed in.

/whois <nickname>—this command tells you if a particular nickname is on, their address, and where they are on the net. If katy wanted to find out if joe was on, she could type **/whois joe**. She then gets a message back telling her that joe is not on, joe: no such nick/channel, or that yes indeed he is on. If he is on, she gets a message that looks like this: **joe joe@domain.net is on #cartoons using server irc.superlink.net** (see Figure 3-2).

/whowas <nickname>—tells you where that nick was just before they left IRC. However, you must type this command within a minute or two of the nick leaving IRC, otherwise the server's memory has lost the information on that nick. This command gives you the same information as a /whois (see Figure 3-2).

/who #<channel name>—tells you who is on whatever channel you choose. If betyboop wanted to find out who was on channel #cartoons before she joined the channel, she would type **/who #cartoons**. She then gets a list of all the nicknames of the people who are on that channel (see Figure 3-2).

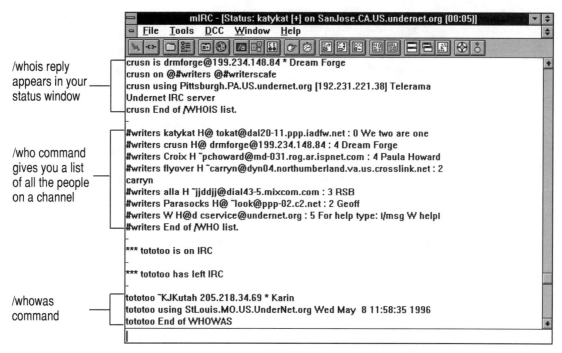

/whois reply appears in your status window

/who command gives you a list of all the people on a channel

/whowas command

Figure 3-2 /whois, /who, and /whowas command examples

/msg <nickname> your message—sends a private message to who-ever you put in the nickname slot. If joe wanted to send a private message to betyboop, he would type **/msg betyboop hi sweet lady, I have missed you**. This message goes to betyboop only; no one else on the channel or the net sees this private message (see Figures 3-3 and 3-4).

IRC users abbreviate nickname to nick, so you see nick used quite often when referring to nickname.

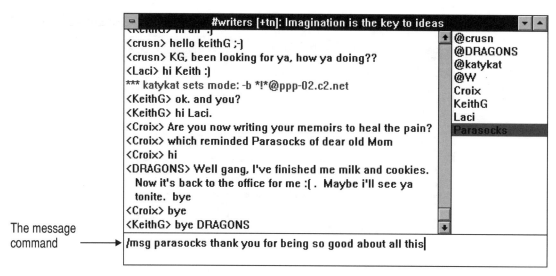

Figure 3-3   /msg command example

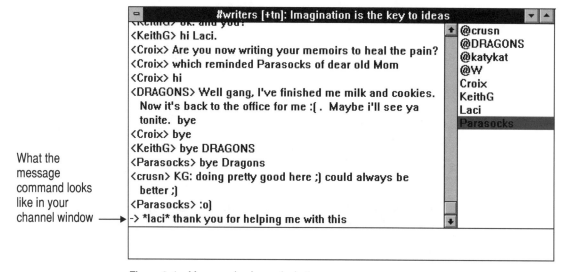

Figure 3-4   Message in channel window

Note: When you type **/msg <nickname> your message**, it appears on your main channel window but offset with stars. It looks something like this: ***betyboop* hi sweet lady, I have missed you**. Do not be alarmed; you are the only one who can see your private message.

/query <nickname>—this does the same thing as the /msg command. It starts a private chat conversation with the nick you indicated. The difference is that you do not have to type the /query <nickname> for each message you wish to send to this person. A query window opens and you simply type your messages in that window. When you are ready to end the private chat with this nick, you simply type **/query** (see Figure 3-5).

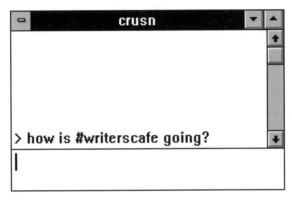

Figure 3-5   Query window

/ping <nickname>—this command tells you how long it takes that user's response or message to get to the channel and be seen by you or the other users. This is also referred to as *lag*. To get a ping reply on someone, you would type **/ping joe**. Then you get a response that looks like this: **ping joe 12 seconds**, or whatever his ping response is.

Note: The ping response is how long it takes between the time someone types their message and presses the return button and the time you actually see it. For instance, it would have taken 12 seconds for the people in the channel to have seen any message that joe typed (see Figure 3-6).

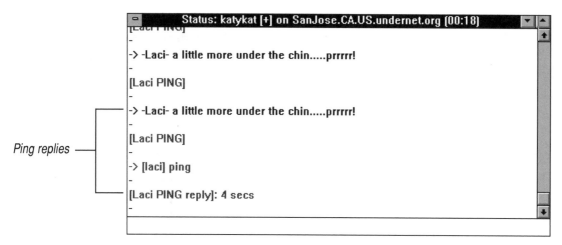

Ping replies

Figure 3-6   Examples of ping replies

/invite <nickname> #<channel name>—invites the nick to the channel you indicate. If joe wanted to invite katy to #cartoons he
would type **/invite katy #cartoons**.

/me <your message>—this command lets you type action type messages. For instance, if betyboop wanted to greet katy after she
joined cartoons, she could type **/me welcomes katy to #car-
toons**. This would appear on the screen as ***betyboop welcomes
katy to #cartoons**.

/notify <nickname>—notifies you as soon as the nick you typed in
joins IRC. If joe wanted to know every time he was on when betyboop joined IRC, he could type **/notify betyboop**. Then whenever she logged onto IRC, joe would be notified. It would appear
to him like this: **betyboop is on IRC**, and when she leaves it
would appear like this: **betyboop has left IRC**.

/ignore <nickname>—this command lets you type in the nicks of people you wish to ignore. There are times when someone makes a
nuisance of themselves and you want to put them on ignore so
that you do not have to see any messages they type, whether in
channel or in private messages. Betyboop has been getting hot
chat messages from bozo and she does not want to talk to him
any more, so she types **/ignore bozo**. Then whenever he tries to
send her a private message he gets a message back that says you
are being ignored by betyboop. When he is on channel she knows
he is there but does not see any messages he types to the channel.

All others in the channel are able to see his messages unless they put him on ignore also.

/away <message>—marks you as being away. This lets anyone who tries to message you know that you are not there. If betyboop has to leave for a few minutes to make herself a sandwich, she can type **/away getting a bite to eat**. Then whoever messages her gets that response. Also, as soon as she types that away message it appears on the channel, letting all there know she will be away for a few minutes (see Figures 3-7, 3-8, 3-9, and 3-10).

This is how you type the away message. →

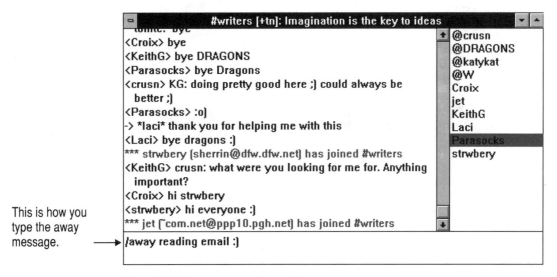

Figure 3-7 /away command example

This is what appears in the channel for the other users to see and it also appears in your status window. →

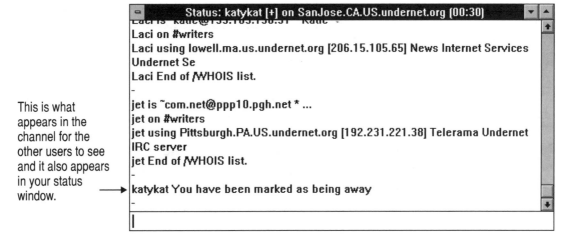

Figure 3-8 Away message example

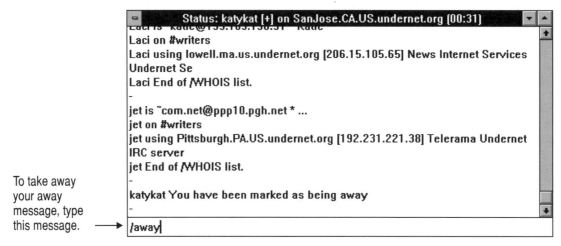

To take away your away message, type this message. ⟶

Figure 3-9   Reversing /away command

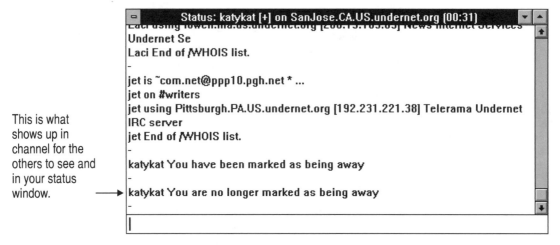

This is what shows up in channel for the others to see and in your status window. ⟶

Figure 3-10   Example of /away command reversal

/help—brings up a list of commands that there is a help file on. At the prompt line you can type in the topic you need help on. If you press Enter on a blank prompt line, you exit help. If katy needs help with the who command, she types **/help**, then in the prompt line she types **who**. The help file appears on her screen. To exit help, she simply hits Enter at the blank prompt line.

/leave #<channel name>—this command takes you out of the channel you are in. If joe is in #cartoons and wants to leave, he types **/leave #cartoons**.

/part #<channel name>—this command also takes you out of the channel you are in.

/exit—takes you out of IRC completely. If katy needs to leave IRC so that she can go to the store, she types **/exit**.

/signoff—also takes you completely out of IRC.

/quit—does the same thing as /exit.

/bye—also takes you completely out of IRC.

/bye <comments>—leaves your parting comments with the channel when you type this command. If betyboop wants to leave IRC and leave the channel with her parting thoughts, she types **/bye I'm off like an old prom dress** (see Figure 3-11).

This is what a bye message looks like when you quit IRC while you are still in a channel. →

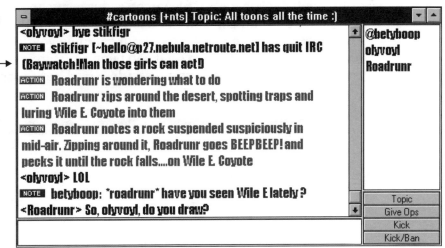

Figure 3-11   /bye command example

/set novice off—this command turns your novice mode off and lets you join multiple channels simultaneously. However, if you are using one of the IRC software packages I include later in this book, you need not use this command. It has been built into the software.

/set hold_mode on—pauses your screen once one screen full of messages has accumulated. This command is very effective when bringing up channels lists. Again, with the newer IRC software, you probably do not ever need to use this command. The newer software lets you scroll back and forth within the window it provides when you call up a channels list.

/set show_channel_names on—lists all the names on the channel when you join the channel. This is a command used with the older IRC programs. All the newer programs give you a names list as part of the window when you join a channel.

Note: DCC stands for direct client connections. It is a direct link between two clients—your machine and someone else's—without using the servers of IRC.

/dcc send <nickname> <filename>—this command lets you send a file from your computer to another person on IRC. While the file is being sent to that nick you can continue your other conversations. If joe wanted to send betyboop a picture of himself that he had in his files, he would type **/dcc send betyboop joe.gif** (see Figures 3-12 and 3-13).

This is how you type the dcc send command. ⟶

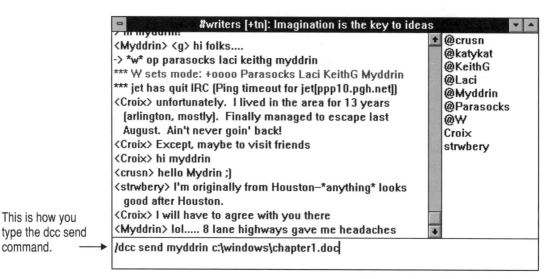

Figure 3-12 /dcc send command example

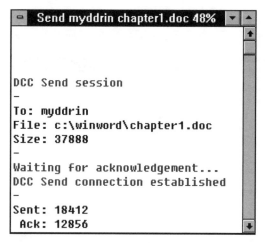

Figure 3-13   DCC send window

Tip: To make it easier and faster on both the sender and the receiver of DCC sends, it is advisable that you both be on the same server. The lag between you two is decreased, and in the event of a netsplit you both remain together.

/dcc get <nickname> <filename>—this is the command the person receiving the file needs to type in order to start the send/receive process. If betyboop wants to receive joe's picture, she types **/dcc get joe joe.gif**.

Note: When the net you are on is experiencing a lot of lag or if the two of you sending and receiving the files are lagged to each other, it may take you several tries before you successfully transfer the file. Or you may have to try again at another time.

/dcc chat <nickname>—lets you establish a private chat conversation with another nick. It works much the same way as /msg, the difference being that often you can chat with this nick using DCC chat no matter if your servers are lagging from each other. It is similar to being able to send messages from your machine to theirs, bypassing the lags. The other nice thing about this DCC chat function is that if one of you splits off, the connection is not lost. As soon as you reappear, you can resume chatting without having to restart a new DCC chat session (see Figures 3-14 and 3-15).

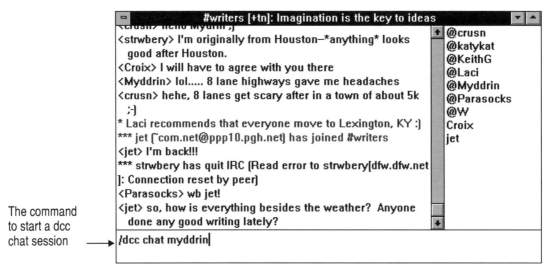

The command to start a dcc chat session ⟶ /dcc chat myddrin

Figure 3-14 /dcc chat command example

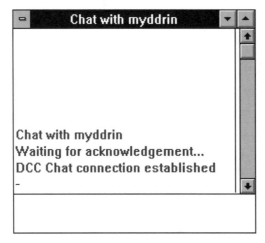

Figure 3-15 DCC chat window

Note: If you have a slow connection with your provider, you will experience lag or other problems with DCC chat.

Note: CTCP stands for client-to-client protocol. It allows you to pose questions to another user's client system, and get an answer.

/ctcp <nickname> finger—gives you idle time information on the nick you fingered. Idle time is how long it has been since that nick last typed a message (see Figure 3-16).

/ctcp <nickname> ping—gives you lag information on the nick you indicated (see Figure 3-16).

/ctcp <nickname> clientinfo—gives you a master index on the user's client information (see Figure 3-16).

/ctcp <nickname> userinfo—gives you information about the user. This is whatever information the user has programmed in for you to know (see Figure 3-16).

/ctcp <nickname> version—gives you information about the IRC software the user has installed (see Figure 3-16).

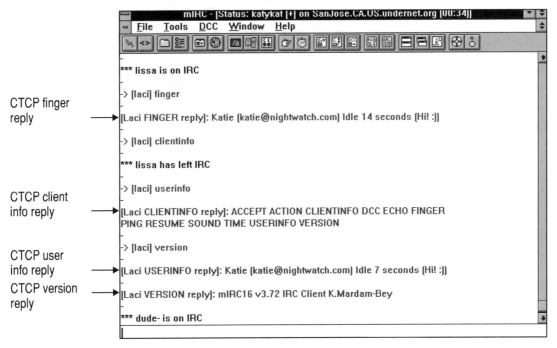

Figure 3-16 /ctcp command examples

What are Mode Commands?

You have seen messages that appear on the channel that are not messages from one person to another. These are messages that seem to have something to do with the channel. Sometimes these messages change the status of a user on the channel. You wonder to yourself, What in the world are these things, what do they do, and how are these people doing them? These are called mode commands.

Mode commands are those commands that change the characteristics of the channel or another person on the channel. Mode commands can only be executed by channel operators. Generally you see the mode commands as follows: **katy changes channel mode to +nt**. They appear as blocked or colored messages on your screen, depending on which IRC software you are using.

Following is a list of the various mode commands and what they do when they are activated.

/mode #<channel name> +o <nickname>—bestows channel operator's status on that nick. If betyboop wanted to give joe channel operator's status, otherwise known as ops in Internet lingo, she would type **/mode #cartoons +o joe** (see Figures 3-17 and 3-18).

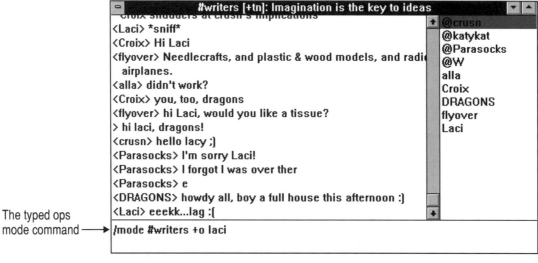

Figure 3-17   Ops mode command

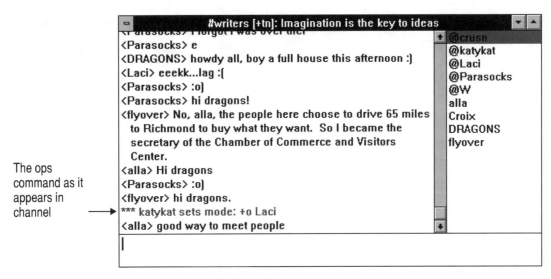

The ops
command as it
appears in
channel

Figure 3-18   Example of granting ops status

☞   ***Tip***:   It is wise to only give ops status to people you know.
There are some people out there who like nothing better than
to cause trouble for others by coming to a channel, getting ops
status, and then kicking everyone off the channel. This is their
idea of fun. So beware of who you give operator's status to.

/mode #<channel name> -o <nickname>—does the opposite of giving someone ops; it takes ops status away. If joe and betyboop
had an argument and he wanted to take her ops status away from
her, he would type **/mode #cartoons -o betyboop** (see Figures
3-19 and 3-20).

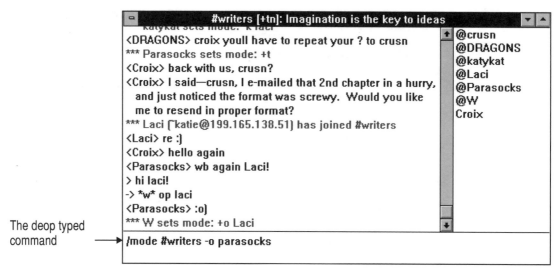

Figure 3-19   Deop mode command

The deop typed command → (points to: /mode #writers -o parasocks)

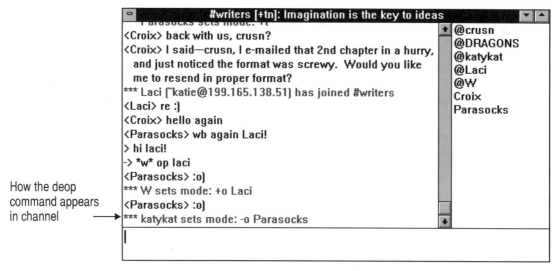

Figure 3-20   Example of deopping user

How the deop command appears in channel → (points to: *** katykat sets mode: -o Parasocks)

/topic #<channel name> <topic>—allows you to set the topic for your channel. If joe wanted to set the topic for his channel #cartoons, he would type **/topic #cartoons All toons all the time** (see Figures 3-21 and 3-22).

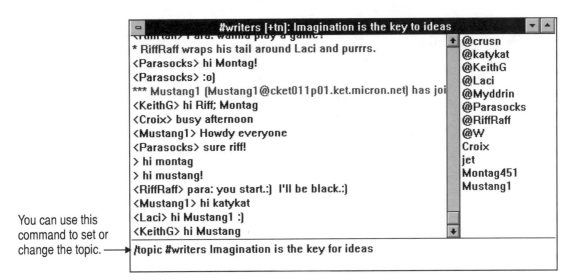

You can use this command to set or change the topic. →

Figure 3-21   /topic command

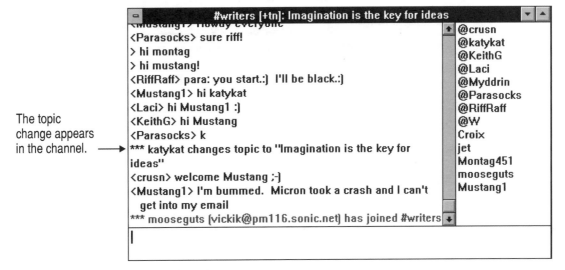

The topic change appears in the channel. →

Figure 3-22   Example of changing topic

 Technique: Any of the following channel modes can be used alone or in combination with others. The optimal protection for a channel would be the +spitn mode.

/mode #<channel name> +i—marks the channel as invite only. When a channel is marked invite only, no one can join that channel unless they are invited first. If katy wanted to hold a meeting between joe and betyboop to help them get over their argument, she could open a separate channel called #peace, then as channel manager with ops she would type **/mode #peace +i**. Then she would need to invite both betyboop and joe over to the new channel before they could join (see /invite command).

/mode #<channel name> +p—marks the channel private. Marking a channel private prevents it from showing up on a channels list.

/mode #<channel name> +s—does the same thing for the channel as marking it private. However, when a channel is marked secret, users do not show as being in that channel if someone outside the channel does a /whois or a /who.

/mode #<channel name> +t—makes it so that only those with ops can change the topic of the channel (see Figure 3-23).

Channel mode command →

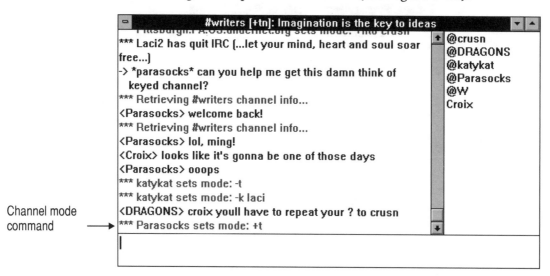

Figure 3-23   Setting a channel mode

/mode #<channel name> +n—prevents outside channel messages from being sent to the channel. This feature is nice because it prevents someone you may have had to kick off your channel from sending continuous, annoying messages to the channel even after they have been booted out.

/mode #<channel name> +m—makes the channel moderated so only those with ops are able to send messages to the channel. This is a nice feature if you have a guest speaker or if you use the channel as a classroom setup. It allows the speaker to have their say without interruptions (see Figure 3-24).

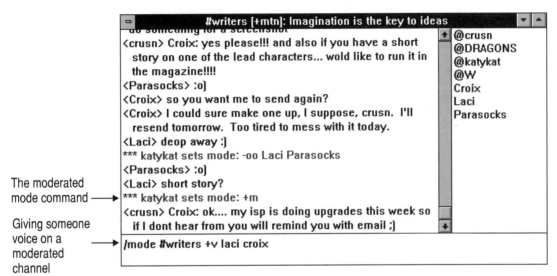

The moderated mode command →

Giving someone voice on a moderated channel →

Figure 3-24   Example of moderated channel

/mode #<channel name> +v <nickname>—this command gives a user without ops on a moderated channel voice. With the command activated for a nick that person can now send messages to the channel (see Figure 3-25).

The voice command as it appears on the channel →

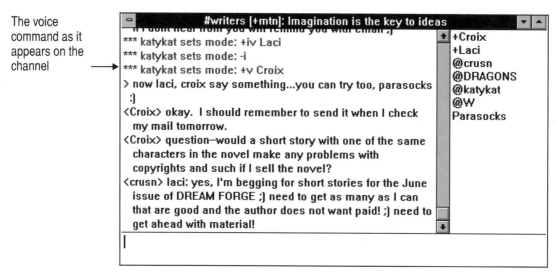

Figure 3-25 Example of giving voice to a user

/mode #<channel name> +l <number>—limits the number of users that are allowed on the channel. Whatever limit number you set, when that limit is met, no one else is allowed to join until someone leaves.

/mode #<channel name> +k <keyword>—marks the channel as keyed. This command does not let anyone in until they enter the correct keyword or password. If betyboop was not able to resolve her differences with joe and wanted to start her own channel and keep joe out, she could key her new channel. Let's say betyboop started her new channel as #cartoonys with a key of sylvester. She would join the channel, then type **/mode #cartoonys +k sylvester**. Now if katy wants to join this channel she has to type **/join #cartoonyssylvester**. Of course, betyboop has to give katy the password before she can join.

/kick #<channel name> <nickname>—this command kicks someone off the channel you are in. Katy and joe are in #cartoons and someone with the nick of jacka comes on and starts calling them names. Katy and joe both have ops, but katy is faster and has less patience than joe. She types **/kick #cartoons jacka**. Jacka is quickly and promptly booted out of the channel. The message that appears on katy's and joe's screens looks like this: ***jacka was kicked from #cartoons by katy** (see Figures 3-26 and 3-27).

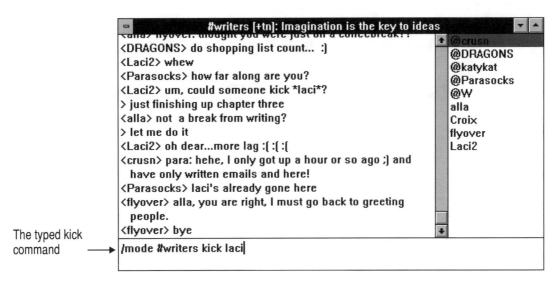

Figure 3-26   /kick command

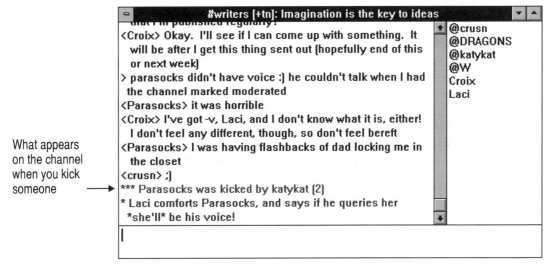

Figure 3-27   Example of kicking someone

/mode #<channel name> +b <nickname>—bans a user from your channel. Jacka has come back and is even more abusive. No matter how many times katy or joe kick him out, he keeps coming back. Now it is time for drastic measures. Katy once again is quicker and the one with the least patience. She types **/mode #cartoons +b jacka**. Then of course she has to kick him again.

This time jacka cannot get back into the channel. He gets a message that tells him he has been banned from the channel (see Figure 3-28).

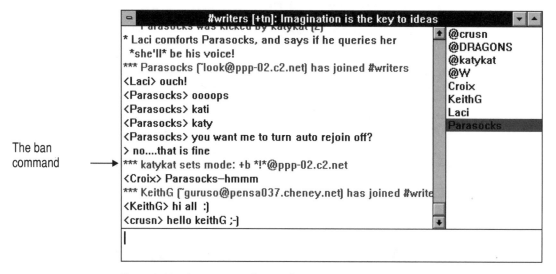

The ban command →

Figure 3-28   /ban command example

 Warning: Banning the nick alone may not be sufficient to keep someone out of your channel; after all, they can simply change their nick and get back in that way. There are two other bans you can use to make sure they do not get back in. One of these is called a user@host ban. You type **/mode #<channel name> +b <nick *!*user@host>**. The *!* is called a mask and tells the servers or the program to ban anyone using that user@host address. The user@host is the address the person uses while they are on IRC. You can get this information by doing a /whois on them. The second way to ban someone from your channel is to do a site ban. This is not advisable since it bans anyone who uses that site. To do a site ban, you would type **/mode #<channel name> +b <*!*@host*>**.

/mode #<channel name> -b <nickname>—removes the ban from the channel (see Figure 3-29).

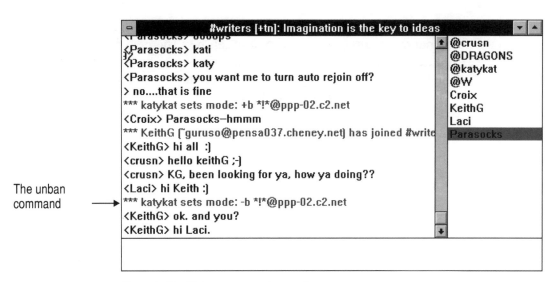

The unban command →

Figure 3-29   Unban command example

Summary

Learn most if not all of these IRC commands. They will be very important to you later as you learn to use your software. They are important to you now because without them, you will not be able to do much more than type your messages to the channel.

These user commands let you get information about other users, find out if your friends are on and where they are, and let you communicate privately to them. They also let you do more than type plain text messages to the channel, like action statements.

Use them to get CTCP information about users and use them to send information to other users. With the DCC send command you can send a friend pictures of your children or pets. Use the DCC receive command to let them send pictures back to you.

The mode command lets you control your channel if you have operator's status. You are able to set the channel modes, change or set the topic, and kick or ban offensive users from your channel. You are even able to give operator's status to your friends when they join you in your channel.

Take what you have learned so far about nets, servers, channels, and commands, and apply it to what you learn in the next few chapters about the IRC software that is available to you. The commands you have learned here will become very important as you learn to use the software that is discussed in Chapters 5 and 6.

Chapter 4

The Software

Now that you have a foundation of commands to work from, let's put that together with software and see what you can do with them.

> **In this chapter you learn:**
> - ☑ What chat software is
> - ☑ What the best chat software is
> - ☑ Where you can go to find this software
> - ☑ What other chat software is available and what it does for you

Let's take a look now at what you can find and learn about chat software.

What is Chat Software and What's Out There?

In early 1993 when I first found the Internet, the software available for IRC was pretty limited. When IRC began in 1988 there was no software. You logged on to the Internet and typed a command to take you to IRC. Then you had to type all those commands I gave you in the last chapter to be able to do anything. Those commands are called UNIX commands, for the UNIX systems that are the backbone of most of the Internet tools like IRC, e-mail, newsgroups, etc.

Some very smart and IRC-savvy people began designing software programs to make using IRC easier. One of these earlier software programs was Telix. Telix was a windows-based software package that took some of the UNIX-based commands and turned them into toolbar buttons or menu items.

Then some computer-smart college men began creating what were called scripts, which were computer programs that could run on top of the UNIX program and automated certain IRC activities. Two of these scripts were called Phoenix and Dreamer. Both of these were loaded or activated once you connected to an IRC net.

Phoenix was the first script that was designed, and it was soon passed from user to user through the DCC send function. Then Dreamer was designed with enhancements of the Phoenix script. Both of these scripts added features that let users activate kicks with a custom designed message for the kickee. They also included a feature that would protect the user from floods. Remember, a flood is when one person sends excessive pages or screens full of information to another user. Usually a flood causes the receiver to get disconnected from their server and, in extreme cases, disconnected from their provider.

In 1994 Caesar M. Samsi designed a new IRC program called WS-IRC. This program, like the older Telix program, provided you with an icon to click on and connect to IRC. WS-IRC went a few steps further than Telix and automated more of the IRC commands and functions. It was a *shareware* program, meaning that you pay a small fee to have the rights to use the full program. The shareware price was $29.95. With shareware programs, the designers sometimes add programming into them that cancels certain functions of the program after the free trial period is over (usually 60 days). Sometimes they program in a special registration message that appears each time you activate the program until you do register it. And sometimes the programmers do nothing special to their programs to entice you to register their program. They trust you to be an honest person and pay the shareware fee to register their product.

In early 1995, Khaled Mardam-Bey in London designed still another IRC program called mIRC. It included enhancements of the WS-IRC program, and he added a few new features. He continues to make improvements to this software, releasing a new version every few months.

This software used to be freeware. Recently Mardam-Bey chose to make it shareware, but he only charges a very minimal fee of $20 for the client—a very reasonable price for one of the best IRC clients on the market. You can find a copy of this mIRC software on the World Wide Web at http://www.tucows.com or at http://www.mirc.com/ and on the CD at the back of this book.

Mardam-Bey added some very nice enhancements to mIRC. He added a feature that lets you send and receive sounds called waves or .wavs. He also added something called a URL catcher. This enhancement saves web site addresses into a separate window. It also opens your browser and lets you view the web page by activating your web browser from IRC. This feature saves you the trouble of writing down these web site addresses every time someone gives them out on IRC. You also no longer have to type them in yourself after you take the time to open up your web browser. Mardam-Bey added several more features that I get into in the next chapter (see Figure 4-1).

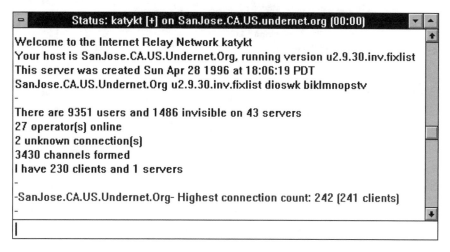

Figure 4-1

Then in November of 1995 Northwest Computer Services created another new software program for IRC called Pirch. This program is similar to mIRC in many ways but has some added features and enhancements. It has the same sound exchange functions and a URL catcher. In addition, the software has added a feature that lets you connect to more than one server at a time, allowing you to be on more than one net at a time. This is all accomplished within the same application window. mIRC only lets you do this if you open the program twice, and then you have more than one mIRC application window for each server rather than one application window with a separate window within it for each server as with Pirch.

Note: mIRC is a fully tested product. That does not mean that it does not have any bugs in it; it just means most of the bugs have been worked out.

Pirch is a shareware program also. The designer asks that you send $10 to register the program. Not a bad price for such an excellent software program (see Figure 4-2).

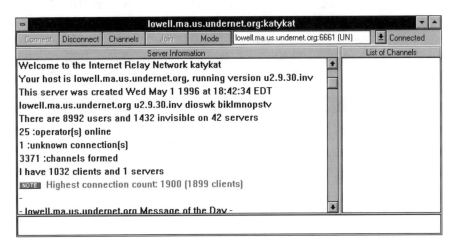

Figure 4-2

Either one of these IRC programs, also called clients in Internet lingo, are excellent. They are equally easy to use and provide you with excellent features to make your time on IRC easier and more pleasant. They come in both 16-bit and 32-bit versions for installation on either Windows 3.x or Windows 95 operating systems.

How Do I Get There From Here?

Both mIRC and Pirch are detailed in the following two chapters.

Installing either of these programs on your computer is relatively simple. mIRC is an executable program. Executable programs are very easy to install on your system.

With executable files, you simply double-click on the .exe file. In this case, it is mirc.exe. You can do this by clicking on the My Computer icon and then clicking on the C folder. When the C folder opens, it displays all your program folders. Find mirc.exe and double-click on it. Once you start the file executing, it installs itself on your hard drive and puts it in your Start menu (in Windows 95). You can use mIRC from there or you can create a shortcut for it on your desktop.

Pirch is a compressed, or zipped, file and requires that you unzip it before you can use it. There are several good programs at the sites I gave you earlier that unzip compressed programs.

When you unzip the compressed program, you are asked where you want to put it. I suggest that you put it in the same program group as the rest of your Internet programs. This makes it easier for you to open it up when you are ready to use it.

In Windows 3.x, mIRC, once it's executed, installs itself on your hard drive and creates a program file and icons for you. Then you simply double-click on the icon once you are connected to the Internet through your service provider.

After you have unzipped the program, you need to create a new program item in your program manager and select an icon for it. Here is how you set up a new program item in Windows 3.x:

➤ In Program Manager select and open the program group in which you want the icon for IRC to reside.

➤ Then click on the File menu item and select New. You get a dialog box that asks you to select either Program Group or Program Item. Select Program Item and click on OK.

➤ You get another dialog box called Program Item Properties. This time it wants to know the filename of the program item. You can type IRC in the Description line and tab down to the Command line.

➤ Now you can click on Browse and search until you find either the mirc.exe or pirch.exe file, depending on which program you are installing. These are in the directory you saved the IRC file in when you unzipped it.

➤ Next, you double-click on that filename, which puts it in the Command line.

➤ Now click on the Change Icon button and select the icon either program has provided for you. After you have selected your icon, click on OK; you are now ready to begin using these programs.

For Windows 95 users, here are the instructions for setting up a Program Item:

➤ Click with the right mouse button on the MIRC32.exe file in your Windows Explorer.

➤ Then select Create Shortcut.

➤ Next click with the left mouse button on the New Shortcut to MIRC32 and drag it onto the desktop background. This is outside all other windows.

➤ Double-click on this new desktop icon to run IRC.

With the 16-bit versions of these two programs you do not need anything extra other than what is needed in order to connect to the Internet. However, with the 32-bit versions you need to have Win32s installed or be using a 32-bit operating system.

Now you are ready to test your new IRC program. Read on in the next two chapters to find out what is available on these two programs and how you can use all the wonderful features they have.

Is There Other Chat Software?

You find as you surf the chat channels that there are many different kinds of chat software available. I have given you the two most popular and more advanced of what is available. Now I would like to tell you about a few others that are offered with a brief description of each. Then, if you find that you truly hate either mIRC or Pirch, which I cannot imagine happening, you have a basis to make a choice from the others that are out there.

Alpha World™ with its Active World software is a virtual reality place populated by real people. It takes social computing to the next level. You become one of its citizens and help to shape it. You acquire and develop property, assume an online persona, and interact in and with a living, breathing, multi-user community. It is not some preprogrammed simulation—it is as unpredictable and unique as the individuals who help create it, the users.

Alpha World is a chat 3-D multi-user community. You are no longer interacting with your computer with this software; you are interacting <u>through</u> your computer. You are represented by your own online avatar, or personification, letting you see and interact with the avatars of other people in the space. With this software you build your dream house, create a new world and experience not only by sight, but by sound and sensory, too. This software lets you claim land, build on it, create commerce applications, and explore ever-changing online environments. You can become part of an online virtual community through this freeware.

The Jumanji Pavilion mentioned in the first edition of this book is no longer available for download from any of the software sites I visited (www.tucows.com, download.com or stroud's software archive). Therefore, I have removed it from the list in this edition.

Internet TeleCafe is an IRC software program that works in conjunction with a membership-based group of users. There are three levels of users with this program: trial member, regular member, and VIP member. There is no fee for the trial or regular members; however, there is for the VIP member.

With the various memberships come certain limitations or privileges. Regular members can move freely through most of the rooms and options of the TeleCafe. As a $29 VIP member you get the following:

➤ Access to the entire TeleCafe (including access to the VIP Lounge)
➤ Access to set up a total of five custom actions for yourself
➤ Custom Entrance and Exit messages

This program is a shareware program; the cost is the membership fee for the VIP members.

The Palace is kind of like a cross between IRC and hypercard, yet completely unique in many respects. You can create and run your own social online environment on your server or visit other people's servers. Using a scripting language, you can create any visual look you want. The Palace offers a lifetime membership at a one-time cost of $39.95. If you prefer to test this software and its offerings first, The Palace also offers a free guest membership with limitations. With this guest membership you can visit all the Palace chat rooms and attend its special events. You can't, however, have a permanent identity or participate in its special events. There are other limitations. You can read more about this product at http://206.79.193.218/discover/try/index.html. You can also download the software from this site.

LOL Chat, formerly known as CyberBabble, is a chat software package that offers many unique and exciting features. It includes rich text formatting; an answering machine that lets you leave a message for someone if they don't answer; unlimited connections; macros for text, format changes, sounds, or any combination of the three; and synchronized sound that lets you send all the sound files you have but that another user doesn't. It also lets you surf the web with multiple leaders and followers. See Figure 4-3 for an example of a chat screen. This is a freeware version of the software. You can download this program and find out more about its features at http://www.lolchat.com/.

Figure 4-3   LOL Chat chat screen

OrbitIRC is another of the newer chat clients available. It is designed for Windows 95 users and gives you easy point-and-click control over all aspects of chat. There are no windows hiding other windows—everything is in the open for you to monitor your IRC sessions. It allows users to keep track easily of their public, private, and DCC chats. OrbitIRC has DCC Draw which lets you activate a picture box and doodle back and forth with other chatters. This chat client also lets you create a bot it calls OrBOT to handle some of the more mundane IRC tasks for you. This software is a $9.95 shareware version. See Figure 4-4 for a view of a chat session with OrbitIRC. Find out more about this program at http://www.dlcwest.com/~orbitirc/index.htm.

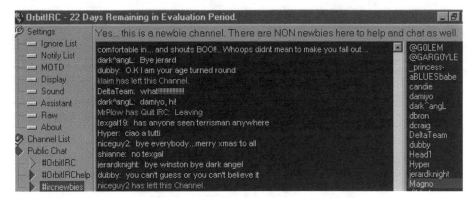

Figure 4-4   OrbitIRC chat screen

Virc lets you format your text with bold, underline, and italics, and allows for seamless integration with your web browser just like mIRC and Pirch. It lets you conduct real-time audio chat with other users and also lets you establish video conferencing supporting any Windows-compatible video camera. This program is a freeware program and is still in the beta testing stages.

Westwood Chat is an IRC client that lets you start or arrange a game of Monopoly CD-ROM or Command & Conquer, discuss strategies, or even talk with some of its tech support and guest speakers. This program is also freeware. You can find out more about this program and download it at http://www.westwood.com/wchome/wcgetit.html.

WinTalk lets you have two-way text-based chats. It is an implementation of the UNIX talk protocols of previous years. Only two users can communicate with each other at a time with this software. It is a freeware program and is not fully supported.

Microsoft's Comic Chat is a new kind of graphical chat program that lets you choose a comic strip character as your avatar. You type your messages or text into Comic Chat and a comic strip unfolds showing the various participants in the conversation as comic strip characters with their utterances in word balloons. This program is shareware and works with Microsoft's servers and net (see Figure 4-5).

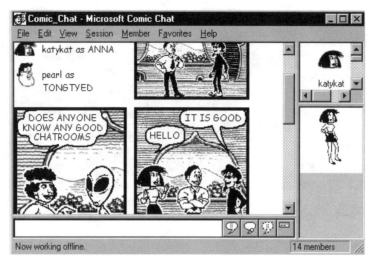

Figure 4-5   Comic Chat chat screen

Speak Freely is a chat client that lets you chat with real voice to users over a network. Speak Freely supports Internet RTP protocol which lets it communicate with other Internet voice programs that use that protocol. It also communicates with programs that support VAT (Visual Audio Tool) protocol. It is a freeware client available at http://www.download.com.

OnLive Traveler is a freeware 3-D virtual world client that gives you an entertaining live community by letting you talk with other users with your own voices through expressive, animated avatars. The avatars which represent users can be customized to lip-synch what the user is saying in real time. This client works as a stand-alone application or as a web browser helper application.

XiRCON is a freeware chat client that boasts it is IRC without limits. It also brags that it is an IRC client with nearly endless configurability and uses. It has a clean, sharp interface that caters to the inexperienced user as well as the veteran.

These are just some of the chat software programs that are available. There are others out there as well as new ones being developed on an ongoing basis. Talk to friends or people you meet on IRC to find out what they are using and how they like what they have. Decide on which of these software programs is best for you from what you hear and what works best with you and your system.

Summary

You now know how IRC clients came into being and how they can make your life so much simpler when you decide to explore IRC. You have learned about two of the better IRC programs being offered and how those two differ from each other.

You also have some information on some of the other IRC clients that have been developed and should be able to make an informed choice about which one of these programs would work best for you and with your computer.

Use what you have learned in this chapter to check out what is being offered on the web sites I gave you and download the software that interests you. If you choose either the mIRC or the Pirch programs, read on into the next two chapters to find out everything you need to know about how they work and how you can set them up to function to your preferences.

Chapter 5

mIRC Software

*T*here are dozens of pieces of chat software for you to choose from, but mIRC is probably one of the best that is offered. It is very easy to use and has many features that not only automate most of the IRC commands but also bring information to your fingertips quickly and conveniently.

In this chapter you learn:

☑ What mIRC is and how you can custom configure it to your preferences

☑ What aliases are and how you can set up your own

☑ What popups are and how to create them

☑ What remotes are and how you can program them to your preferences

☑ What you can do with DCC

☑ What some of the added features are that make mIRC such a superior IRC client

When you signed on with your Internet provider, it probably gave you a disk that had various pieces of software for each of the Internet tools. It may have included Netscape Navigator or Microsoft's Internet Explorer as one of those pieces. Each of these web browsers includes the web browser along with e-mail and newsgroups all in one suite. Or you may have received a disk with separate pieces of software for each of the Internet services including software for e-mail, newsgroups, a web browser, and possibly programs for Gopher and FTP, too.

Your provider may have even given you a chat software program—some do, some don't. If it did, you may like that software, which is great. However, I would like to show you a couple of the newer and, in my opinion, better chat software programs—mIRC and Pirch.

This chapter gives you a detailed description of mIRC. I tell you everything you need to know about this program and how to operate it. In the next chapter, I do the same for Pirch. Then you can decide to stay with what you have or try one of these.

What is mIRC?

You already know that it is a client, or chat software program. Let me tell you some of the features it has. Many of these features were designed to make it easier for you to use IRC or to read the posts on channels. mIRC was created with the aim of giving you total freedom in how you want it to look and operate. Most if not all of the IRC commands can be transformed into mIRC settings.

It is a very good and easily configurable IRC client and offers a nice, clean user interface. It gives you powerful tools and features like the following:

➤ Toolbar—gives you easy access to the most frequently used commands.

➤ Programmable function keys—you can program function keys with every command you frequently use to provide you with quick access to those commands.

➤ World Wide Web (WWW) access—mIRC supports all three of the major web browsers—Netscape, Mosaic, and Microsoft Internet Explorer—to give you easy access to the web pages you run across during your chat sessions.

➤ Multiple instances—lets you access more than one server; however, you have to open mIRC each time you want to access a new net.

➤ Remote CTCP handler—lets you decide how you want to respond to CTCP commands given by other people on IRC.

➤ Events handler—lets you program in automated messages and commands to be displayed in the channels you are on.

➤ Built-in DCC fileserver—gives you a fast, direct client-to-client connection to make sending and receiving files and chats faster and easier.

➤ Perform—allows you to perform certain repeat functions or commands.

➤ Colored text—makes reading and distinguishing between server, control, actions, and other types of messages easier.

➤ Text formatting—lets you bold, underline, reverse, or colorize your text.

➤ A handful of options—let you set mIRC to operate the way you like.

➤ Sound requests—allow you to set up your sound options for receiving and sending sound files.

➤ Uncluttered display—gives you separate windows for your chat channels and your status items.

➤ System menu—contains frequently used functions for easy access.

➤ Aliases—are like macros you can set up to automate many of those commands you frequently use.

➤ Popup menus—can be configured for your personal use.

➤ Drag and Drop—lets you drag files from other programs and drop them to your channel or private message windows.

➤ Menu bar items—can also be programmed to your personal specifications.

➤ Special keys—keys you can use to perform special functions like help.

➤ Full DCC Send/Get/Chat and Resume—unlike most freeware programs in that it does not disable or cripple any of its features, including the DCC function.

➤ Timer—lets you monitor your time online.

➤ Full fonts support—lets you use your favorite font for chats.

➤ Flood protection—keeps you from flooding a server or protects you from floods.

➤ Ident server—lets you access all IRC servers even if they require passwords or other forms of identification.

➤ Finger server—allows you to set up a file containing information you wish someone else to know about you when they do a CTCP finger on you.

➤ Firewall—lets you access IRC servers through a firewall your employer or provider has set up on their server.

➤ Other useful bit and pieces—are included to help you in your chat adventures.

How Do You Custom Configure mIRC?

Before you can even start using mIRC version 5.31, you have to configure at least your personal settings. While you are there you might as well spend the time and configure the rest of the options. All this is pretty simple, and when you get into it you see that it is self explanatory as well.

In this section I take you through the setup configuration. I show you how to get this option configured for you and your account. Then I walk you through the steps to set your general options configurations. With all these settings taken care of you are all set to connect to an IRC server for the net of your choice.

Setup

To begin using mIRC, you must enter basic information about yourself. mIRC provides you with a dialog box under either File/Setup in the menu bar or the File Folder in the toolbar. mIRC does not connect you to any servers if any of these fields are empty.

The first major section of this dialog box that you see when you open the settings menu item is the servers list. Notice that mIRC has given you several servers to start you off. Some of these servers are EfNet servers and some are UnderNet servers. (Remember how I told you to distinguish between the two servers by the address.)

As you use IRC more and more, you may run across servers you want to add to this servers list. You can do this simply by clicking on the Add button in this dialog box. Then you type in the server address, the port number (usually 6667), and a password if one is required to access that server. Generally, you never need to use a password. So, if you do not know if you need one, then you probably don't (see Figure 5-1).

Last server
used

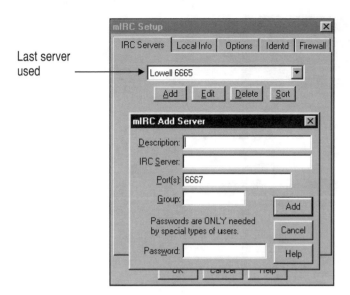

Figure 5-1   Setup dialog box

In addition to entering the required information about a server, you can also include personal information, like a name to identify them. You can give them any name you like, and add comments to them, like personal notes—quick, slow, UnderNet, EfNet, etc.

To use any of the servers in your list, select the one you want by highlighting it and clicking on the OK button (see Figure 5-2). Anytime you want to connect to an IRC server, select the server you want and click on the Connect button. Older versions of mIRC put the last server you used at the top of its servers list. This was also the server mIRC connected you to each time you clicked on its icon.

The newer version leaves the servers where they are but opens the server box with the last server you used highlighted. If you try to connect to a server and you get a message that reads **Unable to resolve IRC server name**, then you have one of two problems. Either your provider's DNS (Domain Name Server) is down or you have an incorrect address for that server. If you get this message on a server that you have used before, chances are good that your provider is having problems. Try reconnecting to your provider. If you get this message on a new server you added, check the address to make sure you did not mistype something somewhere.

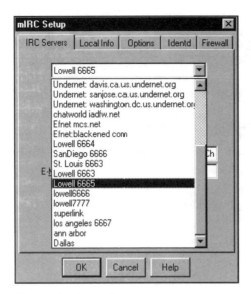

Figure 5-2   Server list

   Tip: If you try to connect to an IRC server that is geographically far away from you, it may take longer for you to get a
connection. Some servers may refuse to allow a connection
from too far away.

In the bottom section of this Setup dialog box, there is a section that
asks for information about you. One section asks for your Real Name.
You can type in your real name here or you can type in a witty saying.
Whatever you type in this box appears whenever anyone does a
/whois on you. Women might want to type in some favorite saying
rather than their real name. This cuts down on the IRC Don Juans
bothering you.

The next box or line asks for your e-mail address. Here you fill in your
complete e-mail address. The user name, the part before the @ sign, is
used to register you with the server you select to connect you to the net
you want to be on. So it is important to fill in this box. You are not able
to connect to any server without this information.

Now we get to the fun part, the Nickname box. This is where you type
in the name you want to go by on IRC. So, pick a nickname you want to
be called, either your first name and last initial, or a variation on this, or
any kind of nickname that suits your fancy. (Remember, a feminine-

sounding nick attracts IRC mashers.) While you're choosing a nick-name, pick an alternative nick to use in the event that someone else is using your first choice when you try to connect to your favorite net. Type that nickname in the Alternate box.

At the top of the Setup dialog box, notice there are five tabs. We have been working in the IRC Servers tab. The next tab in line is Local Info (see Figure 5-3). Generally, mIRC fills in this area for you, however, if you consistently get error messages of **Unable to resolve Local Host**, you may need to adjust some of these settings. So that you can have a better understanding of what each area means and its function, let's define them.

Figure 5-3   Local Info tab

Local Host is used to register you with the IRC servers. It is your iden-tification—your e-mail address. mIRC tries on its own to get this infor-mation, but if you get the **Unable to get the local hostname** message, you can manually type in the information. Notice there is no @ sign. The address is separated by dots instead.

The IP Address is normally supplied by mIRC. mIRC initially (the first time you log on) looks up your IP address and stores it in its mirc.ini file. Then it doesn't have to find it every time you log onto IRC.

The next area in this tab deals with On connect, always get: either Local Host or IP Address. Some providers supply you with a fixed local hostname and IP address while others have what they call a dynamic, or changing, local hostname. A fixed local hostname would appear as your login@domain.name, for instance jsmith@concentric.net. A dynamic local hostname would give you different numerical addresses after the @ sign each time you log onto the Internet. For instance, one time an address might be jsmith@206.104.111.24 and the next time it might be jsmith@207.204.121.35.

If you are unsure of what type of connection you have with your provider, check both these boxes. By selecting Local Host, mIRC automatically selects IP address. In addition, deselecting IP Address automatically deselects Local Host.

In the bottom of this Local Info tab is a box that contains two IP Methods—Normal and Server. When you select Normal, mIRC lets your winsock (your provider) reply with the correct information. The Server method lets mIRC look up your local host through the IRC server you choose. mIRC performs a command /dns on your provider's server and resolves it to an IP address.

The next tab in line is Options (see figure 5-4). When you click on this tab, you get several options you can select or leave deselected. When you select Connect on startup, mIRC automatically tries to connect you to the last server you used. Unless you prefer this method of connecting, leave this option deselected.

Figure 5-4 Options tab

Reconnect on disconnection does just what it says. I advise that you select this option. It makes it easier on you to let the program reconnect you rather than having to do it manually each time you're disconnected from a server. During bad times on any one of the nets or with your provider, this can happen quite often, sometimes as many as five or six times a session.

When you select Pop up setup dialog on startup, mIRC provides you with the Setup dialog box each time you click on the mIRC icon. Then you can choose which server you want to connect to and/or alter any of your other settings.

The next section in this tab is the On connection failure section. This area lets you determine if you want to retry connecting after failures and how often you want to retry as well as the amount of delay between connections in seconds.

The Default Port is always set at 6667 because that is the default port number for most IRC servers. Leave this area alone unless you find yourself on a net that does not use this number for its default ports to servers. To date, I am unaware of any nets or servers that don't use 6667 as the default port number.

The Identd tab is next (see Figure 5-5). Identd server is the local information about you. This information is sometimes requested by servers before you can log on. mIRC can act as an ident server by sending out a specified user ID and system as identification. The User ID is either your account or user name on your provider. Usually this is your e-mail address login. System identifies an operating system. For the purposes of IRC, most systems are UNIX. In the Port section of this tab selection, use port 113. With this setup, mIRC's ident server replies to all ident queries. If you like to see identd requests, select Show Identd requests on. These messages then appear in your status window.

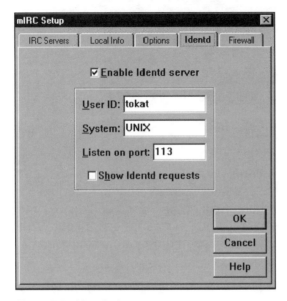

Figure 5-5 Identd tab

Many businesses and some providers set up firewalls on their systems to protect them from intruders and hackers. mIRC provides you with a way around these firewalled systems. mIRC lets you access IRC servers through a SOCKS firewall, set on the Firewall tab (see Figure 5-6). If you are connecting through an account with a firewall, select Use SOCKS firewall. Then type in the machine name of your SOCKS server, which can be either a named address or an IP address. Next type in your User ID, which is either your account or user name on the system. This is the same as for those not connecting through a firewall.

The last piece of information you have to provide is your password. This is the password you are required to use to access the firewall. The port is automatically set at 1080 and should be left alone.

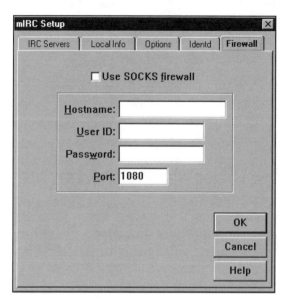

Figure 5-6   Firewall tab

 Warning: The Firewall setup only supports connections to an IRC server. It does not support DCC sends or chats.

Once you have made sure all the boxes and tabs are filled in properly, you can start IRCing simply by clicking on the Connect button. But, since we are already here, let's look at the general options and see what options you have over there. You can get to this section by first clicking on the OK button in the Setup dialog box. Then either click on the toolbar button that looks like it has bulleted sentences, also the one to the right of the file folder toolbar button, or click on File in the menu bar and then Options from the drop-down menu.

General Options

Take a look around and see what you have available to choose from to customize your mIRC. When you open this item, you see that it is arranged with little tabs at the top of the box. Each tab represents a different section that controls areas of mIRC. Within each of these sections you can set the options you want to match your preferences when using mIRC. These sections include:

- IRC Switches
- Notify List
- Control
- Clicks
- Event Beeps
- Drag-Drop
- Sounds

- Catcher
- Perform
- Flood
- Logging
- Servers
- Extras

Let's look at each of these individually and see what you can do with them.

Note: The creator of mIRC lives in England, therefore, some words in this program are spelled using the United Kingdom versions.

IRC Switches

Within IRC Switches, you have the following settings you can either turn on or off. On the left-hand side of this tab window you have these selections: Prefix Own Messages, Iconify Query Window, Dedicated Query Window, Whois on Query, Auto-join Channel on Invite, Rejoin Channel When Kicked, Cancel Away on Keypress, Timestamp Events, and Skip MOTD on Connect. On the right-hand side of this tab window under Show, you have the following selections: Alternative Join/Part/Quit, User Addresses, Quits in Channel, Joins/Parts in Channel, Modes in Channel, Invites in Active Window, Queries in Active Window, and Notices in Active Window. Below this Show section there is another smaller box labeled Strip Codes which includes Bold, Colour, Underline, and Reverse. The previous versions included Connect on Startup and Reconnect on Disconnection under IRC Switches. In this version they are included under Setup. Now let's take each of these settings and see what they mean or what their function is (see Figure 5-7).

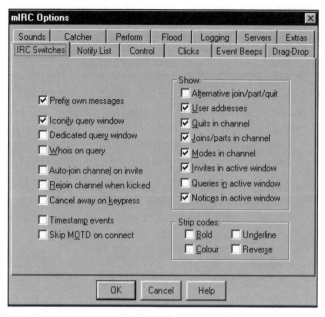

Figure 5-7   IRC Switches tab

➤ Prefix Own Messages—checking this box prefixes all text you enter in the channel with your nickname. For instance, you'll see your nickname in angle brackets before each statement you send to the channel conversation. I recommend you leave this option checked. It will be less confusing when you are in busy channels and trying to keep track of what you say and what everyone else is saying.

➤ Iconify Query Window—when this option is selected, it changes the default on query messages from an open window to an icon. So, rather than getting an open window ready for your input that takes you away from the window you are currently in, you get an icon that you can open at your leisure. My recommendation is to turn this option on. When query messages automatically open a window, they interrupt any typing you are currently engaged in when you receive the query. Therefore, you could find yourself typing a message meant for the channel or someone else into this new query message window. This could prove quite embarrassing.

➤ Dedicated Query Window—when selected, sends all private messages or notices from other users to one single message window. Then you have to use the /msg <nickname> command to reply to each person you are in private message with. I recommend leaving this option off. Having all your messages in one window can become quite confusing and cause you to misdirect posts.

➤ Whois on Query—gives you the whois information on each user who sends you a private message, but it only does it the first time they send you a message. However, if you shut down that message window, the next time that user sends you a private message you get another whois on them. I suggest you turn this option on. It lets you see who you are getting a message from and what channels they are on. Then you can decide if you want to reply to them.

➤ Auto-join Channel on Invite—selecting this option causes you to automatically join any channels that you have been invited to with the /invite command from another user. My recommendation is to leave this option deselected. See the following note.

Note: You may want to keep the Auto-join Channel on Invite option turned off. Otherwise you could find yourself joining channels that you would never go to on your own, like one of the sex channels.

➤ Rejoin Channel When Kicked—when you are kicked from a channel, mIRC tries to get you rejoined to that channel immediately. If you frequent the same channel or channels and the members are prone to playful kicking, select this option on. However, if you channel hop, you want to deselect this option. Regulars of channels get upset and ban you if you automatically rejoin their channel after you have been kicked.

➤ Cancel Away on Keypress—when this option is selected, your /away message is canceled automatically when you type a message to a channel or chat window. Again, this one is a matter of preference. If you have a tendency to forget you have marked yourself away, turn this option on. However, if you only want to respond to certain people and remain marked away, leave this option on.

➤ Timestamp Events—this option prefaces events with the time they occur. If you like to know exactly what time certain events happen or you are logging channels, you should turn this option on.

➤ Skip MOTD on Connect—this option hides the MOTD (Message Of The Day) that the server displays when you log on. If you frequently connect to the same server and that server never changes its MOTD, you want to select this option. However, many MOTDs contain valuable information, so be cautious in selecting this option.

On the right-hand side of this tab window under the Show section, the following selections are available:

➤ Alternative Join/Part/Quit—when you check this option, mIRC displays the join, part, and quit messages in a different and more compact format. If you are not interested in all the information that is displayed when people join, part, or quit channels you are on, select this option on.

➤ User Addresses—you can choose to see users' addresses displayed on your screen whenever they join, part, quit, or get kicked from the channel by selecting this option. Selecting this option lets you know immediately who is joining, parting, or leaving your channels and also lets you learn to recognize impostors.

➤ Quits in Channel—causes the user's quit message to appear in your channel window also when they quit rather than in the status window alone. This option is a matter of preference. If you like to see each person's quit message when they leave IRC while they're in your channel, select this option on.

➤ Joins/Parts in Channel—turning this option off sends all join or part messages for users to your status window, thus saving you the time in reading all those in a busy channel. My recommendation is to select this option on. This lets you get to know the visitors to your channel. Once you become familiar with the regulars on your channel, you can also use this information to monitor for impersonators.

➤ Modes in Channel—when you turn this option off, all channel mode changes are dumped into your status window. This option is a matter of preference. It does, however, free up your channel window for posts. Selecting this option off could cause you to miss important mode changes if you have a tendency to ignore your status window.

➤ Invites in Active Window—sends invite messages to your status window when you turn this option off. If you prefer not to have invite messages interrupt the flow of conversation, leave this option deselected.

➤ Queries in Active Window—puts all query messages in your active window when this selection is turned on. However, if you are not in a channel, you still get a query window. I suggest you leave this option deselected. Combining channel and query messages into one window can be confusing and cause misdirected posts and embarrassment.

➤ Notices in Active Window—when you select this option, any notices sent from other users appear in your active window. I recommend selecting this option unless you are one who checks the status window often. Otherwise you might miss an important message from a friend.

In the smaller box at the bottom right-hand corner of this tab window are selections under Strip Codes. When you select any of these options on, mIRC strips out these codes from any channels you're on or from private messages you receive. Unless you prefer plain text only, I suggest you leave each of these deselected. In addition, if you plan to copy special colored text from logs, it is wise to leave these options deselected.

Some of the options from previous versions of mIRC have been changed and expanded. In those previous versions, many of these were combined. With the newer version of mIRC, some of those combined options have been separated and expanded. Some of these options require a little more thought on your part than simply checking a box to make it active before you decide how you want to customize these settings. But I explain each of the options you have in this tab, what they are, or what you can do with them.

Once you have selected your IRC Switches, move on to the other tabs to finish configuring your preferences. Following are sections for each of the tabs in the Options dialog box along with a description of each and how to configure their setup.

Notify List

This tab has several sections. In the left-hand section is a check box with Notify beside it. Checking this box turns Notify on. In the larger box below this check box is the list of users you want to be notified about. To add names to this list, type their nickname into the Nickname box on the right.

Under Nickname are two other boxes you can insert information into. In the Note box, you can enter a note that will appear beside a specific nick when that person signs onto IRC. In the Play sound box, you can indicate a sound to play when a specific user joins IRC. When your notified user joins, that sound plays to alert you.

This tab also lets you choose several other options. You can select to perform a /whois on the notify nicknames when they join. The last three options tell the program how to notify you when your friends join IRC. You can select to have the Notify window pop up when you connect, Only show notifies in the Notify window, or Show notifies in the Active window. Simply select the options of your preference (see Figure 5-8).

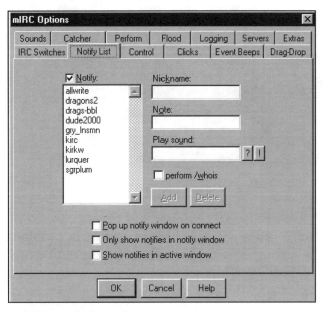

Figure 5-8   Notify List tab

Control

The Control tab lets you choose how you control your friends and other users on your favorite channels. This tab is also broken down into several sections. The first section lets you select the type of control you want to use—Ignore, Auto-Op, or Protect. By checking the Active check box, you activate each of these options (see Figure 5-9).

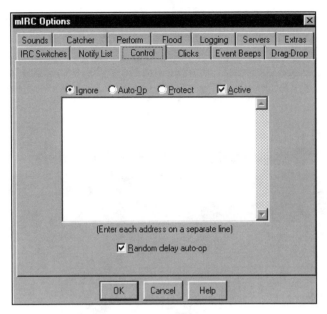

Figure 5-9 Control tab

Under each of these options you can then enter nicknames or user addresses to compile lists. Then you click the Active check box to activate them. Each option breaks down as follows:

➤ Ignore—when you type nicks and/or their addresses in this box and activate it, you no longer get private messages from them and you are not able to see any messages they send to the channel.

➤ Auto-Op—any nicks you add to this list are automatically opped when they join a channel you are already on, provided you have ops status. Since anyone could take on someone's nick, this is not always the best route to take. You can, however, use the person's address instead of their nick in this text box.

➤ Protect—if a user on your channel deops someone you have added to this list, that user is deopped by mIRC. If a user kicks one of your protected nicks, that user is deopped and kicked. However, this only works if you have ops status; if not, nothing happens.

➤ Random Delay Auto-Op—when activated, this option lets you set a random delay on your auto-ops. If a user is on several other users' auto-ops list, then if they get ops from another user, mIRC does not perform the auto-op function for you.

Clicks

Clicks is the next tab in line. This option lets you configure a set of commands that is executed when you double-click in the specified window. For instance, you could type in this option box **/query $1 I've been waiting all day for you. Where have you been?** (The $1 tells the program you are supplying the nickname.) Then when you double-click on a nickname, a query window opens and that user receives that message (see Figure 5-10).

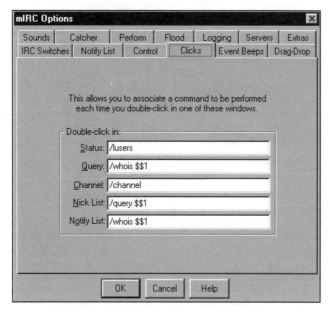

Figure 5-10   Clicks tab

Event Beeps

Event Beeps is the next tab in line under Options. This selection causes beeps to occur to alert you whenever certain events take place. You can indicate the number of beeps and how quickly they are sounded in the boxes provided. In this tab under On Event, you can select the type of event, like DCC Send, and then choose whether to Do Nothing, Event Beep, or Play Sound. If you choose Play Sound, you need to enter the sound filename or use the question mark to locate the file on your hard drive. If you want to turn this option off completely, specify zero beeps or deselect Enable event beeps section. The events you can select beeps for are Beep on channel message, Beep on query message, or Beep on message while in buffer (see Figure 5-11).

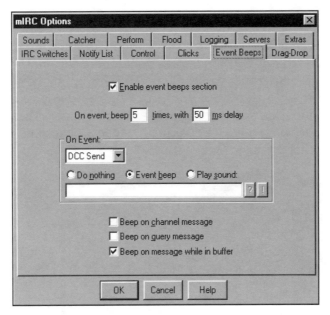

Figure 5-11 Event Beeps tab

Drag-Drop

This drag and drop feature lets you transfer files from your hard drive
to message or channel windows. You can also set up actions to take
place in your aliases to go along with the files you drag and drop. If
you have a text file you created or saved in one of your other programs, you can locate that program, drag it by clicking on it with your
left mouse button to your chat window command line, and drop it by
releasing your left mouse button (see Figure 5-12).

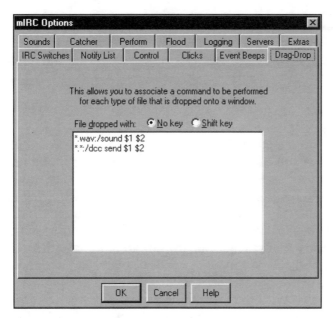

Figure 5-12   Drag-Drop tab

mIRC also lets you set up an alias to perform a certain action when you drag and drop certain files. For instance, if you want mIRC to read text files to a user or to a channel when you drop those files into message or channel windows, you can make an associated alias such as: ***.text:/play $1 $2**. In this alias, the $1 represents the name of the user on the channel, and the $2 represents the name of the file that you are dropping. The /play command tells mIRC to send each line in the specified file to the user. Therefore, if you had a text file named quotes.txt that you wanted to send to betyboop, your alias command would look like this: **text betyboop quotes.txt**.

You can set up this same alias association for dragging and dropping wave files or for DCC sends. The command in your Aliases dialog box would be the same as above, substituting the commands for sound or DCC send. For instance, for a wave alias it would look like this: ***.wav:/sound $1 $2**, and for a DCC send it would look like this: ***.*:/dcc send $1 $2**. Then when you drop a wave file, it is played with the /sound command while any other type of file initiates a DCC send to the user.

Note: When you drop a file that has a space in it, it is automatically encased in quote marks as part of the mIRC program.

Sounds

Sounds tab selections let you select how the sound features work for you. When you turn the Accept sound requests option on, mIRC listens for sound requests from other users. These are the .wav or .midi files I mentioned before. If a sound request is already playing and a new sound request is received, you can tell mIRC to ignore new sound requests by clicking on that option. If you leave this option unchecked, mIRC stops your current playing sound and plays the new sound. You can also indicate if you want mIRC to warn you with notification in your status window when a user is trying to send you a sound that you do not have. With the information in your status window, you can then ask that user to send you that sound. The last box in this tab is where you type in the directory where all sound files are stored (see Figure 5-13).

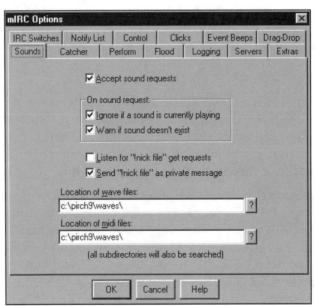

Figure 5-13   Sounds tab

Note: In order for you to hear a sound request that has been sent to you by another user, you must have a copy of that sound file. All sound files end in .wav, .midi, or .mid. To send a sound request to another user, you type **/sound <nickname> <file.wav> <message>**. You also need a sound card on your computer.

Catcher

The catcher is that neat little option I told you about earlier that collects web page addresses for you. It looks for addresses beginning with http://, ftp://, gopher://, www, and ftp. This tab lets you set up how you want your URL catcher to function (see Figure 5-14).

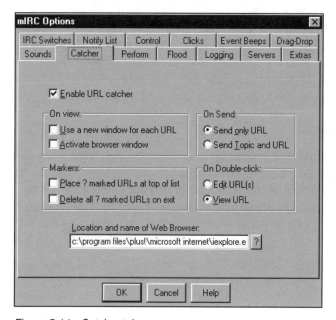

Figure 5-14   Catcher tab

When you activate or enable the URL catcher, it catches references to web addresses and stores them in the URL list box. Within this tab you also see an On View box that contains two more options: Use a new window for each URL, which tells your browser to open a new and separate URL window when you select View from the popup menu within the URL list box, and Activate browser window, which activates your web browser each time a URL is detected while you are in IRC.

You can also indicate in this tab selection how you want URLs sent to channels or other chat windows in the On Send selections. You can select either Send Only URL or you can choose to Send Topic and URL.

When you select the Delete All ? Marked URLs on Exit option in this tab, mIRC deletes all ? marked items in your URL list box when you quit mIRC. Any other addresses that have been changed from the ? mark to something else remain in your list until you delete them yourself. Selecting Place ? Marked URLs at Top of List moves all these URLs to the top of the URLs list.

The last box in this tab selection is the Location and Name of web browser. This is where you type in the directory and name of your web browser or you can click on the ? button to locate your browser on your hard drive. Then when you select View from the popup menu in the URL list box, mIRC activates your web browser. In the Double-click box, you can select how these URLs are treated when you double-click on them. Your options are: Edit URLs or View URL. To make it easier on you, I suggest you select View URL and leave Edit URLS deselected.

Perform

The Perform tab lets you set up commands that execute on certain events or functions in IRC. You can set these options to perform activities pertaining to specific words or your nickname, or to perform specified commands when you connect. This tab also lets you set up your CTCP finger reply and your Quit Message (see Figure 5-15).

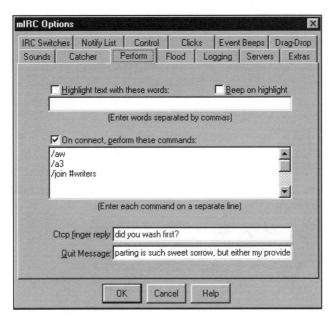

Figure 5-15 Perform tab

These available options are:

➤ Highlight text with these words or Beep on highlight—when any words you type in this text box appear on a channel you are on and this box is selected, they are highlighted in dark brown or red. This was set up to help you locate messages that are directed at you or about you or messages you type yourself. For instance, when you type your nickname in this box, every time someone on a chat channel types your name, their whole message appears highlighted or mIRC beeps at you, depending on which selection you turned on. You may also select both these options on. You can type as many words in this box as you want; just remember to separate them with commas.

➤ On connect, perform these commands—lets you enter a set of commands in the text box so that these commands are performed every time you connect to IRC. For instance, if you type **/join #<favorite channel>** when you connect to IRC, you automatically join your favorite channel. If you type **/names #<favorite channel>**, you get a list of everyone who is currently on your favorite channel when you connect to IRC.

> ➤ Ctcp Finger Reply—when you type a message in this box, any user who performs a CTCP finger on you gets that message.

> ➤ Quit Message—when you quit IRC, the message you type in this box displays on the channels you are on.

Flood

The Flood tab lets you enable flood protection and thus prevent mIRC from flooding a server or to prevent others from flooding you. With this option selected, mIRC counts the number of bytes you send to a server and triggers a flood check if you surpass a maximum number of bytes (see Figure 5-16).

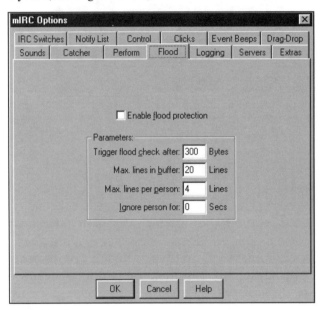

Figure 5-16   Flood tab

In this tab you can designate the parameters for flood protection. In Trigger flood check after, you set the number of bytes mIRC checks for to see if you are flooding a server. Putting in a large number here is not useful to you. The lower the number you use, the more sensitive mIRC is and the slower it replies. The default is 400 and you should not set it over 500. You can, of course, use the default or select a number of your own.

Max. lines in buffer lets you set the maximum number of lines mIRC buffers. Max. lines per person allows you to set the maximum number of messages users can have in your buffer. In the Ignore person for box, you can set how long in seconds you want to ignore users who have exceeded their maximum number of buffered messages. If you do not wish to use this option, set the seconds to zero (0).

mIRC flood protection performs intelligent buffering so that it can handle the maximum number of users possible and prevent a single user from hogging the queue. If you want to turn flood protection on without opening up this Options tab, type **/flood on**. mIRC then turns flood protection on and uses the settings you have set up or the default settings.

Logging

Logging is another handy option within mIRC. With this tab item, you can indicate that you want the log turned on for channels and/or for private chats. You can also indicate in the text box at the bottom of this tab window the directory where you want those logs to be stored. In the larger box on the right-hand side of this tab window is a list of all your logs. You have the option to either view these logs or to delete any of them. There may be times when you want to have a log, or proof of conversations, such as when you hold an online sales meeting or class (see Figure 5-17).

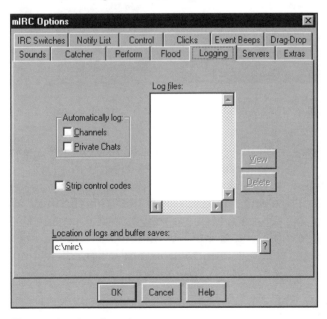

Figure 5-17   Logging tab

Servers

Servers listen and respond to requests from other users or systems. mIRC only supports limited DDE (Dynamic Data Exchange) capabilities. When you check Enable DDE server, you activate mIRC to listen for and reply to server messages. In this application, mIRC acts as the server, therefore, you type in or leave mIRC as the default Service Name. mIRC automatically enables the DDE server and uses its own defaults when you first log onto IRC (see Figure 5-18).

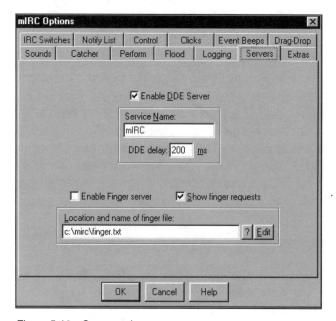

Figure 5-18   Servers tab

When you Enable Finger Server, mIRC listens for finger requests, and if you have Show finger requests selected, it displays them in the status window. In order for this to work, you must specify a finger file under Location and name of finger file. This file must also be set up with names sections which are sent as replies to any finger requests. This is a text file you create and should include the following information: Names sections, information, and a default section. Therefore, your finger file would look something like this:

```
[default]
John Smith
Ask and you shall receive
```

```
[Smith]
John Smith
Boring Corporation
1234 Boring Drive
Boring City, USA
```

At any time, you can go back and edit the finger file and replace it with a new file by clicking on the Edit button beside the Location and name of finger file box.

Extras

Extras is the last tab selection. This tab contains options like Fast screen update, ESCape key minimizes, Pop up colour index, Multi-line editbox, Minimize to tray, Toolbar, Tooltips, Switchbar size, Fixed width buttons, Always highlight, Include DCCs, On top, Line separator, Command Prefix, Scrollback buffer, and Show this text in the application title bar (see Figure 5-19).

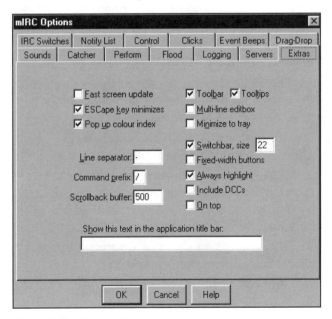

Figure 5-19   Extras tab

➤ Fast screen update—for users with slower video cards, this option updates the screen in batches rather than line by line. It speeds up screen updates for most users.

➤ ESCape Key Minimizes—causes a window to be minimized when you press the Escape key and you have turned this selection on.

➤ Pop up Colour Index—will pop up a color index dialog whenever you press Control-K in an edit box to insert a color code.

➤ Multi-line Editbox—when you turn this option on, the text starts again at the left and scrolls downward versus the text scrolling to the right when you reach the end of the edit box in a single-line mode. This multi-line mode also allows you to paste several lines of text into the edit box.

➤ Minimize to tray—only appears in the 32-bit mIRC under operating systems that have a tray. It lets you minimize mIRC to your system tray.

Tip: The status window is always a single-line edit box.

➤ Toolbar—lets you choose to have these options hidden.

➤ Tooltips—you can choose with this option to have your tooltips showing or hidden.

➤ Switchbar size—lets you choose to have the switchbar shown or hidden. The switchbar is the tabs at the bottom of your mIRC window for each channel or private message you have running at a time.

➤ Fixed width buttons—when this option is on, the buttons don't span the entire length of the switchbar.

➤ Always highlight—when this option is turned on, the switchbar button at the bottom of your window is highlighted when there is activity in a window you have open but is behind another window or non-active.

➤ Include DCCs—lets you show DCC sends/gets in the switchbar; otherwise they appear as normal icons.

➤ On top—lets you position the switchbar at either the top or bottom of your main window.

➤ Line Separator—in this option you can specify a line separator to be used in your status window by using a space to have a blank line. If you leave this box empty, lines in your status window are not separated.

➤ Command Prefix—as I told you earlier, the symbol that indicates a command is the forward slash mark (/). With mIRC and this

option, you can select another character to use in its place. mIRC
still recognizes the / character and uses it internally.

➤ Scrollback Buffer—limits the number of lines in your scrollback
buffer. You may choose the number of lines you are comfortable
with and insert it in the box provided.

➤ Show this text in the application title bar—lets you specify text
that appears in the mIRC application title bar. That is the blue bar
at the top of your application window.

What are Aliases and What Can You Do with Them?

Aliases is one of my favorite commands. They let me create shortcut
keys, or macros as some people like to call them, out of the longer IRC
commands I use most often.

The more aliases you create for those commands, the easier and faster
your adventures in IRC land are. They come in handy when you get to
the point where you feel advanced enough to join more than one
channel. Wouldn't it be so much faster and easier to type one or two
letters versus the long commands that IRC normally uses? I have
found that it does.

First, let me show you some simple aliases. Then I get into the more
involved aliases and how you can set them up for almost any command you use. Then program them yourself and use them to glide
along effortlessly through your IRC channels and messages (see figure
5-20).

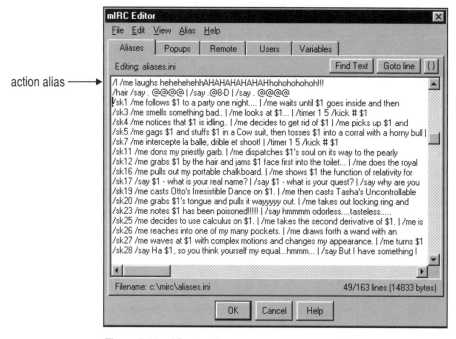

action alias ———▶

Figure 5-20   Alias text box

Before you begin, bone up on the IRC commands I gave you in Chapter 3. They are going to come in handy here. For aliases to work you have to know the proper IRC command you are trying to make the alias for.

Tip: Each alias must be typed on a single line.

Let's take the join command and pretend we are betyboop. Betyboop wants to program an alias that lets her type just two letters (with the forward slash, of course) to join her favorite channel, #cartoons.

Technique: Aliases can be initiated from the command line, from other aliases, or from popups or remotes. They can also work with popups and remotes.

The first thing betyboop needs to do is click on the Aliases toolbar button. This opens up the aliases text box which is where betyboop types in or programs her aliases. Betyboop decides that she wants to use the two letters jc to program her alias for joining #cartoons, so she begins the alias command with /jc. Next she types in the command that /jc executes for her, the /join #cartoons command. Her complete alias looks like this: **/jc /join #cartoons**. When she is connected to IRC and she types in that /jc command in a prompt line, she joins #cartoons. Nice, isn't it?

Note: Aliases cannot initiate themselves.

You can do the same thing with all the IRC commands that you use the most, like /who or /whois. You can even set these aliases up to be generic aliases. For instance, betyboop could create an alias to let her fill in the channel name she wants to join. It would look something like this: **/j /join $1**. Let's pretend betyboop wants to join a channel named #comics. She can type /j #comics instead of /join #comics.

What betyboop has done is set up a parameter string. The parameter in this case is the $1. This $1 lets betyboop pick the channel she wants to join when she uses that alias. Another way betyboop could set up this alias would be to type /jj /join $?. This lets her do the same thing—pick the channel she wants to join but in a slightly different way. When she types in the /jj command, betyboop gets a dialog box that asks her for the name of the channel she wants to join, then she simply types the name of the channel in the box and clicks on OK. The question mark tells mIRC to ask for that parameter, or in this case that channel name.

One other way betyboop could set up this alias would be to type the following: **/jj /join $?="Enter channel to join:"**. This alias does the same thing as the previous alias, but the dialog box has the "Enter channel to join:" line displayed inside it.

You can use these parameter settings for almost any of the IRC commands. For instance, you could set up an alias for an action statement like this: **/wel /me welcomes $1 to our channel**. Or you could set up an alias for your away message like this: **/aw /away checking my e-mail**.

If you want to set up two parameters for the nickname and the channel name or any other combination, you can do that also. You would simply add a second dollar sign and a second number, or as many dollar signs and numbers as you need to make your alias work. It might look something like this: **/wel /me welcomes $1 to $2**. You note that each number you use after the dollar sign (within the same parameter string) is an ascending number. Then when you type this alias it would look like this: **/wel joe #cartoons**. When it appears on channel it look like a regular action statement—***betyboop welcomes joe to #cartoons**.

If you add double dollar signs in your parameter strings, the command is not executed unless you fill in both parameter fields. So in the previous example if you designated the alias as: **/wel /me welcomes $$1 to $$2**, you have to type in two values for the two strings. If you only type one value, the command does not execute.

You can also set up these aliases to include multiple parameters. The star or asterisk symbol tells mIRC that there are multiple values added after it. So, if your alias is **/manyping /ctcp $* ping**, you could ping joe, katy, and betyboop with one command. It would look like this: **/manyping joe katy betyboop**.

Anything you append in the $ parameter is also appended to the final parameter. For instance, if you set up an alias that is an action of you laughing at someone's joke, you could type it this way: **/haha /me laughs at $1's joke**. If betyboop had this alias and wants to laugh at joe, it would appear on channel like this: ***betyboop laughs at joe's joke**.

For multiple command parameters, you insert the vertical line character between the commands in the parameter string. (This vertical line is the character above the backward slash or the shifted character on the backward slash key.) If betyboop set up a command to kick and then ban any intruders on any channel she was on, she could type the alias like this: **/kb /kick # $1 | /mode # +b $1**. Then when betyboop is ready to kick an intruder named jacka out of her channel she can type **/kb #cartoons jacka**. Since the two parameter string identifiers are the same, she only needs to type the channel name and the nickname for that person to be kicked and banned from the channel she is on.

When using aliases there are some other identifiers you can use. Inserting these identifiers in an alias causes mIRC to include that information in your parameter string. These other identifiers are as follows:

➤ $day, $time, $date—gives you the current day, time, and date

➤ $adate—gives you the U.S. style date in month/day/ year

➤ $fulldate—when typed as an alias, gives you a full date such as Tue May 14 13:15:00 1996

➤ $me—refers to your nickname

➤ $cb—brings up the first 256 characters in the current clipboard contents

➤ $server—the server you are connected to

➤ $ip—your IP address

➤ $host—your local host name

➤ $url—inserts the currently active URL in your web browser

mIRC has some other identifiers to help you in programming aliases. These are the $nicks identifier, the $read identifier, and the $file identifier.

You can substitute the $nicks identifier when using multiple parameters such as for the /manypings alias. This identifier inserts the string of nicks you select from your active channel list box. For instance, if betyboop has her alias set up with this identifier: **/manypings /ctcp $nicks ping**, she types **/manypings**, then highlights all the nicks in her channel names list box and presses Enter. Then mIRC pings each of those individuals for her.

The $read identifier picks a line from a file and inserts it for you. Unless you specify a certain line in that file, this identifier picks a random line from the text and inserts it. So if betyboop has a file set up with lines from famous cartoons, she could set up an alias to either select a random line from that file or a specific line and display it on her channel when she typed that alias. For instance, she could have an alias that is programmed as **/say $read c:\cartoons.txt**. Or if she wanted to select a specific line from that file, she could program her alias as this: **/say $read -15 c:\cartoons.txt**. You can add these $read identifiers to any alias command, even kick commands.

The $file identifier lets you select a filename to insert in your alias parameter strings. One area you might use this is with sound files and action statements. If you have a .wav file that you like to repeat often after certain things you say, you can create an alias for it. For instance, if betyboop says, "That's all, folks" a lot, she can create an alias that looks like this: **/say /me says that's all folks $file c:\thats.wav**. Then when she types that alias it appears on channel as **betyboop says that's all folks*** followed by her .wav file playing.

Tip: Do not use $file with the /dcc send command, because it has its own built-in DCC send dialog.

This new version of mIRC has the capability of adding color to your text and ASCII files you send to channels. This feature lets you spice up your IRC chats by colorizing text and creating a form of graphics. Some of these actions you can take can be in the form of aliases or popups, while some combine commands in both aliases and popups.

You can create your own artwork or you can have friends send you text files of art they have created. If you have the time and patience, you can also copy these out of log files you keep on the channels you visit and then add them to either the aliases or popups in mIRC.

To help you get started, here are instructions on how to create these colorful aliases and some examples. In mIRC, when you hold down the Ctrl key and type in certain numbers—from 0 to 15 or combinations of those numbers—you tell the program to add the color associated with that number. These numbers and their corresponding colors are as follows: 0 - white, 1 - black, 2 - blue, 3 - green, 4 - orange, 5 - red, 6 - purple, 7 - pea green, 8 - yellow, 9 - lime green, 10 - turquoise, 11 - aqua, 12 - bright blue, 13 - lilac - 14 - silver, and 15 - gray. When you type these numbers separately with the Ctrl key, whatever text follows appears on the channel as the color for the number you picked. If you use two numbers separated by commas and with the Ctrl key, the first number is the text color and the second number is the background color. Therefore, if you want to use one color and say hello to a visitor, you type **Ctrl k 4 Hello joe**. It appears in the channel as **Hello joe** in orange type. It appears to you as a block, the number, and then your greeting (see Figure 5-21). With this version of mIRC, when you press the Ctrl key and the K key, mIRC pops up a Color Index box that lets you see the colors that go with each number. Then you simply type the number for the color you want to use.

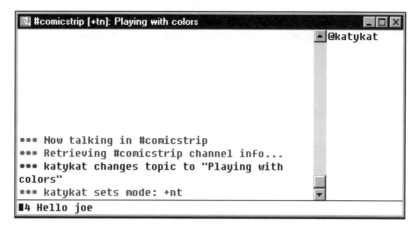

Figure 5-21   Colorized text command—one color

When you use two colors with your text, you type Ctrl k, the first number, a comma, and the second number. Then you follow that with your text. It appears on the channel as words on a background. For you, it looks like a black box or block followed by two numbers separated by a comma and then your text (see Figure 5-22).

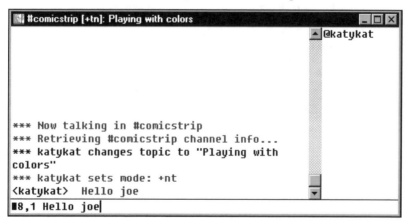

Figure 5-22   Colorized text command—two colors

Now that you have a basic understanding of how to use colors in your text, you can start creating aliases using those color codes. If joe wants to create an alias to give roses to the ladies who come to his channel, he types something like this: **/doz /me gives $$1 a dozen beautiful roses Ctrl k Ctrl k4,1@Ctrl k3}-`-,-`-- Ctrl k Ctrl k4,1@ Ctrl k3}-`-,-`-- Ctrl k Ctrl k4,1@Ctrl k3}-`-,-`-- Ctrl k Ctrl k4,1@Ctrl k3}-`-,-`-- Ctrl k Ctrl k4,1@Ctrl k3}-`-,-`-- Ctrl k Ctrl k4,1@Ctrl k3}-`-,-`-- Ctrl k Ctrl k4,1@Ctrl k3}-`-,-`-- Ctrl k Ctrl k4,1@Ctrl k3}-`-,-`-- Ctrl k Ctrl k4,1@Ctrl k Ctrl k3}-`-,-`-- Ctrl k Ctrl k4,1@Ctrl k Ctrl k3}-`-,-`-- Ctrl k Ctrl k4,1@Ctrl k3}-`-,-`--**. Entering Ctrl k twice tells mIRC to stop the color preceding the first Ctrl k and then to start the new color following the second Ctrl k. Remember, all this has to be typed on one line in the Alias dialog box. Then you simply type your alias and the nickname you want this alias for. In Figure 5-23, you can see how this looks on the channel.

roses (@) are red

leaves (`) and stems (-) are green

background is black

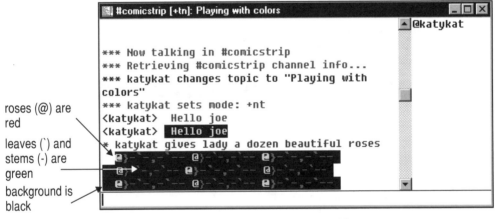

Figure 5-23   Colorized alias text with colorized ASCII art

The possibilities for what you can create using these colors is endless. During my visits to channels I have seen blocks with nicks or quotes in them. I have also seen numerous fancy graphics using ASCII art and these colors as well as some creative users who designed graphics with these colors and text that look like candy wrappers from Lifesavers, Snickers, and many others.

Use your imagination or borrow files from others to spice up your IRC activities. The addition of these colors to text lets you explore all the possibilities (see Figure 5-24).

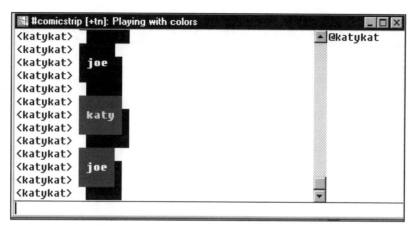

Figure 5-24   Colorized alias text in blocks of color

This Alias text box is also where you can program your function keys
with some of your most often used commands. For instance, you can
program them to work in conjunction with your Shift or Ctrl keys to
perform almost any of the IRC commands. You program them the
same as you do other aliases but substitute the function key for your
alias command. An example is: **/sF2 /msg $1 $?="Enter message:"**. Using the lowercase s for shift and the lowercase c for control
tells mIRC that you are using these keys along with the function key to
activate this command.

Technique: If you are on a channel when using these function
keys as aliases, the function key works with selected names in
the channel names list box. So if betyboop wants to send a
message to joe, she highlights his name and then holds down
the Shift key as she presses the F2 key. Then she types her message to joe in the dialog box that pops up.

So, you see aliases are pretty easy to program and there is so much
you can do with them. They make your life so much easier once you
get the hang of them. Using aliases, you spend less time typing out
tedious commands and more time actually talking and reading the
activities in your channels. Play around with them and have fun.

What are Popups and What Do They Do?

Popups are aliases that have been converted to pop-up or, if you prefer, drop-down menu items. They work in tandem with your right mouse button and your channel names list. So, when you highlight a nick in your channel names list and press the right mouse button, you get a preprogrammed list of menu items to select from. Some of these pre-programmed commands are Give ops, Kick, Whois, CTCP, and DCC.

You can create your own popups and you can create as many levels of popups as you want. These would be menus within menus. And, of course, you have to have a good understanding of some of the basic IRC commands to program these popups. You can create these popups for the three different kinds of windows you have in IRC—the main window, query/message windows, and the channel list box window—as well as for the Nickname List and menu bar. To get to the Popups text box, click on the Popups toolbar button (see Figure 5-25).

accesses popup control areas

menu item

submenus

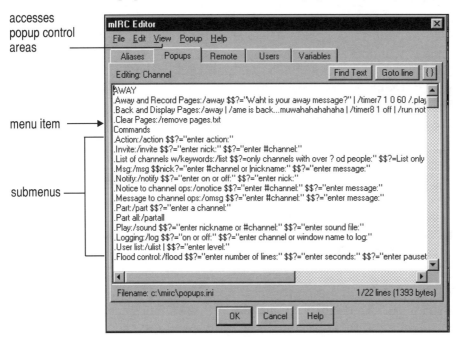

Figure 5-25   Popups dialog box

Let's begin by learning how to set up menus. It is pretty simple actually. You just type the name you want for the menu header, like Join or Modes. Then, to create a submenu, simply type a dot or period preceding the heading you want. For instance, under Join for the main window, you could have two submenus—Social Channels and Professional Channels—with aliases or menu items under each submenu. For the menu items under each heading you type two dots preceding the command and a colon preceding the menu item to distinguish it as a menu item and separate it from the command. Your popup looks something like this:

```
Join
.Social
..Social1:/join #cartoons
..Social2:/join #!webe30+
.Professional
..Prof:/join #writers
..Prof:/join #realestate
```

Note: You can separate menus by placing a single dash (-) on a line by itself.

Remember when you are programming these menu items and commands to type the commands just as you would for aliases. All popup commands are preceded by at least one dot, followed by the Command menu item name and a colon. Then you type the command, leaving no space between the colon and the forward slash.

After you have set up these popup menus and submenus, it's time to start adding popups to them. If, for instance, you want to create a hug to give to your friends when they come to your channel by simply clicking on their nick in the channel names list and choosing your hug, you can create a menu item titled Hugs and add your various hugs to it. Each item is preceded by a dot followed by the name of the hug, a colon, and the command to perform the hug. An example of a hug is: **.darlinhugz!:/say *HUGZ* $$1 darlin' :)** This is how it looks in the Popup dialog box. As you see, with the exception of the first part, the command is the same as you enter for aliases. Follow these steps and create a few hugs of your own.

Some of the colorized text activities we talked about can be created as popups instead of aliases. Follow the steps to create a popup and then add the command for the colorized text you want to use. Here is one of the popup hugs I have colorized: **.HUG:/say Ctrl k4 (¯`'·., (¯`'·.,(¤),.·'´¯),.·'´¯) control k12 ***********($$1) ************ Ctrl k4 (_,.·'´(_,.·'´(¤) `'·.,_)`'·.,_)**. See Figure 5-26 to see how this looks on a channel.

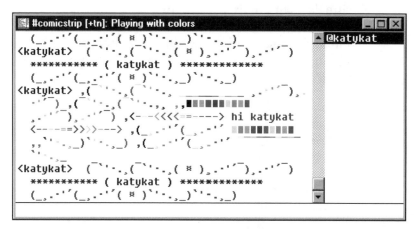

Figure 5-26 Colorized popup text and ASCII art

Try creating a few popups of your own. To create popups for the different areas the popups can work with, you select View and then the area you want to put the popups in. You have five areas— Status, Channel, Query/Chat, Nickname List, and Menubar.

What are Remotes and How Do They Work?

Remotes are replies or commands you program mIRC to use when responding to CTCP queries or in reaction to certain IRC events. This tool lets you respond to almost any remote command you can think of. Actually, any command you type can be programmed to be executed remotely. Just to give you an idea of what you can do with this remote tool, here are a few examples:

➤ Get whois information on anyone who joins your channel

➤ Auto greet all who enter your channel

➤ Send a custom reply to anyone who does a ping on you

These are just a few of the things you can program your remote to do. The mIRC Editor text box, which can be reached by clicking on the

Remote toolbar button, has five areas which includes tabs for aliases and popups as well as three areas you can program remote commands into. These are:

➤ Users—list of all users you specify along with their access levels

➤ Variables—list of defined variables you use

➤ Remote—list of CTCP, events, and raw commands for mIRC to respond to (see Figure 5-27).

accesses remote control areas —

turns listening on for the events

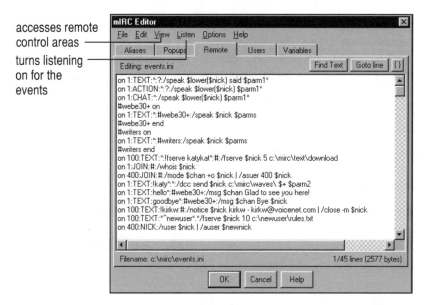

Figure 5-27 Remote tab

Following is a tutorial to help you learn how to program and use remote commands.

It is probably a good idea for you to read the current FAQ (Frequently Asked Questions) for mIRC which is available at: http://www.mirc.co.uk/get.html to get a better understanding of how mIRC works and how the Remote option functions within it. At this site there are links to sites where you can download a current version of mIRC.

Under each of the options in this Remote dialog box you are able to program activities specific to those options. The next few sections of this chapter deal with each of these options and shows you how to program functions and activities into them. These include some basic commands used in IRC that you can program remote commands with to let your client do the work for you.

Users or Friends Lists

The first thing you need to do is click on the Remote icon in your tool-bar. This is the box that has a C and an E in it with two circles underneath them. You get a dialog or text box you use to type in the commands to program your remote commands, events, variables, raw, and users lists.

Select Users, as this is the first section you are going to learn to program. Here you are going to set up your users lists and add yourself to this list and give yourself a level. Just like you, everyone on your users list will have a level. You may choose any number level you like. For simplicity's sake let's use the level 500 for you, 400 for your closest friends, and 100 for others.

Before we begin adding you or other users to this list, you need to be familiar with some of the commands used in this option and what they mean. Following is a list of those commands:

➤ /auser—adds a nick or address with the specified levels to the users list

➤ /guser—works the same as /auser but looks up the address of the user and then adds it to the list

➤ /ruser—removes a user from the users list

➤ /dlevel—changes the default user level

➤ /rlevel—removes all users with the specified level from the users list

➤ /flush—clears the users list of nicknames that are no longer valid

With each of these commands you add parameters and/or names to complete the command. Next we discuss how you use these commands with parameters to set up your users list and add yourself and others to your list.

To add yourself to your users list, type the following command line: **/guser 500 <your nickname> 3**. This command line breaks down to mean the following: /guser is the command, 500 is the level for yourself, and the number 3 tells mIRC the way to log this person to your user list. You can also type the command as **/auser 500 <your nickname> 3**.

Now let's start adding friends to your users list. If betyboop wanted to add roadrunr to her list as one of her better friends, she types: **/guser 400 roadrunr 3** or **/auser 400 roadrunr 3**. Then if she wanted to add WileECoyo to the list, she could wait until he comes to her channel, highlight his name in the channel names list, right-click with her mouse to bring up the popup menu, and then click on Adduser. But first she has to type this command into her popups in the Nicknames List option under Add Users in the Popup dialog text box: **/add50:/guser 400 $$1 3 | /auser 400 $nick**. The last part of this command tells mIRC to grab the nick and add it and the address to your users list (see Figure 5-28).

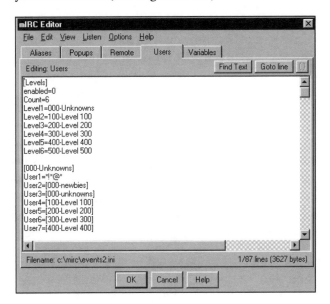

Figure 5-28   Users tab

If you would like to notify people when you add them to your users list, you can do that too by adding the following to the command you just typed in the Popups dialog text box: **/msg $nick You have been added to my friends list**. So the whole command with this message looks like this: **Add50:/guser 400 $$1 3 | /auser 400 $nick | /msg $nick You have been added to my friends list**. If you don't like this message, feel free to customize it to your own message. Now your users list is all set up and you're ready to start adding friends.

As people leave your channel or when you quit IRC, you may want to purge your users list of those nicks. You can remove a nick from your list when they leave the channel with the following command in the Events section of the Remote text box: **400:ON PART:#:/ruser $nick**. To remove nicks from your list when you quit IRC, type the following command: **400:ON QUIT:/flush 400**.

Warning: For some unknown reason, the ON PART and ON QUIT commands do not always work for everyone. If you want to purge your list manually you can do so by typing **/flush 50**.

Variables

Variables are data storage devices that you use in creating scripts. Scripts are a set of programming codes that execute certain activities. Variables are not discussed further in this book because scripts are a more advanced activity and are covered in *Learn Advanced Internet Relay Chat* (Wordware Publishing, ISBN 1-55622-604-7).

Commands

As you get into these other options, you start using identifiers in your commands. Identifiers refer to certain values within mIRC and IRC. These identifiers help mIRC perform your commands and make it easier for you to partake in some of these activities once you get them set up. Following are identifiers you can use and their definitions:

➤ $chan—the channel where an event takes place
➤ $clevel—the command level matched with a triggered event
➤ $nick and $address—the nickname and address of users sending queries or involved in the command or event
➤ $site—the portion of a user's address after the @ sign
➤ $fulladdress—the full address of a user
➤ $maddress—gives back a matching address from the users list
➤ $numeric—the raw numeric being processed in a raw event
➤ $parms—the whole parameter line a user sends with a CTCP query
➤ $ulevel—a user's level
➤ $wildsite—the address of a user containing wild cards (*!* in IRC before an address is a wild card)

Note: CTCP and Raw commands are not associated with a channel, therefore the $chan identifier is never used with commands for these two options.

Some of these identifiers you use with the Commands option and some you use with the Events or Raw options. In this section you learn how to set up a few commands to work with CTCP queries.

One of the common ways to flood someone is to send them recurring DCC or CTCP commands. If you want to only answer legitimate inquiries, yet halt someone who is trying to flood you, add the following lines to your Remote/Command section and make sure the Listening box is checked: **1:VERSION:/whois $nick | /notice $nick I'm using mIRC, of course. | /ignore -ntiu45 $nick 3 | /echo # $nick has been ignored**. Type this as it is here in one long line. It accepts the incoming inquiry for a version check, notifies the person what version you are using with your message, and then ignores them for 45 seconds. Those who try to send you fast repeated version requests are then ignored. If you want to set up other CTCP inquiries, just add lines reflecting the command and alter your message, like so: **1:USER-INFO:/whois $nick | /notice $nick <your text> | /ignore -ntiu45 $nick 3 | /echo # $nick has been ignored**.

Tip: The /echo command tells mIRC to print text in the specified window.

As you travel IRC and do pings on people you notice that some get very creative with their ping replies. You can create and change your own message quickly by adding the following line to the Remote/Commands: **1:PING:/notice $nick <message>**.

If you want to customize your ping replies to certain users you can add this command line to Remote/Commands: **400:PING:/notice $nick <message> :>**. This command instructs mIRC to send this particular ping message only to those people who are level 400 on your users list. Once again, you can substitute any CTCP inquiry and message you want to respond to other users' queries. For instance, if betyboop has joe and katy on her users list, when they try to ping her, they get the ping reply that she programmed for each of them. Betyboop can program a ping reply for joe that says, "yes, I'm still here, joe" by typing this ping command with this in the <message> area into the remote section and then do the same for a different reply for katy. Then when joe pings her, he gets the ping reply back with her message, **yes, I'm still here, joe**.

Tip: Some of the ping replies you might see are: "a little more under the chin . . . prrr," "that tickles . . . giggle," "careful, I bruise easily."

Other commands you can customize to handle CTCP queries are:

➤ 1:FINGER:/notice $nick <your message> |/halt
➤ 1:TIME:/notice $nick my local time is: $time
➤ 1:VERSION:/notice $nick I'm using mIRC v4.7
➤ 1:USERINFO:/notice $nick <your message> | /halt

The number 1 at the beginning of each line is there to specify the access level necessary to make this command work. The word in all caps following the 1: is the CTCP query the user or friend sent you. The /notice is a command that sends your message to the user. $nick is the identifier that lets mIRC send your message to the right nickname or the one querying you. The /halt at the end of the command line stops the normal reply to the CTCP query from being sent and lets yours be sent instead.

Note: All users have a default access level of 1 if they are not already specified differently in your users list.

You can customize any of the commands I have given you here to fit your own personality or copy those of others you meet on IRC. Use your imagination and these commands to create your own unique CTCP replies in the Remote/Commands option.

Events

After you have all your friends added to your list at the level you like, you want to add event commands. Event commands handle certain commands as they pertain to your friends when they enter a channel, like giving them ops or adding them to your protect list. Event commands react to events initiated by friends on your users list or by others. Each event has an access level that it matches to the user's access level. You can also activate normal command definitions in this area that will work with users who aren't on your users list.

Note: In the Remote option, auto-op only works on the user addresses, while the protect feature works on nicks.

The most common events that this option responds to are: ON OP/DEOP, Auto ops, Protect, ON BAN, ON CHAT/SERV, ON FILE-SENT/FILRCVD, ON JOIN/PART, ON KICK, and ON TEXT. Events also respond to other special events you can set up. These are discussed later in this section.

The ON OP/DEOP command lets you set up the type of event that is performed regarding those with ops status. This command lets you remotely op and deop user and friends. If you have a channel where you have set up strict rules for who can and cannot have ops, this event gives you ways to remotely control your channel ops. You can set up an event that will deop those who get ops but aren't on a high enough access level (per your standards) to receive ops. Along with this command you can send a message to the person who opped the lower level user. The command is: **100:ON OP:#:/mode #chan -o $nick | /msg $nick <your message>**. Add your own customized message in place of <your message>. Then when a user who only has an access level of 100, or whatever level you specify, gets opped, you deop them and send the message to the opper.

You can set up a similar command to reop someone who has been deopped and send a message to the offending opper. The command might look something like this: **400:ON DEOP:#:/mode $chan +o $opnick | /msg $nick <your message>**. With this command, you give ops back to your friend and send a message to the opper who deopped your friend.

From time to time you may see people who come onto your channel during a split and get or have ops. They get these ops from the servers. If you want to avoid this and take ops away from them, add the following line to your Remote/Events: **1:ON SERVEROP:#:/mode $chan -o $opnick | /notice $me $nick <your message>**. This command deops anyone who rides a server back to your channel and is holding op status. It also sends a message back to you with the $me and the $nick referring to the server that did the opping.

If you want to auto-op the friends on your users lists, you add the following command into the Events option in your Remote dialog text box: **400:ON JOIN:#:/mode $chan +o $nick | /auser 400 $nick**. This command tells mIRC to give ops to the users in your list who have a level of 400.

If you have friends who like to change their nicks often, you can also set up a command to cover them when they change their nicks. The following command adds them to your users list for the events you programmed. In the Events section of your Remote text box type this: **400:ON NICK:/ruser $nick | /auser $newnick**.

To protect your users when they get deopped, the following command in the Events section of the Remote text box does the trick: **50:ON DEOP:#:/mode $chan +o $opnick**. Then if someone deops them, mIRC reops them for you.

The ON BAN command lets you set up an event response that deops and removes a ban that another user sets. The command looks like this: **1:ON BAN:#:/mode $chan -o $nick | /mode $chan -b $banmask**. If you like, you can use $bnick to refer to the user's nickname but if the banmask does not include the user's nickname, $bnick doesn't have a value.

The next set of commands deals with causing the Event commands to listen for messages in DCC Chat windows. You can set up prearranged responses to certain comments you know your friends send you in DCC chat messages. The command looks like this: **1:ON CHAT:<user's message>:/msg =$nick <your message back>**. This command forces mIRC to send your message back to this nick in response to their message to you. The = sign in front of $nick is there to send your message back as a DCC chat message.

Another command that can come in handy is one that is sent after a chat connection is established. The command is: **1:ON CHAT-OPEN:/msg =$nick <your message>**. In the <your message> area you could include something like "Hi, I'll be right with you..." or something similar.

You can also direct mIRC to listen for messages in fileserver windows. Using the following command, mIRC listens for any messages and sends a message back: **1:ON SERV:*:/msg =$nick <your message>**. You can also send a reply message back to a user when they establish a fileserver connection with you. The command for this is: **1:ON SERVOPEN:/msg =$nick <your message>**.

Note: Because of the way that DCC chat works, the previous commands respond to all users level 1 and above.

When you send and receive files with your friends on IRC, you can use a fileserver and program commands in Events to return messages to your friends when the files complete their send or reception. The commands are **1:ON FILESENT:*:.txt,*.ini:/echo Sent $filename to $nick ($+ $address $+)** for files sent or **1:ON FILERCVD:*:.txt,*.ini:/echo Received $filename from $nick** for files received. Then when any file match of .txt or .ini is successfully sent or received, mIRC sends these messages to the status window indicating the success of the transfer.

As people come and go on your channels, you can set up remotes to automatically greet them or comment on their departure. You can also create a remote that automatically kicks someone you add to a special level of your users list when they join your channel. The command for auto greeting visitors to your channel is: **<ACCESS LEVEL>:ON JOIN:#:/msg $chan <your message>**. The command for commenting on departures is: **<ACCESS LEVEL>:ON PART:#:/msg $chan <your message>**. To auto kick someone who joins your channel, type: **<ACCESS LEVEL>:ON JOIN:#<channel name>:/kick $chan $nick | /msg $nick <your message>**. You can choose the access level you want for any of the <ACCESS LEVELS> preceding these commands. For those you want to auto kick, I suggest you set up a special access level and add their names to it.

Note: The ON KICK event only works on a nickname because IRC servers only send the address of the user doing the kicking and the nickname of the person being kicked.

mIRC also lets you set up commands that execute from ON KICK events. You can kick anyone who kicks someone from your channel or send yourself a note when certain people are kicked. To kick a kicker, type: **<ACCESS LEVEL>:ON KICK:#:/kick $chan $nick | /msg $nick <your message>**. You can also add an invite to this message to invite the kickee back to your channel. The command change is as follows: **<ACCESS LEVEL>:ON KICK:/kick $chan $nick | /invite $nick $chan | /msg $nick <your message>**. To send a message to

yourself every time someone is kicked from your channel, type:
**<ACCESS LEVEL>:ON KICK:#<channel name>:/notice $me
<your message to yourself> $nick was just kicked**.

Note: For any of these commands you can use more than one
channel within the command. You just separate each channel
with a comma only—no space between.

The ON TEXT event lists certain messages that happen in your channel. You specify the text to listen for and the message to send in
response in the event command. You can program responses to hellos,
good-byes, private message queries for information, or anything you
find a need for in this event. To give you an example, here are hello
and good-bye events you can set up: **1:ON TEXT:hello*:#<channel
name>:/msg $chan <your welcome>** or **1:ON TEXT:good-
bye*:#<channel name>:/msg $chan <your message> $nick**.
Notice the * in this command. This star is a key and tells mIRC to listen for this event in both private and channel messages. With these
event commands, any time a user in your channel says hello or good-
bye these messages are sent to the channel in response.

When you are on channels and you play a wave, several of your
friends might not have that wave. They will ask you to send them the
wave. You see this in channel as **!<nick> sound.wav**. You can set up
a command in Events that automatically sends requested waves to
your friends. The command is: **1!:ON TEXT:!<your nick>*:*:/dcc
send $nick <directory for your waves, e.g., c:\mirc\waves\> $+
$parm2**. Then whenever someone in the channel you're on types
!<your nickname> and the name of the wave you played, mIRC
automatically initiates a DCC send to them with the wave they
requested.

Other options you can program to take care of things for you include
the following:

➤ 1:ON CTCPREPLY:PING:/echo $nick <your message>—lets you
intercept CTCP ping replies

➤ <ACCESS LEVEL>:ON INVITE:#<channel name>:/join $chan |
/describe $chan <your message>—joins you to the channel you
specified in <channel name> and sends your message to the channel as an action statement

➤ 1:ON MODE:#<channel name>:/notice $nick changed mode to $parms—holds the actual mode change parameters when a mode change happens on a channel you specified in <channel name>

➤ <ACCESS LEVEL>:ON NICK:/describe $newnick <your message>—lets you tell a user what you think when they change their nick while they're in a channel you're on

➤ <ACCESS LEVEL>:ON NOTIFY:/msg $me <your message to yourself> $nick just joined IRC!—sends a message to you when anyone on your notify list and users list joins IRC

➤ <ACCESS LEVEL:ON QUIT:/notice $me <your message to yourself> $nick just quit IRC—same as ON NOTIFY except that it messages you when one of your notifies leaves IRC

➤ 1:ON TOPIC:#:/describe $chan admires $nick's new topic!—sends this message to the channel when someone changes the topic there

➤ 1:ON SOUND:/msg $nick I don't have $filename—is triggered when a user plays a sound file you don't have

File Server

There may come a time when you want to offer files from your hard drive to some of your friends or other users. mIRC lets you program a remote function to do that. I recommend for your own security that you set those files up in a separate directory and only let designated users or friends into that directory. For instance, you can set up a wave directory and put all your .wave files there. Or if you have some text files that you want to distribute to new users on your channel, for instance, channel rules or guidelines, you could set up a directory for those files for that purpose.

These file server activities are initiated by the /fserve command. This command starts up a DCC chat or send with the user. In order for these file server commands to work, you have to indicate a home directory. And anyone requesting a file server can only access files within your home directory. The command breaks down like this: /fserve <nickname> <maxgets> <homedirectory> <file>. Let's look at an example of a file server command you can set up in your Events.

For example, if you set up a NewUser directory containing rules files, you can share those files with other users at level 100 by letting them ask you for the files. To do this you set up the following command in the Events section of the Remote text box: **100:ON TEXT:*^newuser*:*:/fserv $nick 10 C:\newuser\<name of file>**. When someone on your users list types the /fserve command and the number of files they want, he is DCC sent files from your directory. Notice in this command the number 10; that is the number of files you want to limit users' access to.

Keep your directories to a manageable size. Directories with a large number of files in them can slow down these transfers. Also, if a user is idle too long when receiving files, the file server closes the connection. This can be alleviated somewhat by increasing the time on the idle time-out section in the DCC Options dialog box.

Users are limited to only one file server session at a time. Before they can initiate a second file server session, they have to either wait for the one they are in to time out or for it to complete.

Raw

The Raw option lets you create definitions or scripts that respond to numeric server messages. Since this option uses scripts and is a more advanced feature of IRC, it is covered in *Learn Advanced Internet Relay Chat* (Wordware Publishing, ISBN 1-55622-604-7).

With the users list, commands, and events, you have automated a lot of functions and commands that take up much of your time in IRC. Use the ones I gave you here and add your own flair to them or use them as they are. Although they may look complicated, they are fairly easy to use and will make your time in IRC go smoother and easier.

What Can You Do with DCC?

As I mentioned before, DCC is Direct Client to Client protocol and allows you to send files or chat with other users by establishing a direct connection between your computer and theirs. This connection is established through the use of each of your providers' servers, the one you connect to when you dial in to get your Internet connection. So, if you ever have problems sending someone a file or chatting with him, it could be one or both of your providers experiencing problems.

With the DCC send function, you can send a file or even a prescanned picture of yourself or your family to a user by clicking on the Send toolbar button, then typing in the nick of the person you wish to send the file to. Next you select the directory and filename from the list of your files that appear in this dialog box (see Figure 5-29). Once you have completed this information, click on the OK button; the file is ready for the other person to accept. All the other person needs to do is either type **/dcc get <nick> <filename>** or click on the Get button in the DCC Receive box that appears on their screen.

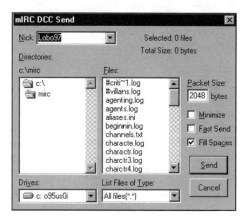

Figure 5-29   DCC Send dialog box

mIRC also allows you to send multiple files, with a maximum of nine files at one sitting. You can also set the Packet Size, which is the number of bytes that mIRC sends to another client in one packet. The minimum size is 512, while the maximum is 4096. Unless you need to change this setting, my advice to you is to leave it alone.

Note: The Fill Spaces option is only available for the 32-bit version of mIRC which is used with Windows 95 operating systems. It is recommended that you leave this option turned on.

When you are on the receiving end of a DCC send, you get a dialog box that asks you if you want to Get or Cancel (see Figure 5-30). If you select Get, mIRC tells the sender client to begin the file transfer and you start receiving the file being sent to you. If you select Cancel, of course, the file is not sent to you.

Figure 5-30   DCC Get dialog box

If someone tries to send you a file that already exists in your directory, mIRC gives you a dialog box with three options to choose from—Overwrite, Resume, or Rename the file. If you choose overwrite, the file downloads from the beginning and erases the existing file. The resume option allows you to resume a transmission where it left off or for the remaining part of the file. It appends to the portion of the file you already have. And, of course, your last option is to rename the incoming file so that it neither overwrites nor resumes. It just creates a new file with a new filename.

Next to the DCC Send and DCC Chat buttons on your toolbar is another button called simply DCC. This is your DCC Options button. You should click on this button after you set up your general options and set your options for DCCs. You have several options there to set (see Figure 5-31).

Figure 5-31   DCC Options dialog box

You have the following options on the Send tab:

➤ In the On Send request box, there are several choices: Show get dialog; Auto-get file and minimize; and Ignore all. By default you must accept all send requests before transfers begin. My advice to you is to leave it set this way. The reason behind this is that there are some people who like to send you things you may not want to have or try to flood you through DCC. If you leave this at the default, you have the option of choosing what you want to receive. Then if someone tries to send you something you are not sure of, you can refuse to accept it. So, always make sure the Show get dialog box is checked or activated. There is also a section that lets you set how you will receive files when you have the Auto-get and files exist option selected. These are: Ask, Resume, and Overwrite. You can also select the Max. DCC Sends you are willing to accept at a time. The default is already set at five for you.

Tip: It is always wise not to accept DCC sends from someone you do not know. People on IRC have been know to try to send other users smutty pictures or computer viruses, or even try to flood them using this tool.

The Chat tab has the following options:

➤ In the On Chat request box, there are Show Chat Dialog; Auto-accept and minimize; and Ignore All settings. The default for this option is Show Chat Dialog. Again, it is wise to leave this option set at default. Then if someone tries to initiate a chat session with you, you have the option of refusing it (see Figure 5-32).

Figure 5-32   DCC Options Chat tab

The Fserve tab lets you set up how you want your file server to handle files. It lets you select the number of Max. Fileservers to use, the Max. DCC Gets per user, the Root Directory to use, the Welcome Text file to use, and whether or not to Display Fileserver Warning (see Figure 5-33).

Figure 5-33   DCC Options Fserve tab

The Options tab lets you choose how you want On DCC Completions handled. You can choose the following: Notify with beep—Send, Get, Chat; and Close window—Send, Get, Chat. When you select these options, mIRC performs them once a transfer is completed. It also lets you select how Time-outs in seconds are dealt with: Get/Chat Dialog; Send/Get Transfer; and Fileserver—the setting here determines how long mIRC waits for you to respond to the accept dialog boxes before stopping the session. The last option you have available under this tab is DCC Ports which lets you specify the first and last ports to use for DCCs. Defaults are already set for you (see Figure 5-34).

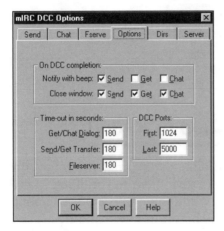

Figure 5-34   DCC Options Options tab

The Dirs tab lets you add, delete, or edit the directories (where the files you receive are stored) that you want to use for your DCC receives.

The final tab is Server. This lets you select how the file servers will perform. You can choose from the following options: Enable DCC Server, Listen on Port, Listen for Send, Chat, or Fserve, and Perform a DNS Lookup (see Figure 5-35).

Figure 5-35   DCC Options Server tab

What Other Things Do I Need to Know?

There are lots of nice little handy tips that you might not find out on your own, so I am going to give them to you here. Many of these little tips are unique to mIRC, while some of them are common to IRC. All of them help you navigate better in mIRC and IRC.

System Menu

When you double-click in the top left-hand corner of a window, you are able to close that window. In mIRC, if you click once in that corner you get a drop-down menu or system menu. It has the usual system menu items, but it also has a few added features like Position, Buffer, Font, Logging, Beeping, Timestamp, and Desktop.

If you click on Position, you can tell mIRC to Reset, Remember, or Forget the Position and Size of the window you are in. When you choose Reset, your windows revert back to previous sizes. If you select Remember, mIRC opens your windows to that position and size every time you open it. If you check Forget, the window opens up in the default position assigned by Windows.

When you click on Buffer, you can clear or save the text in the window you are in. If you select Save, the filename is taken from the name of the window.

The Font option lets you select the fonts you want for that window. You can have different fonts for each window you have open. Whichever font you select is remembered each time you open that window until you select a new font.

When you click on the Logging option, the text in that window is logged to a file. The setting stays on until you click it off, even if you exit and return to IRC. The filename for the log file is taken from the name of the window.

The Beeping option only appears for Channel, DCC Chat, and Message windows. When selected, mIRC beeps any time a message is sent to that window if it is an inactive window. Again, this setting remains constant until you click it off.

The Timestamp option lets you turn timestamping of events on or off for a window. Refer to the IRC Switches section in this chapter for more information on timestamps.

When you select the Desktop option, mIRC lets you position that window outside the mIRC main window. You can then move your chat window to your desktop and work in other applications, toggling back to your chat window when you want to catch up on the conversation or jump in.

Warning: Selecting the Desktop option will cause your windows to minimize each time you select another window to work in no matter whether it's a window in another application or in mIRC.

Timer

mIRC gives you an online timer. This option lets you choose how you want your sessions timed when you are online and you select it. You can choose to let it reset back to zero each time you connect so you can tell how long you stay on during each session. Or you can let it record a cumulative time to tell you how long you stay on between times you reset it (see Figure 5-36).

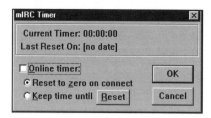

Figure 5-36   Timer dialog box

Smart Tools

If you remember back to the chapter on commands, you remember the command I gave you for listing channels. You might also remember there were parameters you could set to limit your lists. Well, mIRC has turned that command into a toolbar button command. When you click on the List Channels button, you get a dialog box that asks you if you want to set up parameters. It gives you two boxes to add numbers, one for minimum and one for maximum.

Warning: Many servers on the UnderNet no longer let you perform a complete list of channels. Therefore, it is to your advantage to use these parameters when performing lists.

mIRC goes a few steps further; it allows you to define a search for only certain channels by allowing you to use one or more words to match channel names and topics. You can also filter out unwanted channel names or topics by using the Hide function. The Hide function allows you to specify words or substrings you do not want to see. Then when it gives you a list, the list does not have any of the channels listed that match your Hide keywords.

The Hide function does not block out access to those channels; it simply does not display them in a channels list. Another great feature of the Hide function is the Lock button. This button lets you enable password protection. You can then set a password which locks, encrypts, and masks the set of words you selected to hide from the channel list. And of course, it has an Unlock button which lets you disable or change the Hide function settings.

User Central is an option you find under your pop-up menu when you click on a channel names list. It keeps an up-to-date user information database for you. You can store information on your friends using the storage options. It keeps track of their nicks, address, version, and other information for you to refer back to or update at any time.

When you double-click in any channel window, mIRC brings up a dialog box called Channel Central. This dialog box shows you the Channel Modes, Bans, and Topic settings. You can use this dialog box to change or set channel modes or the topic, or add and delete channel bans, saving you time and wear and tear on your fingers typing in all those commands.

The Channel Folder toolbar button lets you store favorite channel names in it. Then you can add or delete channels to this list, use the dialog box buttons to get the names of people in your favorite channels, or join and part those channels just by clicking on the buttons in that box.

Copy and Paste

To copy and paste in IRC, click and drag just like you do in any other windows application. As soon as you release the left mouse button, the text you just highlighted is copied to the clipboard. Notice mIRC does not have an Edit menu item. So, here comes the tricky part. When you are ready to paste the text you just copied, go to the window you want to paste it to. Paste the text by holding down the Ctrl button and the Insert key or by holding down the Ctrl button and the v key on your keyboard. Now, when you press the return button the text you copied displays on the channel you pasted it to.

 Warning: You can only copy text that is displayed in a window. To copy text outside the immediate window area you have to scroll up or down to display it first.

If you are trying to copy from mIRC to another application, you can follow these same instructions and simply hold the Ctrl button and either the Insert key or the v key down in the insertion point where you want the text to go. Or, you can put your cursor at the point you want the text to be pasted and click on Edit in the menu bar and then Paste from the menu.

Special Key Combinations

The F1 key shows help files and is context sensitive. However, remember that if you reprogrammed this key as an alias, it no longer works as the help key. The Shift F1 key combination displays keyword search dialogs for the help file.

When you press Ctrl and Tab at the same time, it toggles you between windows. Pressing the Tab key alone inserts a /msg <nickname> into the prompt line of the window you are currently in. The nickname is the nick of the last person that messaged you. The Shift-Tab key combination switches you between channel windows. Pressing the Esc key minimizes the active window, but it must be turned on in the Extras text box. The Shift key lets you copy text exactly as it appears in a window. The Ctrl key lets you send information that begins with the / command prefix as normal text rather than as a command.

Notify

When you add someone to your notify list while you are on IRC, mIRC notifies you when those people come and go by putting a notice in your status window. It goes a step further by adding a Notify toolbar button. When you click on this Notify button, you get an alphabetized list of everyone from your notify list who is currently on. If you highlight any one of those names and double-click on it, mIRC does a /whois on them and displays the information in your status window (see Figure 5-37).

Figure 5-37   Notify List

This toolbar button with its own window makes it very fast and easy for you to find out where your favorite people are hanging out. It also gives you that nice neat little list of every one of those people who are on. No more having to scroll back and forth through your status window just to find out if one of your friends has come on or left.

URL

When I had you go through and customize all your general options, one of the ones you customized was the URL catcher. I told you this URL catcher would grab web site addresses and store them in a database for you. But I did not tell you how you get to that database. Well, now I will. Next to the Notify toolbar button is the URL toolbar button.

```
URL List [urls.ini]                                    _ □ ×
* mIRC Homepage at Geopages
* mIRC Homepage at mIRC Co. Ltd.
* mIRC Homepage at Nijenrode
+ AltaVista Search: Simple Query PGP cookie.cutter
+ What's cooking at Strouds?
- Yahoo! IRC Clients, FAQs, Server lists, etc.
- Yahoo! list of popular IRC Channels
? http://www.newsinternet.com
? http://www.undernet.org
? http://www.getset.com
? www.sabrina.org...
? http://www.vannet.com/vanecho/magazine.htm
? www.ninc.com/selfed.htm
```

Figure 5-38   URL List box

If you click on this URL button, a window opens (see Figure 5-38). Inside that window are listed all the URLs, or web site addresses, mIRC has caught for you. When you click to highlight any of those addresses, you can then click anywhere in the window and get a drop-down menu. You see that you have several choices here. The first choice is View and when you click on it, your web browser is activated and it loads that address for you to view.

The second selection you can make is Send To. If you click on it, you can send that URL to the channel or any window you have open. You get another box listing any channels or message windows you have open as your choices.

After these two choices, note a separate section with Add, Edit, and Delete as items to select. If you click on any of these items, you get a dialog box asking you to complete information depending on which selection you choose. If you select Delete, you get a box asking you if you really want to delete that URL.

The last option in this drop-down menu is the Option menu item. When you click on this item, you are taken to the Options window where you can change any selections to the URL catcher options.

Multiple Instances

Multiple instances means you can be on more than one server or more than one net at a time. With mIRC, you have to open it up twice in order to do this. Then you can move your channel windows to your desktop by checking Desktop on in the System menu we discussed earlier.

Address Book

This version of mIRC has added a new feature—an Address Book. In this address book, you can keep track of all your online friends. It lets you save information about your friends on IRC, such as name, e-mail address, personal web site, IP address, and other notes. You can also display information that your IRC server has on a user.

When you add e-mail and web page information on a user, mIRC lets you start your e-mail program or your browser from it and lets you send an e-mail to that friend or go directly to their web site. Clicking on the IP address in this address book connects you directly to that user with a DCC connection. This added feature saves you a few steps when trying to communicate with your online friends and family.

mIRC Specific Commands

mIRC has many of its own specific commands. You can find a list of these in the mIRC help files. You can either click on the Help toolbar button or you can type the command **/help <command>** while you are in mIRC. This might be something you want to review at your leisure. Since they are mIRC specific, I am not going to list them all here. The commands I gave you in Chapter 3 are the most frequently used or important commands to you in your IRC adventures. But please do review mIRC's commands. You just might find some in there that would be of use to you.

Summary

You should be able to load this program, custom configure it to reflect your preference, and set up a few of the servers from Chapter 1 in the servers list for this program. Once you have done that, you are ready to set up your nickname and identifier, or whois tag as some people call it.

Then as you find the channels you like best, you can add them to your favorite channels list and use it to find out who is on those channels and join from there if you like.

You are able to set up your auto-ops, and protect, notify, and ignore lists from what you have learned in this chapter. You are also able to program or set up your own aliases to shorten some of those long IRC commands into either function keys or abbreviated keyboard functions.

You have the best popups in your channels once you have mastered how to program them in your popups options. Remotes are no longer a secret to you nor as hard as you thought when you take the tutorial offered in this chapter. Follow the instructions and set up your own users lists and custom replies, auto-ops, etc.

You now know how to configure your DCC functions so that you receive and send those files to your friends and family in the fastest possible way. You are a wizard at mIRC after reading and applying what you learned from this chapter. Go out there and tackle the world of IRC!

Chapter 6

Pirch Software

*I*n the last chapter, I told you all about mIRC. With this chapter, I am going to do the same thing with Pirch version .90.

In this chapter you learn:

- ☑ How to connect to a server with Pirch
- ☑ How the channel windows differ in Pirch from mIRC and how you can configure them to your preferences
- ☑ How to edit or add servers to your server list
- ☑ How to set up and save profiles for each person in your household so that each one can have their own custom Pirch setup
- ☑ How to use the menu bar items—what they are and what they do—as well as their corresponding toolbar buttons
- ☑ How to set up custom Events and Controls
- ☑ How to set up your own bio

Pirch is another user-friendly interface, or client, to use with IRC. It has many of the same features that mIRC does, plus a few additional ones. The developers who designed this program knew very little about how IRC functioned, they claimed. They also say that the name, which stands for PolarGeeks IRC Hack, is a little deceiving since no actual hacking took place. The creator of Pirch says he just watched how messages were sent between the client (the software) and the server and built upon that information.

Remember I told you in an earlier chapter that Pirch is a shareware piece of software. And I gave you an address where you can go to find it. Well, if you think after reading this chapter that this is the IRC client you want to use, go to that web site, and download Pirch. Using the same instructions I gave you in Chapter 4, install it on your hard drive and create an icon for it. Then you are ready to start playing with Pirch and exploring IRC.

So, let's get down to the nitty gritty and find out what this IRC client is all about. Let's find out what it can do and how you can customize it for yourself.

How Do I Connect to IRC with Pirch?

After you click on the icon for Pirch, the application window opens up. Pirch does not automatically try to connect you to an IRC server or even pop up a server list. It gives you a window with a menu bar and items and a toolbar with toolbar buttons (see Figure 6-1).

Figure 6-1   Pirch application window

All of the toolbar items are also included as selections in various Menu bar options. Pirch set these up this way to give you the options of working the way that is more comfortable for you. In this section, I tell you how to use both the toolbar and menu bar items to perform activities.

When you click on the first menu item, IRC, you get a drop-down box with several more menu items in it. These are New IRC Server Connection, Server List, Auto Connect Setup, Proxy Setup, Printer Setup, Printer, and Exit. Clicking on New IRC Server Connection gives you a Server Connection dialog box. This dialog box is similar in some ways to the setup box in mIRC. You can also click on the Login button in the toolbar to get to this same Server Connection box.

To get connected to IRC, you must get to the Server Connection dialog box either through the IRC/New IRC Connection menu or through the Login toolbar option. Here you choose your server, and the creator of Pirch was nice enough to provide you with a list of nets and some of their servers to get you started. In this Server Connection box, you also find fields for Nickname, Alternate nickname, real Name, and e-mail address just like you did in mIRC. And you can select your Initial User Modes here. Let's look at each of the areas (see Figure 6-2).

net list 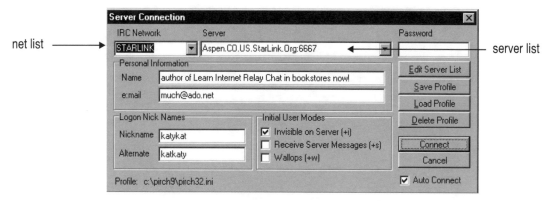 server list

Figure 6-2   *Server Connection dialog box*

The first line you see is the IRC Network/Server/Password line. Each of these has a box for you to either choose an option from a drop-down menu or fill in a word. The net and a server, usually the last one you connected to, appears on this line. If you click on the down arrow next to either the IRC Network or the Server boxes, you get a drop-down menu box listing all the nets or servers in the database. If you don't want the one that is displayed, simply highlight the one you do want and it will replace whatever is in either of these boxes. Also note next to the Server line is a line where you can type in a password if one is called for. (Remember in the chapter on mIRC, I told you that if you are unsure whether you need a password, you probably don't.)

The next area in this window is the Personal Information area. This is where you enter your real name or your custom tag line. You also enter your e-mail address. If you do not have these two areas filled in, you are not able to connect to IRC.

Next, you have the Logon Nick Names area. Here is where you type in your favorite nickname and an alternate nickname. Beside this area is a box called Initial User Modes. There are three choices here, and you can select all three or just the ones you want. The first one in the list is Invisible on Server (+i). What this mode does is make you invisible, in a way. If someone does a /whois on you, he gets the normal /whois information in his status window on you. But if someone does a /who on a channel you are on, your name does not appear on the channels name list. Likewise, if he does a /names on the net, your name does not show up. It gives you a bit of anonymity, but not complete anonymity. The second choice in this list is Receive Server Messages (+s). This allows you to see all the server messages. Server messages are those messages the servers send back and forth to each other. Sometimes these messages can be quite interesting to read. They appear in your status window, so they do not interfere with your chat window conversations. The last selection you have is Wallops (+w). Wallops are the messages that IRCops send back and forth to each other. These are often quite amusing. It is almost like listening in on the bosses talking about the employees. Again, these messages are sent to your status window, so you have to go there to spy on what the IRCops are saying to each other (see Figure 6-3).

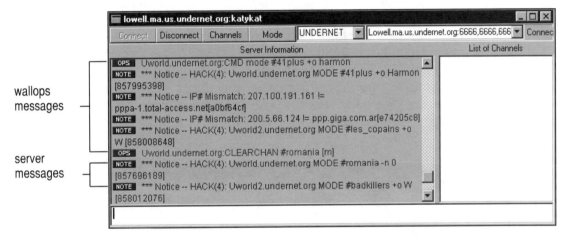

Figure 6-3 IRCops messages

Tip: IRCops are net or server operators. These people are responsible for ensuring the servers are functioning at optimal capacity, and if necessary they step in to deal with some of the more severe user problems. For instance, if a user is flooding others or hacking into accounts, you can complain to one of the IRCops and they have the power to ban that user from all the servers for that net. IRCops have that title as part of their address.

To the right of all this user information are a few buttons that you do not have in mIRC. You have Edit Server List, Save Profile, Load Profile, Delete Profile, Connect, and Cancel. You also have a box you can check to auto connect you when you get disconnected from a server. Let's take a look at each of these and what they do.

When you click on Edit Server List, you get a Servers dialog box (see Figure 6-4). In this box you see a list of the nets and servers you already have in your database. To add, delete, or change the properties of any of these nets or servers, first you have to select the net you want to work with by highlighting it. Then you either right-click on the net or the server you want to alter. You get a menu that lets you select if you want to add a new net or server, delete a net or server, or change the properties of a net or server. Notice that when you are adding servers you can add all or some of the various ports for each server all on one line. Pirch is set up to allow the program to try each port for a server until you get a connection. Therefore, if you put all the ports to a server on one line, Pirch cycles through each port when it gets disconnected until it finally gets a connection. Once it finishes with one server and all its ports, Pirch moves on down the line to the next server and its ports until it reaches the end of your list. If it reaches the end of a list and still has been unable to connect to a server, Pirch stops trying to connect until you tell it to start all over again. It is a rare occasion that you will ever have to do this, though.

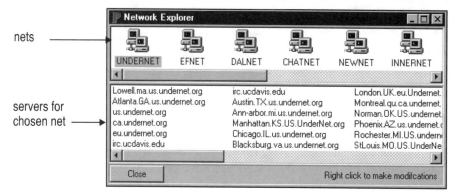

nets

servers for chosen net

Figure 6-4   Nets and servers list

When you select the Add New option for a net, you get a dialog box that asks you to provide the address for the server and its ports. If you want to add a new net to your database, right-click on the nets part of the Servers list box and choose New from the menu. Pirch gives you a new icon for a net and a box under it with New in it. Just enter the name of the net you are adding. Then add new servers by right-clicking in the lower server list box and selecting New from the menu. See Figures 6-5 and 6-6 for examples of what these look like in Pirch.

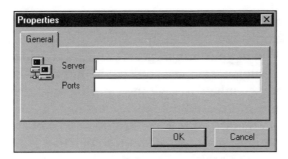

Figure 6-5   Dialog box to add a new server

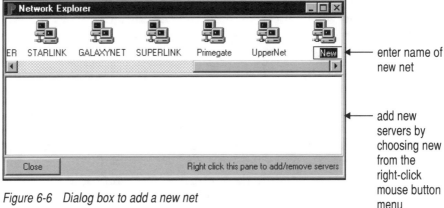

Figure 6-6   Dialog box to add a new net

When you want to delete a net, simply highlight the net, right-click, and choose Delete Network. You can do the same to delete servers—select the server, right-click, choose Delete Entry, and it's done. If you select a server and press the Delete key, you can change the server address of the server. Pirch eliminates the server address but not the server space. It leaves you an edit box where you can type the new server address. When you are finished adding and deleting nets and servers, click on the Close button to save your changes and exit this servers list.

If you are already connected to a server or have a Server Connection box open, you do not see these changes. To see the changes you made, close down either of these you have open and reopen them. Click on the down arrows in IRC Networks and Servers to see your additions or note the deletions you made.

The next two buttons in this Server Connection box after Edit Server List are Save Profile and Load Profile. Once you have this Server Connection box set up to your preferences, you can save them under any name you like. I suggest you use your name and then use the names of your other family members to save their profile preferences. Then each time any of you want to use Pirch, just select Load Profile and choose your profile from the list. After Save Profile and Load Profile is the Delete Profile option. Anytime you want to delete a profile, select this option and choose the profile you want to delete from the list.

Technique: If you just want to update information in the Server Connection dialog box or edit, add, or delete servers, you can do this in Pirch without actually connecting to a server. Once you are finished, click on the Cancel button to take you out of this box.

Pirch lets you create multiple profiles that contain user preferences. So, if there is more than one person in your household who uses Pirch, like at my house, this makes it easier for you to set up your own profiles. Then you don't have to get irritated with each other for changing fonts or window sizes, etc. Just make a profile for each of you and store your individual preferences there. Then when you log on, load your profile and take off into IRC land.

Now that you have filled in all this information, it is time to connect to your server. Click on the Connect button. When you do, you get a Status window (see Figure 6-7). If you have Auto Connect checked in the Server Connection dialog box we just finished with, Pirch automatically starts trying to connect you to a server and displays that information in this Status window. If you chose not to select Auto Connect, you get a blank Status window because you are not connected yet. Click on the Connect button in this window's toolbar and Pirch tries to connect you to your selected server.

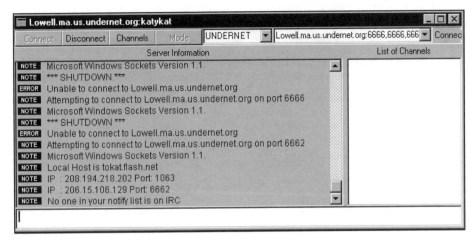

Figure 6-7   Status window

Once the screen scrolls past the MOTD, Message Of The Day, you get a message telling you that you are logged on. Now you can start joining channels, do a list, or just lurk. Pirch lets you call up a channels list by providing you with a toolbar button. If you look at your Status window, you see a few buttons—Connect (now faded), Disconnect (which you use when you are ready to leave), Channels, Join, and Mode. When you click on the Channels button, Pirch performs the channels list command and put the list in that little box on the right-hand side of the Status window (see Figure 6-8). You noticed, I'm sure, that the box is rather small. How in the world are you supposed to see all of these channels' names, much less the topics, in that little bitty window? If you put your cursor on that window and right-click on it, you get a drop-down menu box with several items in it—Zoom Channel List, Channel List Filter, Reload Channel List, Join Channel, List People on Channel, and Report Channel Mode.

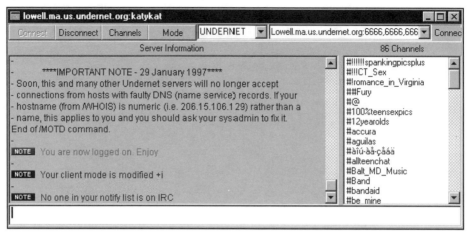

Figure 6-8 Channels list

When you click on the Zoom Channel List menu item, the list window enlarges, letting you view more of the channels list information (see Figure 6-9). With the Channel List Filter, you can set parameters to limit your list, just like you do with mIRC. When you click on the Reload Channel List item, Pirch reloads the channels list.

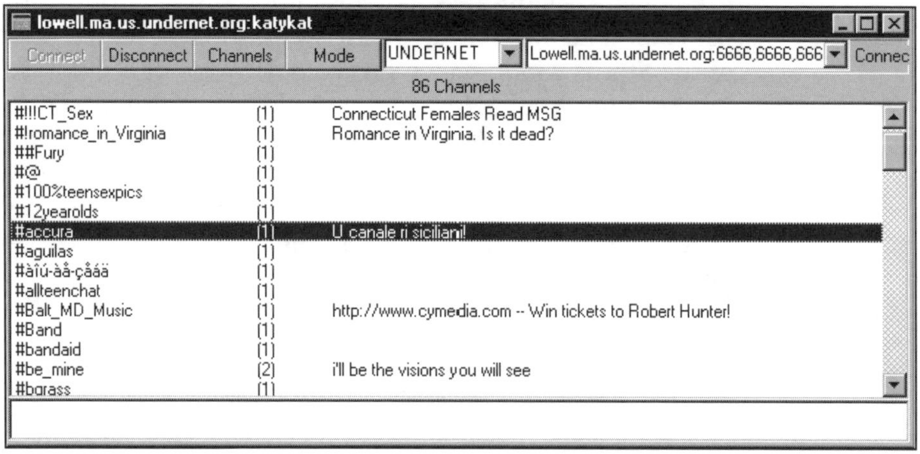

Figure 6-9 Zoom Channel list

You can even join channels from this list. Just highlight the channel you want to join, right-click on the list window, then click on the Join Channel item. Another great feature of the Pirch channels list is that you can also get a names list of people on a channel or the channel mode. Simply highlight the channel name, right-click in the list window to get the drop-down menu, then click on List People on Channel or Report Channel Mode menu items. These last few added features can save you a lot of time and wear and tear on your fingers and wrists by not having to type out all those commands yourself.

What is Going on with These Channel Windows?

Once you start joining channels, you are going to notice that the channel windows look a little different than they do in other IRC programs. Pirch has added some distinctive features for you. Notice the boxes at the lower right-hand corner of the window—Topic, Take Ops, Kick, and Kick/Ban (see Figure 6-10). This is called the Operator Control Panel. This box only appears if you have ops status. If you join a channel and you don't get ops status, the right-hand side of your channel window is blank other than the channels names list.

Figure 6-10   Channel window with Operator Control Panel

Pirch has set up its program to make it easier for you to do a lot of your channel operations quicker and easier. To set the topic, you click on the Topic button, a drop-down dialog box opens, and you just type in the topic you want to give the channel. If you want to give someone operators status, kick, or kick/ban someone, just highlight their name in the names list, then click on whichever one of those options you want to use. Of course you have to have ops status yourself before you can use these controls. Boy, that was easy, wasn't it?

There are some things you can do with your channels that Pirch does not make readily apparent to the naked eye. All of these channel options are accessed using the right mouse button. You can click in either the display window or in the edit line and then right-click.

One of the things Pirch does is support special text attributes, like bold, italics, colors, symbols, and underline. When you right-click on the edit line of any channel window, a menu pops up. In this menu are several selections. Following are explanations of those options:

➤ Multi-Line Editor—changes the edit or input line into multiple lines rather than a single line.

➤ Bold—bolds all text following where you inserted this format.

➤ Underlined—underlines text following where you inserted the format until you turn it off or deselect it.

➤ Italics—italicizes all text following its insertion point until you deselect it.

➤ Color—turns the color on and lets you insert color code numbers following it to create colorized text. However, each time you want to change color in a line of text, you have to select the color option from this right mouse button menu.

➤ Symbol—turns your text into special symbols. Only you or others using Pirch can see those special symbols. Others see plain text.

➤ Fixed Pirch Font—converts your text to this special Pirch font.

➤ Paste—pastes anything you have in your copy buffer to your edit line.

➤ Page up—scrolls up a page in your channel text buffer.

You can also use many of these special attributes by holding down the Ctrl key and other keys or combinations of keys to get the same effects. Holding down the Ctrl key and the b key gets you bold formatting, Ctrl and u gets you underlined formatting, Ctrl i is for italics formatting, and Ctrl with the k key and one of the number codes for a color gets you colorized text. You enter these control key combinations before and after the words you want to give these special attributes to, similar to an on/off switch. This is a really nice feature, but let me warn you, not everyone sees these attributes. It depends on their client. Pirch and mIRC are the only two clients that I am aware of that do support these special attributes.

When you click with your right mouse button in the channel window anywhere but the names list, you get a drop-down menu with the following: Keep on Top, Set Font, Save as Default Window Size, Multi-

Line Input Editor, Clear Window, Rewrap Text to Fit, Show Window Tag, Edit Notes, and Channel Options.

If you click to check the Keep on Top menu item, then that channel window remains or reverts back to the forefront or top window. This means that if you have more than one window open, when you are finished typing in one of the other windows, the one you have marked to be on top returns to the forefront.

When you click on the Set Font menu item, you get a dialog box with various fonts you can use with Pirch. Simply highlight the Font, Font Size, and Style you prefer and click on the OK button. This new font replaces the old font including anything in your buffer.

The Save as Default Window Size item does what it says—saves the window setting as the size you made it. When you click on the Multi-Line Input Editor, it changes the size of your input line, giving you more room to type out your messages. Nice feature, especially if you tend to be a long-winded person. The Clear Window item clears everything off your main message window when you click on it. This feature comes in handy when you get garbled messages or just want to have a nice clean slate to work on.

The Rewrap Text to Fit menu item rewraps your text to fit within the new window size when you have resized your window. For instance, if you make a window larger, the text remains as it was when the window was smaller, unless you click on this item. Then it rewraps itself to match the window size.

When you click on the Show Window Tag option, Pirch displays your nickname and the server you are connected to in a special window tag at the top of your window. This appears under the title bar of the chat window.

When you click on Edit Notes, you get a blank clipboard to copy and paste into or to compose text to copy and paste into your chat window. (Remember in the last chapter I showed you how to copy and paste in IRC.) The last option in this drop-down menu box is Channel Options. When you click on it, you get another menu box that includes: Set Channel Topic, Set Channel Mode, Open Channel Banlist, Names List on Other Side, and Show Op Control Panel.

The Set Channel Topic item does the same thing as the Topic button in the Operator Control Panel. It lets you set the topic. Set Channel Mode lets you select the modes for the channel. When you click on this menu item, you get a dialog box that lets you click to mark the channel modes you want. Refer back to Chapter 3 to refresh your memory about commands and channel modes.

When you select the Open Channel Banlist option, a dialog box opens listing all channel bans for that channel. You can add other addresses or current addresses from this list if you like. If you click on Names List on Other Side, Pirch moves the channel names list from the right-hand side over to the left-hand side of your channel window. Last in this list of menu items is Show Op Control Panel. By default it should be checked if you have ops status; otherwise it is unchecked as default if you do not have ops. If you uncheck it, the Operator Control Panel disappears, leaving you with a channel window that looks similar to other channel windows in other IRC clients.

If you remember back to the last chapter about mIRC, I told you all about creating Popups and Remote commands and menus. Both mIRC and Pirch allow you to click on a user's name in the channel names list, then right-click to get to the Popup menu. In that Popup menu both programs share some commonalities. They both let you do a /whois (Whois) on someone, Query someone (private message), get a user's user information (Ucentral in mIRC and CTCP User Info in Pirch), Ping (CTCP in both) a user, Give Ops, Take Ops, Kick, Kick/Ban (Control in both), and DCC Send and Chat (DCC in both). But Pirch takes some of those Remote and Popup commands I taught you about in Chapter 5 and automates them for you.

Pirch already is set up to let you do some of your most often used commands by using the Popups menu. For instance, in User, you can put someone on Ignore, Protect a user, Add them to your Auto Ops List, Add them to your Notify list, Add them to your Users List, or Lookup their User IP. All this can be done simply by highlighting their name and then clicking in the names list with the right mouse button to pull up the Popups menu. Then just click on the option you want to use. With Pirch you don't have to worry about setting up these activities in remotes; it has done it for you as part of the program.

The next section in these Popups is Control. Pirch adds one feature here that you do not have with mIRC. It is the Give Voice command. If you remember the chapter on commands, you remember that voice is a command you use with a moderated channel. Now, rather than having to type out the command to give or take voice, you simply have to highlight the name and pull up the popup menu to do it. Much easier than typing in those commands for each person.

With both mIRC and Pirch under the CTCP menu item of the Popup menu you can get a Ping, User Info, Client Info, Client Version, Finger, and Time on any user in your channel. You just highlight their name, pull up the Popup menu, and pick your poison. With the DCC menu item in mIRC and Pirch you can start a DCC Send or DCC Chat session with another user quickly and easily with the Popup menu.

Of course with Pirch, just like with mIRC, you can add your own popups also. I will cover that in more detail later in this chapter. For now that about covers everything to do with the channel windows. Now let's move on to the menu bar items and the toolbar buttons for the Pirch application window.

What Do These Menu Bar Items Do?

One of the first things you notice if you compare Pirch with mIRC is that the menu bar and toolbar items and buttons are very different. However, although they may have different names, they share some common features. Notice in Pirch that all the menu bar items contain in their menus all of the toolbar buttons. Let's see what you have.

IRC and Login Menu and Toolbar Items

We have already discussed the IRC menu item. Let's highlight it again here. When you click on this menu bar item, a drop-down menu appears with these items: New IRC Server Connection, Servers List, Auto Connect Setup, Proxy Setup, Printer Setup, Print, and Exit. When you click on the New IRC Server Connection, you get a Server Connection dialog box. As noted before you can get that same login dialog box by clicking on the Login toolbar button.

When you click on the Servers List menu item, you get a dialog box listing all the nets and servers and giving you the option to add, edit, delete, etc. This is the same dialog box you get if you click on the Edit Server List button in the Server Connection dialog box. The Login toolbar item gives you the same Server Connection dialog box.

The next item in the IRC menu is Auto Connect Setup. This option gives you an Auto-Connections Setup dialog box. In this box you can add or remove user profiles. When you add a profile to this dialog box, that profile will automatically load each time you start up Pirch. See Figure 6-11 for an example of the Auto-Connections Setup dialog box. There is no corresponding toolbar item for this option.

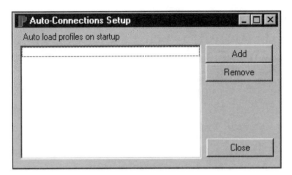

Figure 6-11   Auto-Connections Setup dialog box

Next in the menu list is Proxy Setup. Just as mIRC lets you connect to IRC through a firewall, so does Pirch. This option lets you set up your proxy information. Pirch supports IRC connections through SOCKS proxy. If you are connecting to the Internet through a firewall, click on the Enabled check box in the SOCKS & Proxies dialog box that appears. Then fill in the User ID, Password, SOCKS Host, and Port information and click on OK to save and exit (see Figure 6-12). Again, there is no corresponding toolbar item for this menu option.

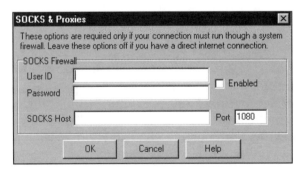

Figure 6-12   Firewall and proxy setup dialog box

In this new version, Pirch has added a feature, the Print option. With Printer Setup you can designate your printer type just as you do with other Windows applications. When you're ready to print, select Print from this IRC menu item. The last menu option in this IRC menu item you can select is Exit. When you click on this menu item, you exit from Pirch completely. If you have any channel windows or server windows open, Pirch closes these and exits.

Server Menu Item

This menu item has no corresponding toolbar buttons, but it contains some menu items that are useful. When you click on this menu option you get a drop-down menu with the following: Get Server Administration Info, Get Message of the Day (MOTD), Get Server Information, Get Server Links Information, Get Server Map Information, Get List of Valid Server Commands, Get Server Time, Get Server Version, Get List of All Users, and Log Server to File.

When you click on Get Server Administration Info, you get the names and addresses of the server and the names of the server administrators along with an e-mail address to address mail to. This is nice information to have if you ever have real serious problems with another user on that server and need to report them to one of the server administrators. Depending on the severity of the offense and your records, or logs, the administrators could ban that user from their server.

Get Message of the Day displays the MOTD for that server. If you have been on IRC for awhile, the MOTD may have scrolled out of your buffer and this option lets you call that MOTD back up for review.

If you click on Get Server Information, it gives you information about the type of server you are on. It tells you who designed it and other pertinent information. This may or may not be of interest to you. If you are a computer whiz, this might be valuable information. But for us average Janes and Joes, it does not mean a lot.

Get Server Links Information gives you all the other servers that are linked to the server you are on. It also tells you all or most of the servers on some of the smaller nets. This is useful in the case of netsplits. It lets you know who your server is linked to so that if you want to change servers and get out of the split, you know which servers to choose or not to choose.

Get Server Map Information maps out how your server is linked to the other servers. This information just backs up the link information you already have.

Get List of Valid Server Commands gives you a list of all the commands you can use with that server. This information comes in handy if you are having problems executing a command. Check this to see if it is a valid command for this server.

Note: Notice when you bring up a list of these server commands that there are a lot of commands we have not discussed here. These are not any of the more common commands and we do not discuss them in this book.

Get Server Time gives you the current time on the server you are connected to. Sometimes it is nice to know what time it is where your server is located. This can also explain the lag and/or splits. During busier times or peak periods, you see more lag and splits on at least the two major nets—EfNet and UnderNet.

Get Server Version gives you the version of the server you are on. This is the same information that the Get Server Info item provides.

Get List of All Users gives you a list of all the users on the server you are on. It gives you their nicks and what channel they are in. Some people like to use this command to see who is on their particular server and where they are hanging out. It can be interesting to pull this command up and see what it reveals.

Log Server to File creates a log file of all server activities. It places this information into a text file you can open in WordPad and read. I've never used this information. But there may be times when you feel the need to log your server activities, especially if you need proof of problems to present to the server administrators.

Channel Menu Item

When you click on the Channel menu option, you get a drop-down menu with the following items: List Channels, Join Channel, Show Channel Occupants, and Show Channel Mode.

If you click on the List Channels menu item, it gives you a list of all the channels on the net you are connected to. It displays these channels in the channels list box on the right-hand side of your status window. If you highlight a channel name and click on the Channel menu option and then on Join Channel, you join that channel.

When you do a list, you can highlight a channel and click on Show Channel Occupants in the Channel menu options. This gives you a list of all the people in that channel, unless they have marked themselves invisible. And if you click on the Show Channel Mode under the Channel menu option, it gives you the modes for the channel you have highlighted in the channels list.

After you join a channel, the options under the Channel menu item change to: Part this Channel, Log Channel to File, View Log File, Show Channel Banlist, Show Channel Topic, Show Channel Mode, and Keep on Top. No matter how many nets you are on, Pirch will perform each of these functions on whichever channel you select by making it your active window—the window in the forefront. The results are displayed in your status window. Let's look at each of these functions more closely.

When you choose Part this Channel from the Channel menu options, it will part you from the channel you have active at the moment. This lets you part a channel without having to type out the /part #channel-name command.

Log Channel to File lets you begin logging a channel when you click on this option. Then when you want to view the log, click on the View Log File and the log displays for you.

When checked, Show Channel Banlist gives you a list of all the current bans for the channel you have active. Show Channel Topic and Show Channel Mode gives you the topic and the modes for the channel you have active when you check these options.

Keep on Top does the same thing here as it does in the channel options from the right mouse button menu when you click on the channel window—it keeps the window you indicate in the forefront.

Tools Menu Item and Corresponding Toolbar Buttons

The Tools menu item contains several of the toolbar buttons in its menu drop-down box. These include: **Favorite** Channels, **W**orld **W**ide **W**eb Links, **Finger** Client, Ident Server, **Media** Control Panel, Bio Viewer, Notify Window, File Server, Video Viewer, **Aliases**, **Events** and Controls, **Popups,** and **DCC** File **Send**er. The bolded words equal the corresponding toolbar buttons. Now let's see what we can do with these menu and toolbar items.

When you click on the Favorite Channels menu item or Favorites toolbar button, you get a Favorite Places dialog box. In this box you can type in the names of your favorite channels. Be sure to include the # symbol before the name and make sure you type the channel name exactly as it appears on the channels list. Otherwise, you could get taken to a channel you never intended, maybe even create a whole new channel. Notice that you can join a channel or find out who is on a channel from this dialog box. You can also add, edit, or delete channels in this dialog box (see Figure 6-13).

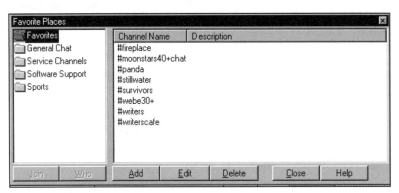

Figure 6-13   Favorite Places dialog box

Previous versions of Pirch only performed a /who on channels for the first net that you connected to. This new version will perform the /who on any channel no matter how many nets you are connected to. Just make sure you have the net with the channels you want to do a /who on designated as active or in the forefront. You can do this by either making the channel the active channel or the status window for the net the active channel. Then select the channel from the list that you want to do a /who on and click on the Who button. The results show up in the status window for the net you indicated.

Add, Edit, and Delete work here just as they do anywhere else in Pirch. And, of course, when you click on the Help button, Pirch brings up the help file for that particular function you are trying to do.

The next menu item under Tools is World Wide Web Links which also corresponds to the WWW toolbar button. If you click on either of these, you get a dialog box that lists all the URLs or web sites Pirch has collected for you. At the bottom of this box you again notice several buttons—Goto, Add, Edit, Remove, Options, and Help (see Figure 6-14).

Figure 6-14   WWW Links list box

If you highlight an address in this dialog box and click on the Goto button, Pirch executes your web browser and inserts this address into the Goto line there, causing your web browser to load that address for you to view. Of course, with the Add, Edit, and Remove buttons you can add, edit, or delete URLs from this database.

The Options button in this dialog box lets you tell Pirch which web browser you are using and where that browser is located on your hard drive (directory and file name). It also gives you a couple of options to choose from—Catch URLs From Chat and Purge Unused URLs. These are on/off switches that you turn on by checking the boxes beside them (see Figure 6-15).

Figure 6-15   WWW Links options

The next option in the menu list is Finger Client with its corresponding toolbar button Finger. When you click on either of these you get a Finger & DNS Lookup dialog box asking you for the address of the person you want to finger. Beside this line to enter the address are three buttons—Finger, DNS, and Clear (see Figure 6-16).

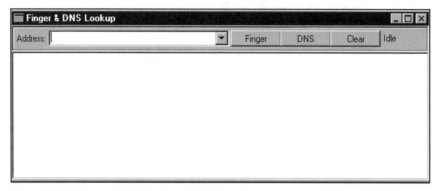

Figure 6-16   Finger & DNS Lookup dialog box

If you click on the Finger button in this dialog box, notice that Pirch puts up a line in the large white box the words **connecting to: <their provider's connection>**. When it has made contact, Pirch responds back with pertinent information in that same box. If you click on the DNS button, Pirch gives you information about that Domain Name Server (DNS), like its name and IP (Internet Provider) address. If you click on the Clear button, Pirch clears all information from this response box. One other thing you notice about this dialog box is the word Idle to the right of the Finger, DNS, and Clear buttons. When you click on the Finger button after you indicate an address, Idle changes to Looking up address. It changes to Connecting once it finds the address and to Closed if it has made the connection and gathered the information or if it is unable to make a connection. This is a status line to let you know how the finger is progressing.

Next in line in this Tools menu item is Ident Server. When you click on this item, you get an IdentServerForm dialog box that asks you for server identification information that Pirch does for this item. Usually this is already filled in for you (see Figure 6-17).

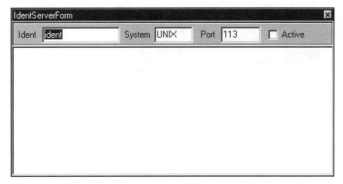

Figure 6-17   IdentServerForm setup box

Next in this Tools menu item is Media Control Panel with its corresponding toolbar button of Media. If you click on either of these options, you get a Media Player dialog box similar to Figure 6-18. You use this item to play various multimedia files like: Wave—Waveforms Audio File (the most common you run across in IRC), MIDI—Musical Instrument Digital Interface Audio File, RMI—a variation of the MIDI file, and AVI—a Video File. The status panel (the area in this figure that says NO FILES QUEUED) shows the name of the sound file being played, the name of the person playing it, and time remaining on that sound.

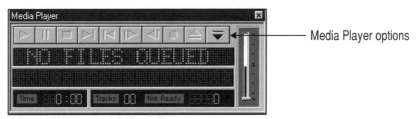

Media Player options

Figure 6-18   Media Player dialog box

When you click on the darkened down arrow in this dialog box, it gives you another Media Player dialog box which is a sound directory list. This area lets you choose which files you want to play. The first line in this box indicates any files that contain sound files on your computer. The next line lets you choose which type of sound you want to play. You have the following options: Uninitialized, All Sounds, Wave Files, Midi/RMI Files, and All Files *.* (see Figure 6-19).

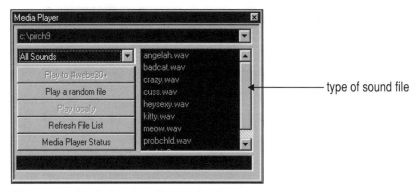

type of sound file

Figure 6-19   Media Player options

Below the directory of sound files, there are several buttons you can choose from. They are: Play to #, Play a random file, Play locally, Refresh File List, and Media Player Status. The Play to # button changes to show the active channel/chat window name; by clicking it, you play the selected sound file to that window. Play a random file randomly selects a sound file from the directory and plays it to the active chat window. Play locally plays a selected sound file that only you can hear. Refresh File List makes the media player reread the directory; you use this if you add new sound files to your directory. The Media Player Status button returns the media player to its original state as seen in Figure 6-18.

The next menu item is the Bio Viewer. When you click on this item, you get a Bio dialog box that lets you view this Bio information on other users. It contains Real Name, Age, Location, Occupation, and About Me (which is really about them) fields. They can also tack on a picture of themselves. Later in this chapter I show you how to create a bio on yourself. This feature is unique to Pirch and lets you send this information back and forth to other users of Pirch. You can also use this Bio Viewer option to view your own bio (see Figure 6-20).

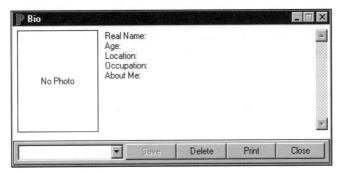

Figure 6-20   Bio Viewer

Three new options in the Tools menu item were added to this version of Pirch. They are: Notify Window, File Server, and Video Viewer. Each of these adds some very nice enhancements to an already fine IRC client.

Notify Window lists each of the nets you are on with any people on your notify list under each of those nets (see Figure 6-21). When you highlight a name in this list and right-click with your mouse, you have several options to choose from—Whois, Query, DCC (which lets you start a DCC chat session with the user), CTCP (which lets you get Ping, User Info, Client Info, and Version information on the user), and Update (which updates this notify list if you've had it open for awhile).

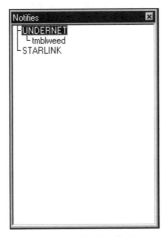

Figure 6-21   Notifies list box

File Server lets you make available some of your files for others to download. This option lets you do this without a lot of interaction on your part. To set up a file server, select File Server from the Tools menu and select the file server options (see Figure 6-22).

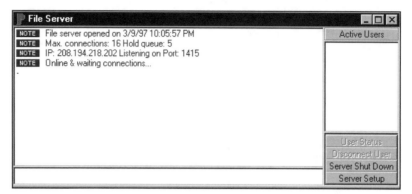

Figure 6-22   File Server setup dialog box

To set up the file server, the first thing you need to do is specify the default options by clicking on the Server Setup button. Then you enter the desired values for each of the options—Idle Disconnect in minutes, Default Max Gets in files, Default Home Dir, and Sign-on Msg File (see Figure 6-23). Indicate by using the up and down arrow keys the number of minutes you want the File Server to wait before it disconnects from a user. You use the up and down arrows to also specify the maximum number of files you want to allow users to get from you at a time. The Default Home Dir (directory) is where you have your file server files that you want to offer to users. It is the root directory that users can access and are allowed to browse through its subdirectories. Set up a special directory for the files that you want to offer for download and put that directory address in this line. If you want to create a special sign-on message that is displayed to users when they log onto your file server, create a standard text file with your message in it. Then include its address in the Sign-on Msg File line here.

directory for file server file

location of sign-on message file

Figure 6-23   File Server Options dialog box

After you get these options set up, you are ready to let users access your file server. You can automate this function in the Events of Pirch. I go into detail about how to do this later in this section under Events and Controls.

The Video Viewer in Pirch lets you send and receive live video. There is no special hardware or software required to receive videos, aside from Pirch (see Figure 6-24).

Figure 6-24   Video viewer box

To send a live video to another user, you must have a digital video camera or camera and video capture board of some sort. Since this is a new option and a more advanced feature of IRC, it is not covered in detail in this book. You can find out more about it in *Learn Advanced Internet Relay Chat* (Wordware Publishing, ISBN 1-55622-604-7).

Now we get to aliases in Pirch. There is a menu item and a toolbar button for it. If you click on either of these, you get an Aliases dialog box. It looks a lot different from the dialog box in mIRC and the aliases do not look the same. The Aliases dialog box is divided into three parts: the Aliases list that contains the names of all the aliases defined, the Command Definition pane where you enter the alias commands, and the control panel that has several buttons to let you add and delete aliases, save changes, load alias files, cancel, and get help.

Pirch handles aliases a little differently than mIRC does. The actual alias is separated into a box of its own and the alias command is in a Command Definition box to the side of the aliases. Aliases in Pirch take the form of <alias name> <command> <message if there is one>. For instance, if betyboop wants to set up an alias in Pirch to join channel #cartoons, this is how she enters it in this dialog box once she clicks on the Add button: **jc** in the Aliases list box. Then in the Command Definition pane, she types: **/join #cartoons**. Or, if she wants to have a welcome message for people who join her channel #cartoons, she can type the alias command this way: **wel** in the Aliases list box, then **/me welcomes $1 to #** in the Command Definition pane (see Figure 6-25).

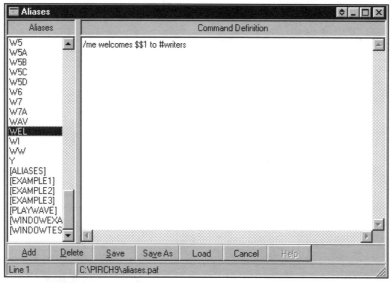

Figure 6-25   Aliases dialog box

The main difference between how you set up aliases in Pirch and how you set them up in mIRC is the beginning part. In mIRC you type the slash and the abbreviation you want to use. In Pirch you type the abbreviation you want to use, then put the command in the Command Definition pane.

Pirch also uses all the same parameter identifiers as mIRC, like the $read identifier; $day, $date, and $time for current day, date, and time; $nick for nickname in a channel; and $ip and $host for the IP and host identifiers. It also uses standard alias definitions like $$1 for nicknames, # for channels, and so forth. Pirch also lets you set up function keys as aliases just like you do in mIRC. Following are some aliases you can include in your aliases files:

➤ bye /me waves good-bye to $1—sends this action command to the channel waving good-bye to the nick you indicate

➤ chat /dcc chat $1—initiates a DCC chat session with the nick indicated

➤ away /away I am away from my computer. . . leave a message—sets you as away

➤ ping /ctcp $$1 ping—pings the indicated nick

➤ send /dcc send $1 $2—establishes a DCC send connection with the two nicks indicated

These aliases give you an idea of how to set up aliases in Pirch. Now try your hand at a few of your own. In addition to these simple aliases, you can also add aliases that use the colorized text and ASCII art you see flowing on channels. Here are a few samples of those aliases:

➤ balloons /me gives a bunch of balloons to ya :) k3~O**~ O**~ O**~Ctrl k4,,ø¤°` Ctrl k10 $$1 Ctrl k4`°¤ø,, Ctrl k13~O**~ O**~ O**~`Ctrl k4¤ø,, Ctrl k10 $$1 Ctrl k4,,ø¤°Ctrl k14~O** O**~ O**~Ctrl k4,,ø¤°` Ctrl k10 $$1 Ctrl k4`°¤ø,, Ctrl k6~O**~ O**~ O**~Ctrl k4`°¤ø,, Ctrl k10 $$1 Ctrl k4,,ø¤°`Ctrl k8~O**~O**~O**~Ctrl k4,,ø¤°` Ctrl k10 $$1 Ctrl k4`°¤ø,, Ctrl k9~O**~O*~ O**~Ctrl k4`°¤ø,, Ctrl k10 $$1 Ctrl k4,,ø¤°Ctrl k2~O**~ O**~O**~ Ctrl k4,,ø¤°` Ctrl k10 $$1 Ctrl k4`°¤ø,, Ctrl k11~O**~ O**~O**~~—wraps this ASCII art of balloons around the nick you indicate. (Remember to type this all on one line.)

➤ doz /doz /me gives $$1 a dozen beautiful roses Ctrl kCtrl k4,1@3}-`-,-`-- Ctrl kCtrl k4,1@3}-`-,-`-- Ctrl kCtrl k4,1@Ctrl k3}-`-,-`-- Ctrl kCtrl k4,1@Ctrl k3}-`-,-`-- Ctrl kCtrl k4,1@Ctrl k3}-`-,-`-- Ctrl kCtrl k4,1@3}-`-,-`-- Ctrl kCtrl k4,1@Ctrl k3}-`-,-`-- Ctrl kCtrl k4,1@Ctrl k3}-`-,-`-- Ctrl kCtrl k4,1@Ctrl k3}-`-,-`--

Use these aliases I have given you here to get you started. Then copy other aliases from log files or get your friends to send you their text files of these aliases and copy them into your aliases. Use them to spice up your adventures in IRC.

Pirch has its equivalent to mIRC's remotes. It calls them events and controls, which you can access by either the menu item or the toolbar button. When you click on either of these items, you get an Automated Events & Controls dialog box. Notice that this dialog box looks very different from the mIRC Remote dialog box (see Figure 6-26).

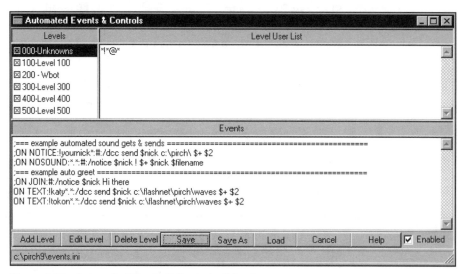

Figure 6-26   Automated Events & Controls dialog box

These events and controls let you customize automatic responses to a variety of events that happen on IRC, like people joining the channel you are on. Just like with mIRC, the first thing you need to do is create a user list. This user list lets you determine which users are affected by the event handlers and have access to the custom CTCP commands you set up. The user list is set up alphabetically, but the order of the entries in the list is important. Pirch searches through events starting at the highest level and working down to the lowest levels. Since Pirch already has this event programmed into the client, you can add users through the popups menu. Remember, in mIRC we talked about giving the people on your user list a level. You are doing the same here. When you set up this list you should put the lowest level users on top and the highest level users on the bottom of your list.

Note: You need to have correct addresses for users in order for these remotes to work.

There are only a few event commands that Pirch recognizes. Anything other than these event commands are treated as CTCP commands. The event commands that Pirch recognizes are as follows:

➤ ON ACTION
➤ ON BAN
➤ ON DEOP
➤ ON IGNORE
➤ ON DCCDONE
➤ ON INCOMING
➤ ON INVITE
➤ ON JOIN
➤ ON KICK

➤ ON KICKED
➤ ON MODE
➤ ON NOTICE
➤ ON NOTIFY
➤ ON OP
➤ ON PART
➤ ON QUIT
➤ ON TEXT
➤ ON TOPIC

Also notice that these commands all start with ON and that the command itself is capitalized. The CTCP replies do not, however, have the ON preceding the command. The following instructions are not capitalized. With Pirch it is very important to capitalize the event command.

For example, if betyboop wants to get a /whois on people as they join the channel, she can enter the following in the events box of the dialog box for this option: **ON JOIN:#:/whois $nick**. In the user section, she types ***!***. This is the universal mask symbol.

Now if betyboop wants to create a ping reply she sets up her users' list under one of the levels, 000 to 500, then she needs to enter the command and her response. It looks something like this: **PING:/notice $nick that tickles....hehehe**. Then whenever someone on her users' list pings her, he gets that reply.

If betyboop wants to send the standard CTCP reply, the time lagged, she can type the same command and add :+ at the end. It looks something like this: **PING:/notice $nick that tickles...heheheh :+**. Then when one of the people on her users' list pings her, he gets her reply and the ping response in seconds lagged.

Here are a few events you can add to your Events and Controls:

➤ ON TEXT:!yournick*:#:/dcc send $nick <directory> $+ $2—lets you set up automatic DCC sends for your sound files. You can also use the ON NOTICE command here.

➤ ON JOIN:#:/whois $nick—does a /whois on everyone who joins your channel

➤ ON JOIN:#:/notice $nick Welcome to # $nick $+ , <your custom message>—sends your welcome message to everyone who visits your channel

➤ PING:/notice $nick <your ping reply message> followed by :>+—sends your ping reply message and the ping time to who-ever requests a CTCP ping on you

Events and controls is also where you include your file server com-mands. When you set up the events for file server functions, the user can then type HELP to get a list of available commands. With this file server event, when a user requests a file, it is sent to them using DCC send. Before someone can access your file server, however, you must first give them permission using the /faccess command. In Events under any of the user level lists, enter the following command: **/faccess <nickname> <directory of your files> 5**. The number at the end of this command tells Pirch and the file server how many files that user has access to from your file server directory.

To automate access to your file server you need to add this command to the events under any user level: **ON NOTICE:*!fileserver:*:/fac-cess $nick <your fileserver directory> 3**. Then when a user types **/notice younick !fileserver** to access your file server files, Pirch tries to initiate a DCC connection with the user via a DCC chat. Before a user can access any files on your file server, they must log in using their nickname. Pirch then tries to match that nickname against its internal security list and your user list. Once it has made that connec-tion and the login passes inspection, Pirch lets your user issue certain commands to get information and files from you. These are as follows:

➤ HELP <command>—lets the user issue this command to get a list of available commands or to get specific help on a command

➤ GET <filename.ext>—lets the user retrieve filenames through DCC

➤ TGET <filename.ext>—lets the user retrieve filenames through a TDCC connection. In order for this to work, however, both the users' clients must have TDCC capability

➤ READ <filename.ext>—lets the user view the contents of a text file while online with the file server

➤ CD <directorymask> or CHDIR <directorymask>—used to change directories

➤ EXIT or BYE—closes the file server connection

Use these event commands to set up your automated events and controls and free up more of your time for chatting. Take what you have learned here and try your hand at creating a few of your own.

Next in line under the Tools menu is Popups and its corresponding toolbar button. Popups work here the same way they do in mIRC. You can set up your menus and submenus the same as you do in mIRC. Remember that popups are aliases that have been converted to pop-up, or if you prefer drop-down, menu items and work in tandem with your right mouse button and your channel names list.

To set up your menu headers, just type the name you want for the menu header. I use all caps to designate these are menu headers, but you don't have to do that if you prefer not to. For anything that you want to fall under the menu header—submenus or pop-up items— just put a period in front of it. With subheadings, put two periods in front of the pop-up items you want to include under that heading, and so on.

Also, remember when you are programming these menu items and commands to type the commands just as you do for aliases. All popup commands are preceded by at least one dot, followed by the command menu item name and a colon. Then you type the command leaving no space between the colon and the forward slash (see Figure 6-27).

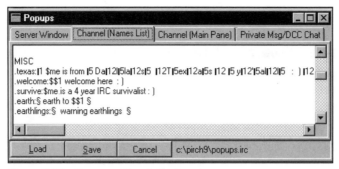

Figure 6-27   Popups editor dialog box

Here are a few examples of some popups you can add to your Popups menus. Some of them are general popups and some of them utilize colorized text and ASCII art:

➤ .welcome:$$1 welcome here :)—when you click on a user's name and then this popup, this message is displayed on the channel with the user's nickname inserted.

➤ .YRoses:Ctrl k9,1 ^ ~+*<Ctrl k3,1{Ctrl k8,1@ Ctrl k9,1 ^ ~+*<Ctrl k3,1{Ctrl k8,1@Ctrl kCtrl k0,1 $$1 Ctrl kCtrl k8,1@Ctrl k3,1}Ctrl k9,1>*+~ ^ Ctrl k8,1@Ctrl k3,1}Ctrl k9,1>*+~ ^

➤ .Slam!:$me slams a 60 lb UNIX manual on $$1's head. That's gotta hurt... but then again... where there's no sense... there's no feeling!

➤ .Hugs: {{{{{{{ $$1 }}}}}}}

➤ .Smiles:/me Ctrl k1,14:) Ctrl k1,8:) Ctrl k1,4:) Ctrl k1,5:) Ctrl k1,6:) Ctrl k1,8:) Ctrl k1,6:) Ctrl k1,9 $$1 Ctrl k1,11(: Ctrl k1,12(: Ctrl k1,7(: Ctrl k1,9(: Ctrl k1,10(: Ctrl k1,9(:Ctrl k1,8(:

Once you have all the Popups set up, go to a channel and check them out to make sure they are working the way you want them to. If they are not, just go back to the Popups option and work with them until you get them the way you want them.

Now for the last item in the Tools menu, DCC File Sender and its corresponding toolbar button—DCC Send. When you click on either the menu item or the toolbar button for DCC Send, you get a DCC Send dialog box. This box is broken into two sections. The left-hand section includes all the files on your hard drive and the right-hand side lets you indicate who you are sending to and has a space for files you want to send. Once you select the file you want to send and click on the left pointing arrow, the filename is copied and moved to the right-hand side for sending.

When you are ready to send a file to someone, you can click on the user's name in the channel names list. A DCC Send dialog box opens and you simply use the left-hand box to scroll through and find the file you want to send. Then you can either double-click on the highlighted file or click on the right arrow button to move the file over to the send section of this dialog box. Next, tab over or click your cursor over to the To line and make sure the nickname of the person you want to send the file to is in this line. If it is not, enter the name of the person you want to send the file to. When you have this dialog box completed to your specifications, click on the Send button at the bottom of this box (see Figure 6-28).

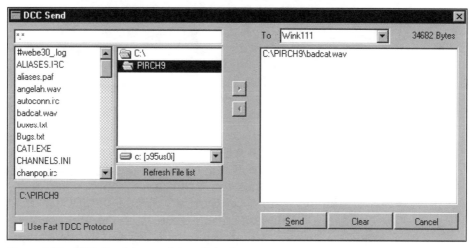

Figure 6-28   DCC Send drag and drop dialog box

Next you get a window that gives you the status of the send you are doing. It tells you who you are sending to, the status, the filename and its size, and the transfer rates. It also gives you a status bar at the bottom of the box that fills up as the file gets sent. You can keep this window open until it is finished or you can click on the down arrow in the upper right-hand corner and hide it.

That covers all the options under the Tools menu bar item. Now let's move on to the next one in line, Options.

Options Menu Item and Corresponding Toolbar Buttons

Under this menu item you have the following choices: Preferences and its corresponding toolbar button, Pref; Colors; Download Extension Map; Personal Bio; Text to Speech; Autoexec Commands; and Desktop Options.

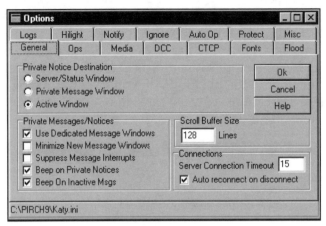

Figure 6-29   Options dialog box General tab

When you click on the Preferences menu item or the Prefs toolbar button, you get an Options dialog box that lets you set up your preferred options (see Figure 6-29). For instance, this Options dialog box contains the following tabs: General, Ops, Media, DCC, CTCP, Fonts, Flood, Logs, Hilight, Notify, Ignore, Auto Op, Protect, and Misc. Take a moment and go through these with me and get your options set up to your preferences.

The General tab lets you select how you want Pirch to handle your IRC sessions. This tab is broken down into four distinct areas—Private Notice Destination, Private Message/Notices, Scroll Buffer Size, and Connections. Under Private Notice Destination you can select where you want your notices to go—Server/Status Window, Private Message Window, or Active Window. My suggestion is to check the Active Window option. This ensures that you don't miss any important messages from your friends. With the Private Messages/Notices options you select how your messages and notices are handled. Your options are:

➤ Use Dedicated Message Windows—sends messages to separate message windows rather than displaying them in the active channel window

➤ Minimize New Message Windows—when new messages are sent to you, Pirch minimizes the message windows rather than automatically sending them as opened

➤ Suppress Message Interrupts—prevents new incoming private messages or notices from popping up and becoming active immediately. Instead, the window is created and the input goes to the active channel window.

➤ Beep on Private Notices—beeps when a user posts to a private notice window you have open and inactive

➤ Beep on Inactive Msgs—beeps when a user posts to a private message window you have open and inactive

Scroll Buffer Size lets you designate how many lines you want in your scroll buffer—how many lines to keep in memory. Lastly, Connections lets you select a Server Connection Timeout in seconds and whether you want to Auto reconnect on disconnect.

Under the Ops preference options, you choose how you want the Channel Operator Control Panel handled. You can select to: Show Op Control Panel when Ops are granted—gives you the operators control box in the right-hand bottom corner of your channel window; Always Confirm Kicks—displays a dialog box asking you to confirm that you want to kick the specified user and only works through this Kick button; Always Prompt for Kick Message—gives you a dialog box to type in your personal kick message; Deop User Prior to Setting Ban—takes ops away from the user before he is kicked. You can also set up a Default Kick Msg that is sent to the kickee in a private message after you kick them. Ban Method lets you choose the way you want Pirch to ban someone. You have choices like: User—nick!ident@port.server; Ident, Port & Server—*!ident@port.server; Ident, Server—*!ident@*server; Port, Server—*!*@port.server; Nick—nick!*@*; or Server—*!*@*server. You just pick the one that works best for you. See Figure 6-30 for a peek at this Ops tab and the settings you can choose.

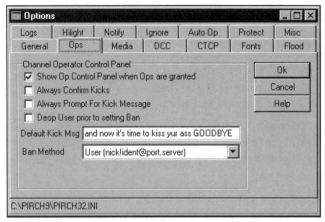

Figure 6-30   Ops tab

The Media preference option lets you choose how you want sound options set up. Here you can select to:

➤ Enable Sounds—allows you to receive sounds

➤ Ignore if already playing sounds—ignores new sound requests if a sound file from a user is already playing

➤ Display error message when media file not found—sends an error message to your status window telling you which file was sent that you do not have and the user who sent the file

➤ Display media events even if no message is attached—lets you hear sound files even if the user does not attach a message to the file when he sends it

Along with setting these options, you can also designate your default sound path. Type in the directory and filename in this box or use the down arrow to find your sound files in your directory. I suggest you create a separate directory for your sound files. You will be collecting quite a few of them during your travels on IRC. They can be such fun! See Figure 6-31 for an example of what this Media tab looks like.

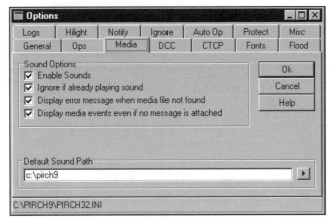

Figure 6-31   Media options

Under the DCC preference option you can select how you want DCC sends and gets handled. This tab is broken down into four areas— DCC Options, Packet Size, Timeouts, and Default DCC Paths (see Figure 6-32).

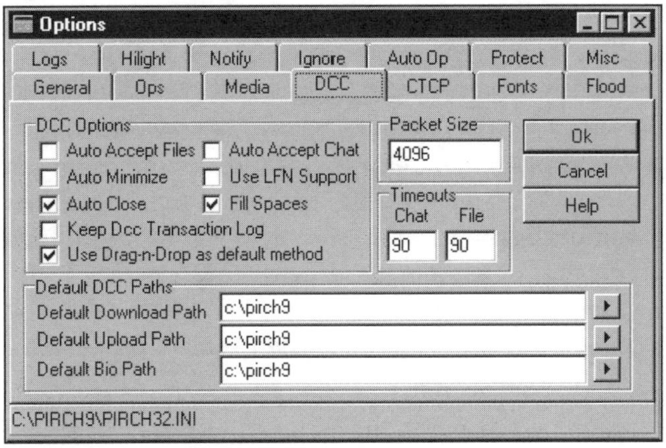

Figure 6-32   DCC options tab

Under the DCC Options you select the options for sending and receiving DCCs:

➤ Auto Accept Files—I suggest you leave this option turned off. Then you can choose what gets sent to you rather than accepting everything anyone wants to send you. Remember we discussed the pitfalls of leaving this option selected in the previous chapter.

➤ Auto Accept Chat—Again, leave this option deselected for the same reasons as above.

➤ Auto Minimize—automatically minimizes DCC windows once the connection has been established

➤ Use LFN Support—sends files that have the Windows 95 or Windows NT long filenames. However, not all IRC clients are capable of receiving files with long filenames.

➤ Auto Close—automatically closes DCC windows when the connection is canceled or lost, or the transfer is complete. I keep this option checked because it saves me time by automatically closing these windows for me.

➤ Fill Spaces—only available when the Use LFN Support option is enabled. This option replaces the space character in filenames with an underscore character. I suggest that you select this option on if you select the Use LFN Support to give you greater compatibility with other clients and operating systems.

➤ Keep Dcc Transaction Log—gives you a log of all DCC transactions. I personally never use this because it ties up space on my hard drive that's better used elsewhere, like for waves.

➤ Use Drag-n-Drop as default method—is the dialog box containing the directory, drive, and file lists from your hard drive. Selecting this option lets you send a file by clicking on the desired filename, holding the mouse button down, and dragging it to the target person's name in the channel names list. Then you drop it by releasing the mouse button. The file is then sent to that user.

The next two areas of this DCC tab deal with packet size and timeouts. Packet Size determines the buffer size used to perform a file transfer. Larger buffer sizes can yield faster transactions. However, if you have problems transferring files, try to lower the DCC Packet Size. The Timeouts area sets up the length of time Pirch waits when trying to establish a DCC connection to another user. When Pirch does not connect within this length of time, the transaction fails and the window closes.

At the bottom of the screen you can also set up your Default DCC Paths. You can set the Default Download Path—where files you send are stored, Default Upload Path—where files you receive are stored, and Default Bio Path—where your bio is stored. You can leave them blank or you can give them a destination by typing in the path name or using the down arrows to locate the directories and files on your hard drive.

With the CTCP preference option you can designate your Default CTCP Responses—Finger and User Info. Use the lines provided to enter the responses you want users to get when they perform either of these two CTCP events on you (see Figure 6-33).

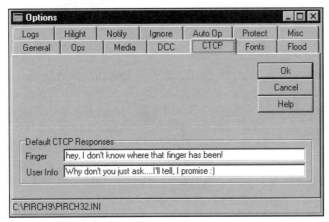

Figure 6-33   CTCP options

Under the Fonts preferences you can select the type of font you want to use for the various areas of IRC. You can set up a different font for each area or set them all up alike. Pirch gives you several different fonts to choose from and lets you see what those fonts look like with samples (see Figure 6-34).

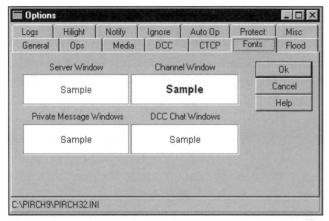

Figure 6-34   Fonts preferences

The Flood preference option lets you set up your flood control options. I advise you to fill this area in and check Enable Flood Control. There are some users out there who like to try to flood others off of IRC, especially when they get angry with someone for kicking them from a channel. Protect yourself with this option. The default settings are sufficient to protect you from floods. In this option you can also set up your CTCP Flood Control. Again, enable this option to protect yourself from CTCP type flooding (see Figure 6-35).

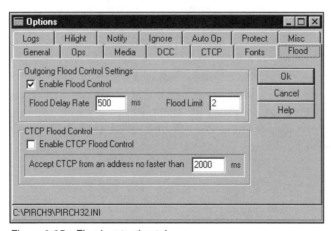

Figure 6-35   Flood protection tab

Logs is the next options tab. Here you select how you want to handle logging. This tab is broken down into two sections: Auto Log and Auto Reset Logs. Under Auto Log you select what you want to log—Channels, Private Messages, Server Messages, or DCC Chats. Under the Auto Reset Logs area you select when you want those logs reset—Never (Manual), Daily, or Monthly (see Figure 6-36).

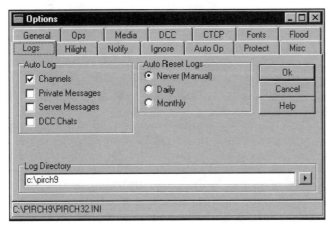

Figure 6-36   Logging options tab

Next, you can use the Hilight tab to select the words you want highlighted every time some other person on the channel uses them. Type in the names or words you want highlighted in the Highlight any messages that contain the following words box. Then select from the two options below this box—Highlight Own Messages and Beep on Highlighted Message—if you want to enable either of those activities for the highlighted words and click on OK. The next time you are on channel any messages with those words in them appear in red (see Figure 6-37).

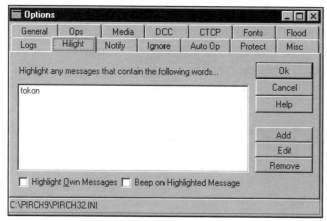

Figure 6-37   Hilight options tab

You can choose who you want to be notified about when they come onto IRC and your net with the Notify tab. Use the Add button to add users' nicknames or addresses to this notify list. Then select Enable Notifications to turn this option on and Notify to Active Window to send the notify notices to your active window when they log onto IRC (see Figure 6-38).

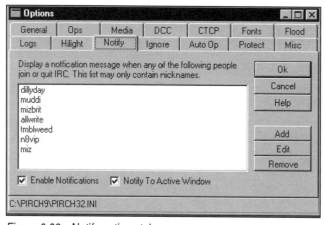

Figure 6-38   Notify options tab

The Ignore tab works similar to the Notify tab in that it lets you Add and Remove users you want to ignore. Type in the names and/or addresses of those users you want to ignore and select Enable Ingore (which is a typo, I believe, for Ignore) to activate this option. As long as you keep these people on this Ignore list, you will not see messages from them either in channels or in private messages. This is a very good way to prevent obnoxious people from bothering you (see Figure 6-39).

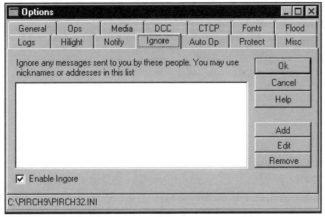

Figure 6-39   Ignore tab

The Auto Op tab lets you set up users you want to receive Auto Ops from you when they join a channel you are on. Enter their names and/or addresses in the box provided. I suggest that you type in nicks and addresses. Anyone can imitate a nick, but few can imitate someone's address. Then select Enable Auto Ops to turn this option on. However, I suggest that you do not use this option if you are on nets that give you channel bots. It is best to let the bots op people on channels. It gives them more control of the bot and therefore the channel (see Figure 6-40).

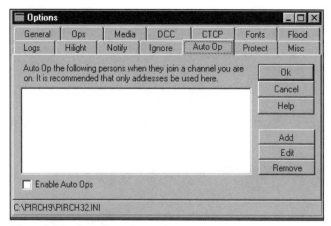

Figure 6-40   Auto Op options tab

On the Protect tab, you Add and Remove users you want Pirch to protect from deopping and bans. Just add their names to the box provided and select the options—Enable Protection and Enable Ban Protection—at the bottom of the tab window. Then when someone on channel tries to deop or ban any of the nicks on your list, that person is deopped and kicked from the channel while your friends are given ops back and unbanned (see Figure 6-41).

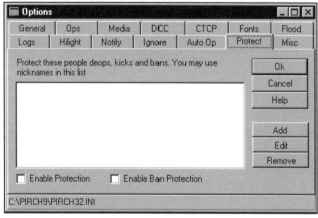

Figure 6-41   Protect options tab

The Misc preference option lets you select how you want to interact with the channels, the servers, and the status windows. The following are your options and what they do:

➤ Hide Server Ping/Pong—suppresses the server ping messages from being sent to you. Pirch still responds to the server pings; it just does not display them to you when this option is checked.

➤ Enhanced Events Format—displays the event glyphs, like NOTE:, CTCP:, etc., when you check this option on. I personally prefer to know what kind of event is being responded to. Set this up to your personal preference.

➤ Auto Join Channel on Invite and Auto Rejoin if Kicked—lets you rejoin channels if either of these events happen to you. I suggest you leave these disabled so that you don't end up in channels you do not wish to be on or you don't end up offending other users to the point where they ban you from their channel.

➤ Hide Own Nickname in Chat—leaves your nickname, in your windows only, off the messages you type

➤ Auto Tile Windows—all your windows tile when you join channels

➤ Whois on Private Msg—gives you a whois automatically on anyone who messages you

➤ Auto Rewrap Text—automatically rewraps text to fit windows when you resize them

➤ Hide Joins/Parts/Quits—does not display joins, parts, and quits in the channel window

➤ Multi Line Editor—does the same thing here as it does when you select it from the right mouse menu options from the window

➤ Wide Nickname List—gives you a wider nickname or channel names list area

➤ Nickname List on left—moves channel names list to the left-hand side of your channel window

➤ Use Window ID Tags—displays your nickname and the server you're on below the channel title bar

➤ Timestamp Activity—gives you date and time for events

At the bottom of this Misc preference options box, you can type in the message you want to leave the channel with when you quit IRC in the Default Sign Off Message line. This message only appears on the channel when you use the /quit, /bye, or other commands that take you out of IRC completely. See Figure 6-42 for a better view of these selections.

Figure 6-42   Misc options tab

Next in line under the Options menu item is Colors. This option lets you choose how you want your chat windows to look. When you click on this option, you get a Color Setup dialog box. This box lets you select what colors you want for your background, various types of posts and messages, CTCP Queries and Replies, and so forth. This is a nice option and lets you add a little color and spice to otherwise dull-looking channel and message windows (see Figure 6-43).

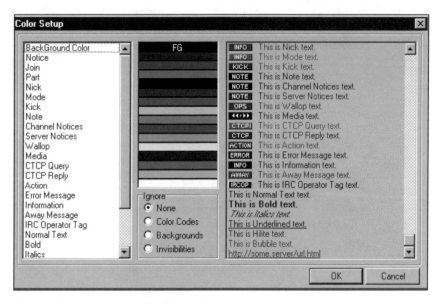

Figure 6-43 Color Setup dialog box

Under the Download Extension Map option for this Options menu item, you can choose to have your DCC downloads stored to different directories based on the type of file. When entering items in the DCC Extension Map, these items should be separated by a semicolon for similar type files. All extension types not found in the extension map are automatically stored to the default DCC download directory you set up in your DCC preference tab (see Figure 6-44). Some examples of items you can place in this Download Extension Map are:

➤ bmp;gif;tif;jpg to c:\images
➤ mid;rmi;wav to c:\sounds
➤ txt;doc;wpd to c:\docs
➤ zip to c:\archive

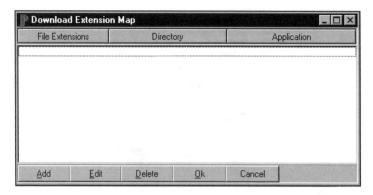

Figure 6-44   Download Extension Map dialog box

When you want to add items to this extension map, click on the Add button and a Download Extension Map dialog box opens. Fill in the appropriate areas and choose your Download Action options. Then select OK to add these items to the extension map.

The Personal Bio option under this Options menu item is similar to the Bio Viewer item under Tools. However, this option lets you fill in your personal information and include a picture of yourself. See Figure 6-45 for an example of my bio.

Figure 6-45   Bio setup box

The Text to Speech option turns any text you type to speech. You can copy what you want to hear spoken into Edit Notes clipboard or you can hear what was said in DCC chat windows. It only vocalizes your words and it is very dull and dry. The Text to Speech is fun to play with, but that's the only advantage I can see to it (see Figure 6-46).

*Figure 6-46 Text To Speech Options
dialog box*

Autoexec Commands are commands that can be executed automatically each time you log onto an IRC server. You can set these up to automatically join you to your favorite channel. To set these up, select Autoexec Commands from the Option menu and then type your command in the IRC Autoexec dialog box that appears. Only type one command per line. Let's say betyboop wants to join #cartoons each time she comes to IRC. She can set up the autoexec command by typing in the dialog box: **/join #cartoons**. Then every time she logs onto IRC, she automatically joins #cartoons (see Figure 6-47).

Figure 6-47 IRC Autoexec dialog box

Desktop Options lets you set up how you want your Pirch desktop to look. You can select a Wallpaper—the default or one from your hard drive; Layout—n/a, Tiled or Centered; Color—from a palette selection; and how you want your Tools and Toolbar Properties to look (see Figure 6-48).

Figure 6-48   Desktop Options setup box

Under Tools you can Show Toolbar, Show Window Tabs (those tabs for channel and message windows at the bottom of your Pirch application window), and Show Hint/Status Bar. For Toolbar Properties you can choose Text Only, Icons Only, or Text and Icons (see Figure 6-49).

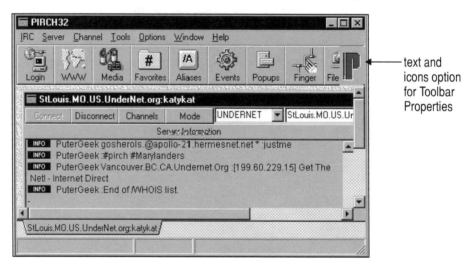

text and icons option for Toolbar Properties

Figure 6-49   Pirch Status window dialog box

One last Toolbar item remains that is not covered directly under any of the menu items. This is DCC chat. When you click on this option, you get a DCC chat dialog box that asks you to enter the nickname of the person you want to chat with (see Figure 6-50).

Figure 6-50   DCC Chat initiator

Once you enter the nickname and select OK, Pirch tries to establish a DCC chat session with that person. When the connection is established, the two of you can begin chatting.

That takes care of all of the menu bar options and the toolbar buttons. You should have a good understanding of all that Pirch has to offer and how it compares to mIRC. It functions like mIRC in many ways. There are a couple of differences but nothing that should be too hard for you to learn to overcome. It is still a fairly easy program to master.

One of the best advantages to Pirch over mIRC is the ability of Pirch to let you be on more than one server at a time. This allows you to be on more than one net and have all your chat windows within one application window. Pirch puts tabs at the bottom of your application window and highlights them in red each time a message appears in an inactive window. This makes it much easier for you to keep up with multiple channels and chat windows.

If you want to join more than one server or net, simply click on the Login toolbar button or New IRC Server from the IRC menu option. Then select your server and connect. If you select another server on the same net you are already on, you need to give yourself another nickname for the second server. Otherwise, you could collide with yourself and get dumped from either or both servers. Some servers, like lowell.ma.us.undernet.org on the UnderNet, do not let you connect to them twice. It monitors all logins and refuses the second connection attempt.

Summary

Now that you have finished this chapter you have a good basis to compare Pirch to mIRC. You can see the differences and the similarities between the two programs. They share a lot of common features and also have features that are unique to each of them.

Pirch lets you choose your server before you log into the net. You can customize your Pirch preferences for you and also for each member of your family. Save a profile of your favorite channel settings and preferences for each family member.

Many of the channel operator's commands are built into the channel's window in a custom Operators Panel. This lets you quickly and easily perform those ops commands that you use most often. Those that are not included in the Operators Panel have been added to your pop-up menu for easy access.

You can now choose between the menu bar or toolbar items and perform those particular tasks in IRC. Set your preferences, program Events and Controls, or set up your own bio. You have the information here to get this program working the way you want it to.

Then, when you get more comfortable with IRC or if you are real brave, try your hand at logging onto more than one net. Just click on the login for the first server and net you want to be on, join your preferred channel, and then click on login again to select another server for another net and join the channel of your choice there.

With what you have learned here you should be able to use this software in confidence and sail your way through IRC fun and games.

Chapter 7

Netiquette

One of the pitfalls that I see many IRC users falling into is not knowing or understanding proper usage or behavior in IRC. This chapter was included to give you a head start on those who just leap before looking.

> **In this chapter you learn:**
> - ☑ What netiquette is
> - ☑ What you should and should not do or say in IRC channels
> - ☑ What the common sense rules and guidelines for proper behavior in IRC are
> - ☑ What emoticons are and how and when to use them
> - ☑ What all those acronyms are and what they mean

IRC is probably the only communication medium in the world that lets you get to know the person, the personality of the individual. With IRC you do not have the prejudices the eyes send to the brain. Everyone on this medium looks the same—there are no races, many times you do not know the true sex of the person you are talking to, and there are no other sight indicators that we use each day to discriminate in our choices of people to talk to.

Unless the other person gives you that information, you may never know if they are tall or short, skinny or fat, what color their hair or eyes are, or even what they look like. All you have to go on is how they communicate to you in words. And those words, the medium of communication, let people from all over the world get to know each other—the real person, not the person that you might see walking down the street or sitting in a cafe somewhere—the true personality of the person.

Because this is a written or text form of communication, the very things that let you get to know the personality of someone can also hinder some of your communications. In a face-to-face conversation you have facial expressions and body language to help you get your thoughts, meanings, and ideas across. You can wave your hands about in excitement or agitation, you can frown or smile to convey displeasure or joy, you can cross your arms over your chest to let the other person know you are not open to what they are saying. But, on IRC, you have none of that to help you. You just have the black on white of typed words. Many times things you intended to say are misconstrued because of this.

The people who began using this medium long before it was opened to the public realized this was one of the flaws with it, so they came up with some tricks to help get their messages across. They also formed their own rules and guidelines for proper use and conduct while using the various communication tools of the Internet, like e-mail, newsgroups, and IRC.

What is Netiquette?

The Internet society came up with some common practices, customs, and conventions to make communicating within their medium more pleasant and to cut down on what are called flame wars. *Flames* are emotion packed or incitive type messages sent to other users or in response to another user's message. Often they are written in anger with little thought or concern for the consequences of the meaning of the message.

These rules and guidelines the Internet society came up with are called *netiquette,* for Internet etiquette. Many of them are pretty common sense or common courtesy guidelines, but they were all designed to keep strife under control in this rapidly growing community of users.

Just because you can do a certain action on IRC does not necessarily mean that you should. Depending on the severity of your actions or inappropriate use of this medium, you could lose your access to the Internet. So, if you follow netiquette, you can get along better and make more friends in this wonderful communications medium. This society is just like any society in real life. Inappropriate behavior is frowned upon as much here as it is out there in the real world.

> **Warning**:   It is not a very good idea to enter a channel issuing insults like, "What's up, lamers?" It could get you kicked off the channel before you have a chance to type anything else.

One thing to keep in mind when you are on IRC is that while English is the most widely used language, it is not the <u>only</u> language. There are some channels that restrict the language used there to the language native to the name of the channel, like in #france the people there are only using French or in #germany they are only typing in German.

Another thing to keep in mind is that some channels find it very annoying for a user to join a channel and greet everyone there individually. It takes up a lot of time and space to do that and interrupts any conversations that may have been going on before you entered. So, keep the greetings to a minimum. I usually enter and greet everyone at once with a simple, "hi, everyone."

Begging for ops on a channel, especially if it is your first time on the channel, is frowned upon and can get you kicked from the channel. Most of the users on IRC feel that ops status is something you earn by becoming a regular of the channel and letting the people there get to know you. As the regulars on the channel start to accept you as part of the "family," they eventually bestow ops on you.

Be yourself on IRC. There are many people who already know this and they act on IRC the same as they do in real life. However, there are some who see IRC as a big game or a fantasy world. They pretend they are someone they aren't. Remember that the only thing others on IRC have to go by to form their opinions are your typed words, the personality you put forward. You run across both types of people as you use IRC more and more—the real people and the game players. The users that have been on IRC for several years can usually spot the game players eventually.

One of the best things you can remember is not to harass another user. Harassment is behavior towards another with the purpose of annoying them. With the ignore command at your fingertips, there is not much else you can do about it. None of the IRCops come to your aid; they simply do not have the time or the resources to help with every harassment complaint. The best thing for you to do is to put the annoying person on ignore. Then you do not get any more messages from them, either in private or on the channels you are on.

Here are some basic core rules of netiquette for you to keep in mind:

➤ Remember the human—behind every monitor and every keyboard there is a real live human being with feelings and emotions. Treat everyone on IRC as you do friends, family, and relationships whether they be professional or personal.

➤ Adhere to the same standards of behavior online as you follow in life. At first this may not seem real to you, but it is real, as real as real life. You find all the same kinds of people here as you do in real life.

➤ The use of profanity should be avoided—remember that many of these channels are open forums. There may be minors present or you could be talking to a potential client, customer, business associate, or even employer. Not to mention, profanity is grounds to get you kicked and banned from some channels.

➤ Respect other people's time and space—especially in the professional channels. One or more of the people there may be the experts, the moderators, or the channel founders. These people are usually very busy keeping the channel flowing smoothly, answering questions, or giving advice, so try to limit your private messages to them. Be courteous of their time; try not to waste it on frivolities.

➤ Make yourself look good online—just like in an office setting, word does spread through the ranks in IRC. If you act inappropriately in one channel, before long the word spreads to others about how you acted. Present yourself in your best possible light and others go out of their way to help you whenever you need it. And remember, you never know who might be on the other end of that screen. It could be your next boss or client.

➤ Share expert knowledge—this is a tight-knit community of users. They go out of their way to help out a fellow user. If you have knowledge that can help another, share that knowledge.

➤ Help keep flame wars to a minimum—people come to IRC channels to have fun, relax after work, and let their hair down. They do not like to be involved in controversy or online battles.

➤ Respect other people's privacy—if someone tells you something in confidence, keep it to yourself. Do not be the spreader of gossip and rumors. Many flame wars can be prevented by following this advice.

➤ Respect the channel operators—if you are on a channel and you have been asked to change the topic of discussion or to curb your behavior, do not argue; just abide by the operator's wishes. They are trying to maintain order in their channel. If you do not like the way the channel is run, find another channel or create your own.

➤ Be forgiving of other people's mistakes—everyone has been a newbie at one time or another. People make mistakes. Understand that and let them slip by; everyone is better off if you do.

➤ Do not bring your private conversations to the channel—if you are involved in a heated debate in private message with someone, keep it private. The other users on the channel probably do not want to be involved in your private matters. However, if you are new to IRC and you are having problems with another user, you can message a channel operator for assistance, but keep it private.

➤ Do not give out personal information or passwords to anyone online—there are times when someone will ask you for the password to your account, or for credit card or other personal information about yourself. Do not give this out to anyone you do not know and trust personally.

These are some of the more general and important of the IRC netiquette rules. Keep them in mind when you join channels and you will find your way much smoother and happier.

How Can I Avoid Social Faux Pas?

One of the best ways to avoid making a fool of yourself in IRC is to think before you type. This is especially true when you are angry. I know that is something that is hard for some of us to do, but it is necessary on this medium especially.

Because the other people on the channel cannot see your face, hear the inflection in your voice, or see the way you are holding yourself, they often miss some of the true meaning behind your typed words. What you typed and intended to be sarcastic or humorous could be seen in plain type as hostile or antagonistic. So think carefully before you type something like that and see if there is a way to rephrase it so that it does not look so harsh or belligerent.

How Do I Get My Meaning Across?

Just as the Internet community came up with netiquette to give this very anarchistic society some guidelines and common practices to go by, they also came up with some symbols to help you convey emotions in your typing. These are called emoticons.

Emoticons are ASCII art symbols that you can use to add emotion or to ease the impact of your typed words. If you place your head on your left shoulder and look at these symbols, you are able to see that they look like faces. Some people try to be a little different and reverse the angle of these symbols. In that case you want to lay your head on your right shoulder to see the face. Eventually you come to recognize these symbols without having to turn your head.

Following are a list of many of these emoticons and their meanings. Use them in your typing to help you convey those meanings or emotions your body and voice do not get to express in IRC.

Emoticons

:-)	smiley face to express humor
:)	smiley face without a nose; variation of above
:(	frowning face used to convey sadness or displeasure
:-(	frowning face with a nose
;-)	winking smiley face used to convey humor or flirtation
8-)	wide-eyed smile used to convey shocked pleasure
:*)	someone with a cold
:p	sticking tongue out used in fun
:-p	face with nose and tongue stuck out
:-p~	raspberry
:-o	a look of shock

These are just a few of the basic emoticons. You run across variations of these and a few innovations. If you are not sure what the emoticon someone uses means, ask them. They are more than happy to tell you.

If betyboop is on #cartoons and joe says something to her that makes her smile, she can end her message with one of the smiley faces. So if she were to reply back to joe, it might look like this: **how sweet of you, joe :-)**.

I think you can use your imagination here and see how these emoticons can help you to convey some of the emotions you might feel. Try them out with some of your messages or just watch for awhile and see how some of the other users are using them.

Another way that users have found to emphasize some of their words or to let you know how they are feeling is to use the * key or the _ key preceding and following certain words. Since this is a text-only format, none of the other users can see bold or underlined words unless they have a program like Pirch. Therefore, there is no other way to put emphasis on certain words. I sometimes use *smile* instead of the smiley face, especially if that is all I want to type on a line. You see some users using the * symbols to set off certain phrases they are fond of using or use them to surround their attempts at using dialect.

What Do All These Acronyms Mean?

You may notice a lot of the users on IRC typing two-, three-, or more letter abbreviations. They often look like some kind of new language. Many times I get asked by newbies what certain letters mean that a user has typed. Well, I am going to give you a list of some of the most common acronyms used on IRC and what they mean. Then you can start using them without fear of appearing foolish and without having to ask someone on channel or in private what they mean.

Abbreviations

BRB	be right back
BBL	be back later
BBIAF	be back in a few
BBIAB	be back in a bit
TTFN	ta ta for now
LOL	laughing out loud
PPL	people
ROTFL	rolling on the floor laughing
ROTFLMAO	rolling on the floor laughing my a** off
IMO	in my opinion
IMHO	in my humble opinion
IMNSHO	in my not so humble opinion
AFAIK	as far as I know

BTW	by the way
OTOH	on the other hand
FAQ	frequently asked questions
RTFM	read the &*^%# manual
WB	welcome back
RE	regards or re hi or hi again
LTNS	long time no see
AFK	away from keyboard

Again, you see these bandied about quite often. These are the most common acronyms used in IRC. You also see some variations on these. If you run across one you are not familiar with, ask the user who typed it. Sometimes it is their own variation and only they know what they mean.

The netiquette guidelines, emoticons, and these acronyms should help you to glide your way through most conversations in IRC and come out looking less like a newbie and more like an expert. These too should help you to navigate around much more comfortably. Use them well, wisely, and often. Save wear and tear on your nerves and fingers and those of others out there in IRC land.

Summary

The Internet community is relatively old compared to the personal and business community that has only come online in the past few years. For over 25 years these academicians, the military, and researchers and scientists have had free reign over the Internet. Through their years of experience and use of the Internet they came up with some basic rules and guidelines to help assure that everyone's time on any of these tools is not wasted or abused. These rules and guidelines are called netiquette.

If you follow the guidelines set out in this chapter you find that you have a much happier time. You find yourself accepted in more channels and make many friends and acquaintances. Avoid social faux pas while in IRC by following these common sense guidelines.

Using emoticons, you are able to express your true feelings in this typewritten, text-only medium. The special character keys on your keyboard also let you show emphasis or emotion if you learn how to use them.

Use the acronyms and abbreviations to save wear and tear on your fingers and wrists and still get your meaning across. The basics that are included in this chapter give you a start in understanding what people mean when they type these in your channel conversations.

When you apply this chapter to all the others you have learned, you look like an expert when you get on IRC and start surfing the channels.

Chapter 8

The Nitty Gritty

We have gone over a lot of material up to this point, and I imagine you are wondering to yourself whatever do you do with all this information. In this chapter we put it all together.

In this chapter you learn:

- ☑ How to take all this from step one through to the end
- ☑ How to select a server, how to join a channel, and how to get your messages across
- ☑ How to use some of the commands, how to make your own channel, and how to operate as the administrator of a registered channel
- ☑ How to use a personal bot and where to get it

This chapter takes you step by step through most of the things you have learned in this book. It is meant as a guide to get you started, then you can take what you learned from the other chapters and apply them to this chapter and experiment with the commands or with your IRC software.

Now What Do I Do?

Back in Chapter 4 I explained to you where to get an IRC client (the software) and how to install it on your computer. I hope you have done that already. If you have not, you need to do that now. We will learn how to navigate around IRC using both of the clients I have covered in this book—Pirch and mIRC. If you have chosen not to use either of those programs, not to worry. Most if not all of the commands I gave you in Chapter 3 work with most of the IRC clients that are out there.

The first thing you need to do is connect to your provider. This is usually done by clicking on the icon for your provider or your connection, or if you have a Slip/PPP account, clicking on the Winsock icon. Once you are connected, click on the icon or shortcut for your IRC client or access it through your Start menu in Windows 95.

The client opens and tries to connect you to a server. Refer back to the chapters for the client you chose to get instructions on how to set up your client. mIRC uses the last server that you were connected to on your previous visit or the first one in the list, unless you chose a different option during the setup process. If this is not the server you want to connect to, simply click on the Disconnect toolbar button (the one that looks like a broken chain) and then open your setup folder, highlight the server you want, and click on the Connect button.

For Pirch, click on the Login toolbar button, then in the Server Connection window select the server you want to connect to and click on the Connect button. If you have selected Auto Connect, Pirch automatically tries to connect you to a server once you click on the Connect button. If you don't have that option selected, when the Server Status window pops up, click on the Connect button there.

Both of these programs give you a status window; in Pirch it is the Server Status window, which tells you that you either are or are not getting connected to the server you selected. At the top of the status window you see your nickname and the name of the server you are connected to. See Figure 8-1 for a mIRC status window and Figure 8-2 for a Pirch status window.

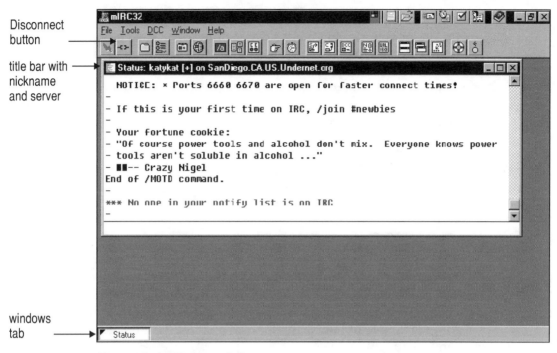

Disconnect button

title bar with nickname and server

windows tab

Figure 8-1   mIRC status window

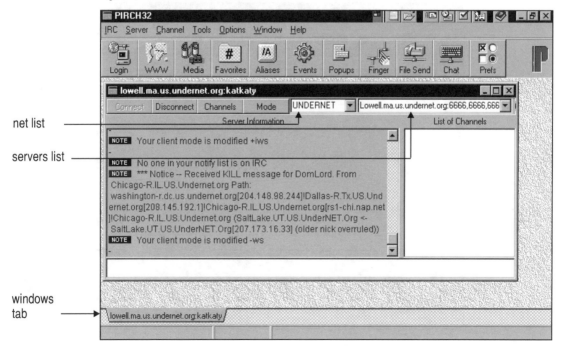

net list

servers list

windows tab

Figure 8-2   Pirch status window

Now you are connected to a server for the net you want to be on. At this point you can do one of several things. You can call up a list by typing **/list** or **/list <your parameters>**. Beware, many servers on the UnderNet bump you off when you try to do a /list. If you know the channel name you want to join, you can do a **/who #<channel>** to find out who is on the channel before you join. Or you can just join the channel you want without doing either of these.

Tip: With both of these programs you can set up a favorite channels list and join or get the names of the people on those channels. So, if you do not already have this set up, do that now.

To keep it simple here, let's just join a channel. Type **/join #<channel name>** in the prompt line at the bottom of your status window. When you press the Enter or return key, you are joined to that channel. Your channel window has its name at the top in a title bar. See Figure 8-3 for an example of how a channel looks in mIRC and Figure 8-4 for a Pirch channel window.

channel
names
list

join
message

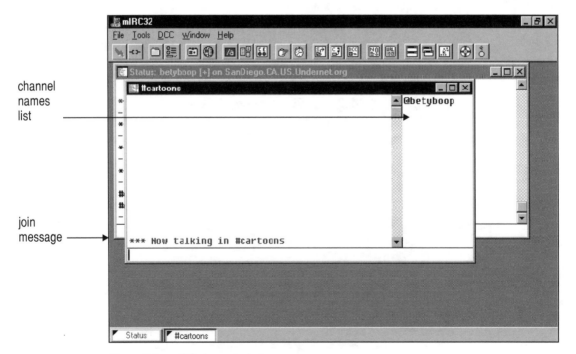

Figure 8-3   mIRC channel window

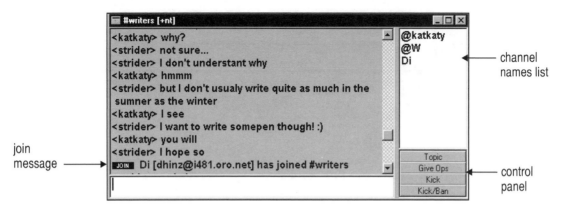

join
message ⟶

channel
names list

control
panel

Figure 8-4   Pirch channel window

Notice in Figure 8-3 that betyboop has joined #cartoons and she is the only one there. Since she was the first one to join the channel, she has operator's status. Now she can set her channel modes and topic. In mIRC betyboop double-clicks in the channel window to bring up the channel information or Channel Central box. Then she can set her modes and give her channel a topic. In Pirch, she right-clicks in the channel window and selects her channel mode. Then she can click on Topic in the Control Panel and type in her topic. At the top of this channel window appear the modes for the channel along with the topic she set. In both mIRC and Pirch, the title bar looks the same.

If betyboop does not like her fonts, she can change them by right-clicking in the window for Pirch and choosing Set Fonts. Then she chooses her font from the list available and clicks on OK (see Figure 8-5).

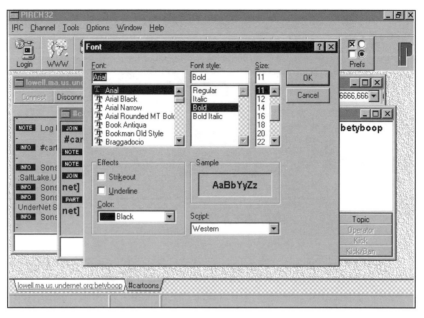

Figure 8-5   Pirch Font dialog

With mIRC, she can click on the box in the upper left-hand corner of her chat window. Then she selects Font and chooses the font and style she wants to use (see Figure 8-6).

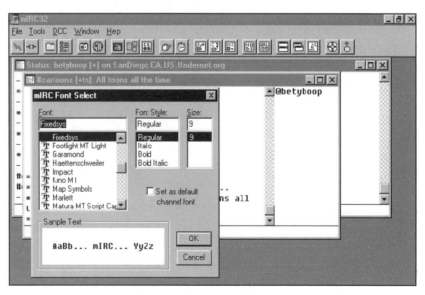

Figure 8-6   mIRC Font Select dialog

Both of these programs let her see what the font looks like in a sample window. Then if she does not like the way a font looks, she can choose another before leaving this dialog box. When she clicks on the OK button, her window fonts change immediately.

When you join a channel in either of these programs, the first thing you notice on the channel is the message **Now talking in #<channel name>** for mIRC or **<nick> [signon@userhost] has joined #<channel name>** in Pirch. Everyone else in the channel gets the message **<nickname> has joined the channel**. Refer back to Figures 8-3 and 8-4 to see how these messages appear in both mIRC and Pirch.

As others begin to join you on your channel, you get to know them and eventually you want to let some of them share ops status with you. Remember the command for that is **/mode #<channel name> +o <nickname>**. In Pirch you simply highlight the name in the channel names list and then click on the Give Ops button at the bottom right-hand corner of your chat window (see Figure 8-7). In mIRC, you highlight the name in the channel names list, right-click to generate the pop-up menu, and select Control and Give Ops.

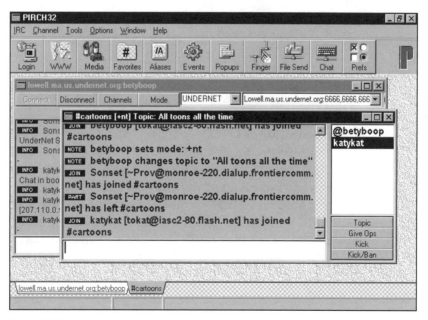

Figure 8-7   Pirch ops

Now that you have people in your channel, you can begin to carry on conversations with them. You type messages and press Enter to display them on the channel (see Figure 8-8).

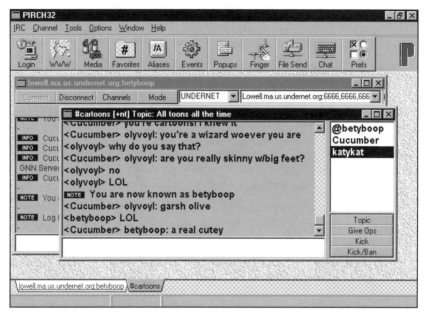

Figure 8-8   Conversation in Pirch

You may even want to carry on a private conversation with one or more people in the channel. You can either type **/msg <nickname>** and then your message or you can select their name from the channel names list and select DCC Chat from the popups menu (right-click after you select the nick). With Pirch you get little iconified boxes for your private chats. These you can resize to any size you like. You also get a tab at the bottom of the window that turns red each time the person in that chat window types a message. This works the same for both mIRC and Pirch. See Figure 8-9 for an example of a private message and a DCC chat in mIRC and Figure 8-10 for a private message and a DCC chat in Pirch.

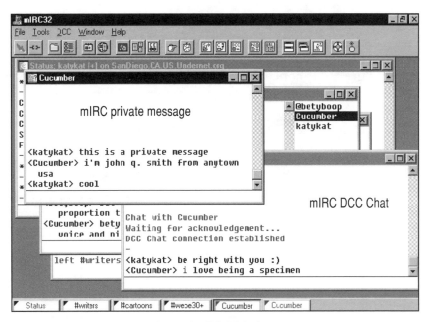

Figure 8-9 Private conversation and mIRC DCC chat

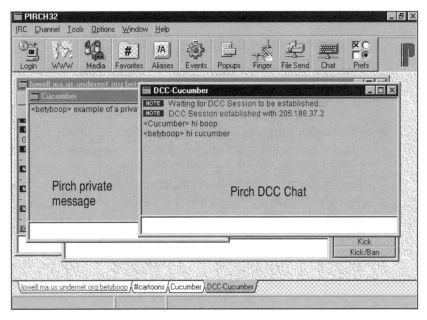

Figure 8-10 Private conversation and Pirch DCC chat

Occasionally, you notice some of the people in your channel change their nicks. You may even want to do this from time to time. Remember the command to change your nick is **/nick <nickname>**. In Figure 8-11, notice that olyvoyl has changed her nick to betyboop. The nick change notice appears the same in both clients.

nickname
change

Figure 8-11   Conversation in mIRC

The longer you stay in a channel or the more you travel the roads of IRC you notice certain things going on in these channels. Some of these are the actions we talked about in earlier chapters. Remember, you can create an action statement by typing **/me <does something>**. Figure 8-12 gives you an example of what these actions look like in channels. Although these actions appear in black text in the figure here in this book, once you get to actual channels, these actions appear as purple in mIRC and blue in Pirch unless you change the color in the Colors Setup.

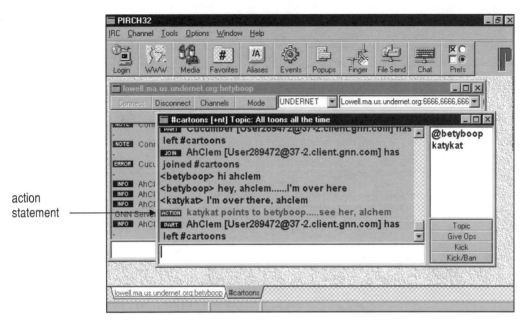

action
statement

Figure 8-12   Conversation in Pirch

On the social channels you often see the participants cutting up and
enjoying themselves. When you type something, note that in both
mIRC and Pirch your nick appears in front of anything you type and
the other people in your channels have their messages preceded by
their nicks too. In both these clients you can select to not preface your
own messages with your nick by clicking the Prefix Own Message off
in mIRC's General Options or leaving Hide Own Nickname in Chat
under Pirch's Misc Preferences. See Figure 8-13 for an example of
unprefixed messages.

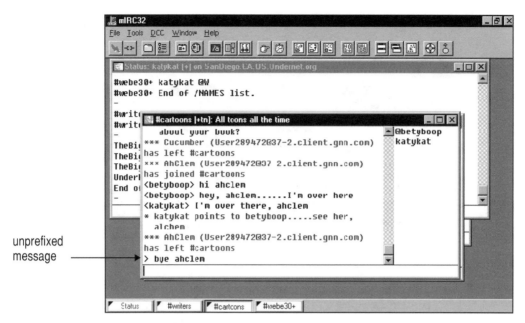

Figure 8-13   Conversation in mIRC

Before we go any further, let me put this into a step-by-step chart for you, so that you can reference each step you need to take to connect and talk in IRC. Use the following chart to help you get where you want to get connected and get where you want to go in IRC.

Step One:	Connect to your provider
Step Two:	Click on your icon or shortcut for IRC
Step Three:	Select the server for the net you want to be on and click on Connect. Be sure to give yourself a nickname.
Step Four:	Once you are connected to a server, select the channel you want to be on and type /join #<channel name>.
Step Five:	Give your channel a topic and set the modes. The mode command is /mode #<channel name> +<mode(s)>. The command to set the topic is /topic #<channel name> <topic>. (Only ops can change or set the modes for the channel.) If a channel is set at mode +t, only ops can change the topic.
Step Six:	Start talking to people who join you on the channel.
Step Seven:	If you want to talk privately to someone, type /msg <nickname> <your message> or click on their name and choose DCC Chat from the Popup menu.

Step Eight:	Give ops status to anyone you like by typing /mode #<channel name> +o <nickname>. Or follow the instructions above for whichever software package you have.
Step Nine:	To create an action statement, type /me <action you want to do>.
Step Ten:	Have fun and enjoy yourself!

This chart should help you get started with IRC. Next we are going to talk about some of the intermediate things you can do in IRC. Then we go into some of the more advanced things that can be done there, like bots.

What are Some Intermediate Things I Can Do?

There are all kinds of characters on your keyboard that you can use to spice up your typed messages to make them more interesting and less dry. And there are special characters that are recognized throughout the Internet to help you get your meaning across—acronyms and emoticons.

Acronyms help you type faster by letting you use fewer typed characters to say what you want to say. Refer back to the previous chapter for some of the basic acronyms. As you travel IRC, you find others that you can add to this list. See Figure 8-14 for an example of how one of these acronyms is used in a conversation. Notice that betyboop found the messages from cucumber amusing so she typed LOL (laughing out loud) and again later she ended a statement with LOL. This is an example of how acronyms are used in messages. In Figure 8-15 betyboop smiles at cucumber with the colon and close parenthesis at the end of her statement. This is an example of how you can use emoticons.

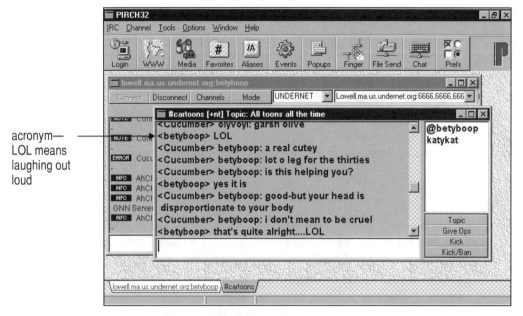

acronym—
LOL means
laughing out
loud

Figure 8-14   Using acronyms in IRC

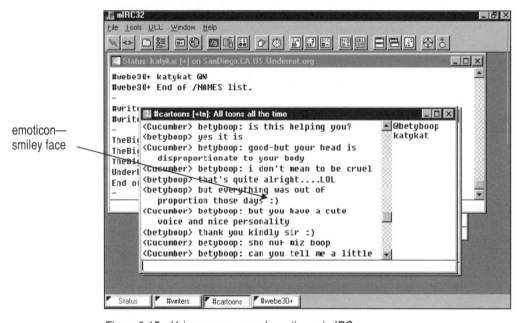

emoticon—
smiley face

Figure 8-15   Using acronyms and emoticons in IRC

Another way that you can add oomph to your typed messages is to use stars to offset words or phrases. These stars or the underline mark are also good ways to show emphasis. In Figure 8-16 notice how DaisyDuk and katykat use stars to show expressions. You can also use special formatting in both these programs like bold, underline, and italics to create emphasis.

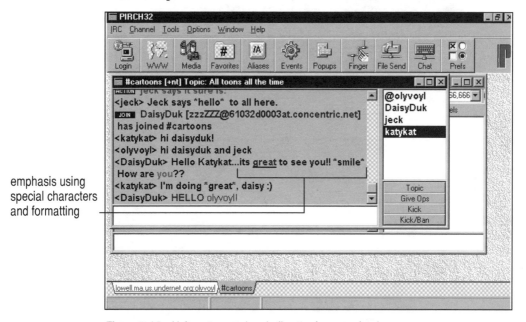

emphasis using
special characters
and formatting

Figure 8-16   Using stars and underline to show emphasis

You cannot physically touch people you talk to online, but the people there like to pretend that they can. You often see hugs passed around. Sometimes you see people say they are hugging another person or persons.

Other times you might see something like what olyvoyl typed to katykat in Figure 8-17. This is another way the online IRC community shows hugs. See how these people use the characters on their keyboard to help them express themselves? With these newer versions of mIRC and Pirch, you can now add fancier hugs. See Figure 8-18 for an example of one of these fancy hugs.

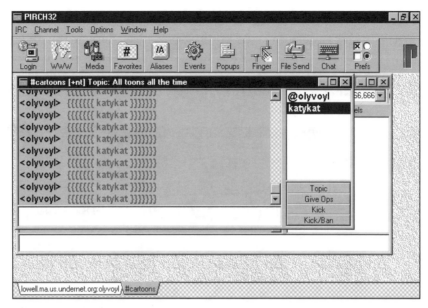

Figure 8-17   Giving hugs in IRC

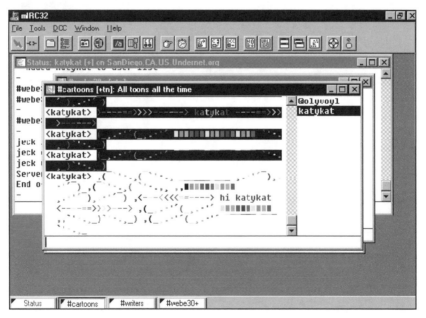

Figure 8-18   Fancy hugs in IRC

From time to time you may want to be on more than one channel at a time. You may even prefer to chat this way each time you are on. The more channels you are on, the more difficult it may become to keep track of all the conversations, especially if any of those channels are busy channels. But it can be done. I have seen people who were on as many as ten channels at one time. I have often wondered how they kept up with all the conversations on all those channels. I certainly can't.

Warning: Having too many chat windows open can cause a General Protection Fault or similar error, and get you dumped from IRC and the Internet and lock up your computer.

To be in two or more channels at the same time, simply join your first channel, get it set up the way you like, and then join the second channel. You get two separate windows, one for each chat channel. You can now tile, cascade, or arrange them any way that you prefer. In both mIRC and Pirch, the windows cascade automatically and you also get tabs at the bottom of your screen for each window. When someone types a message in an inactive window, the tab turns red. Then you simply click on the tab to bring that window forward. See Figure 8-19 for an example of mIRC's channel tabs and Figure 8-20 for an example of Pirch's window tabs.

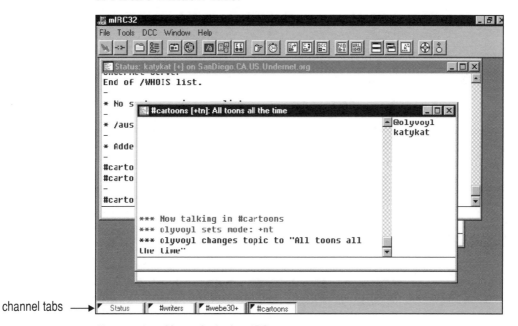

channel tabs ⟶

Figure 8-19   Channel tabs in mIRC

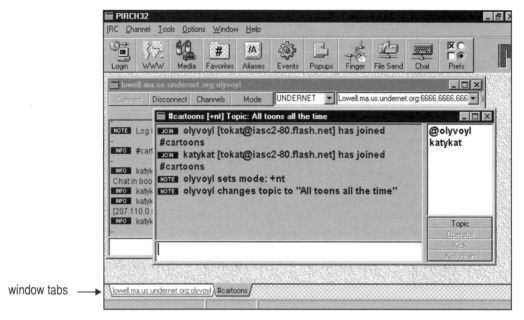

window tabs →

Figure 8-20   Window tabs in Pirch

At some point in your Internet adventures you may want to get your photo or family photos scanned as a GIF (Graphics Interchange Format), a BMP (bitmap), or a JPG or JPEG (Joint Photographic Expert Group format). Once you have these photos converted to a binary file, you are able to pass these back and forth to the friends you meet on IRC, much like you do at a party or other gathering. DCC Send is the option in IRC that lets you send these photos or other files. (Refer to the DCC Send instructions for the software you are using.)

When you are ready to leave IRC altogether, type **/quit**. If you just want to leave the channel, type **/part #<channel name>** as shown in Figure 8-21. If you want to leave the channel with a message, go to General Options/Action Lists and type in your message in mIRC, or to Preferences/Misc in Pirch to type in your quit message. You need to do this before you exit if you want it to appear in the channel window for the others to see. However, this part message does not show up in the channel unless you quit IRC completely. No messages show up if you simply part a channel other than a simple message telling the channel that you left. See Figure 8-22 for an example of the message that's left when you part a channel and Figure 8-23 for an example of what the message looks like when you quit IRC.

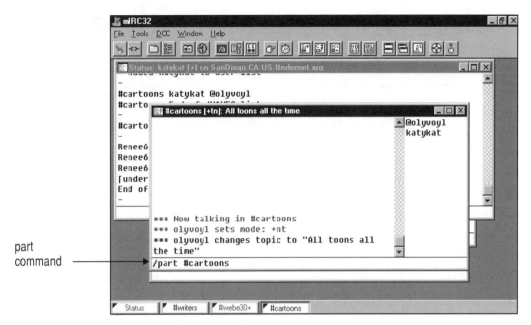

part command

Figure 8-21   Part command

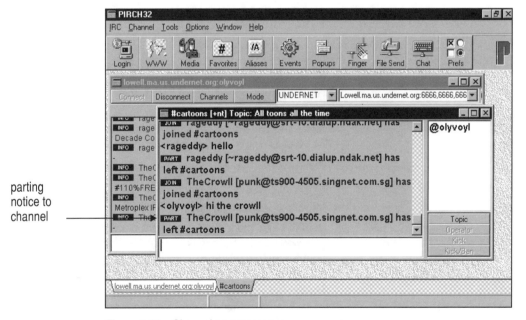

parting notice to channel

Figure 8-22   Channel part message

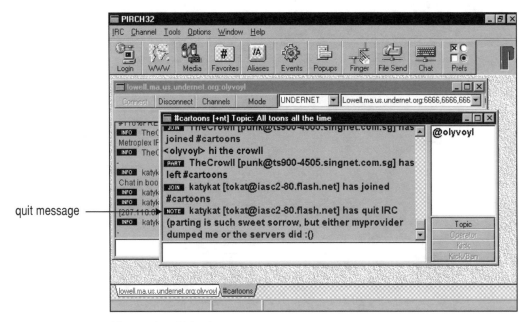

quit message

Figure 8-23   IRC quit message

Let's put these intermediate functions in a chart for easier reference.

Acronyms	Use these to get your point across faster. Refer to the most commonly used abbreviations listed in Chapter 7.
Emoticons	You use these to convey emotions. Refer to the emoticons listed in Chapter 7.
Emphasis	Stars and underlines can be used to show emphasis or to set words or phrases apart from the other words you type.
Hugs	Use the special characters on your keyboard to indicate hugs. Use special colors and ASCII art to create fancier hugs in Popups and Aliases.
Multiple Channels	Join the first channel that you want to be on. Get it set up the way you want, then type /join #<channel name> to join the second channel.
Parts & Quits	If you just want to leave a channel, type /part #<channel name>. If you want to leave a parting message before you quit IRC altogether, type your quit message in the area provided in your software and then type /quit.

What are Some of the Advanced Things I Can Do?

As you become more comfortable with your IRCing, you may want to try some of the more advanced functions. These might include joining more than one net, adding a bot to your channels, or creating your own channel and registering it on the net you want it to be on.

Let's talk about trying your hand at joining two nets and channels in those nets. The easiest way to do this is with Pirch. Pirch allows you to join more than one server, no matter which net that server belongs to. It keeps all your windows in one application window with tabs at the bottom of the window to help you keep track (see Figures 8-24 and 8-25).

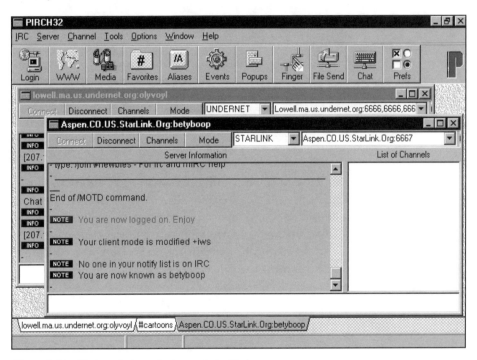

Figure 8-24   Status windows for two nets in Pirch

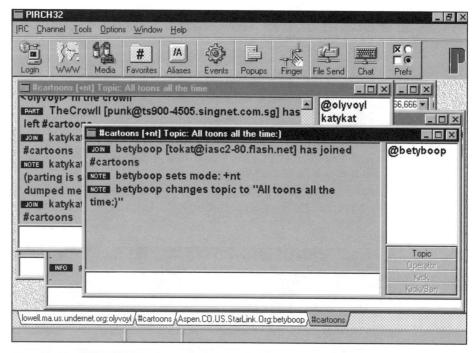

Figure 8-25   Pirch with two nets and two channels

With mIRC you have to have two copies of the program open. You can open mIRC the first time, connect to your first net, and then go back and open it a second time and connect to your second net. Then you can join your channels on each net. I suggest you then mark the channels Desktop from the System menu so that you can move them to your desktop and make it easier to manage (see Figure 8-26).

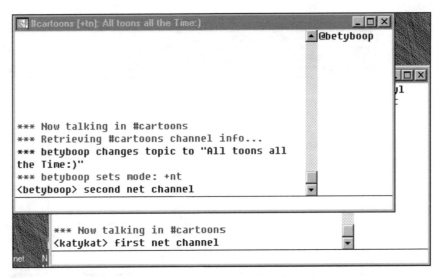

Figure 8-26 mIRC with two nets and two channels on the desktop

We have not really talked about bots before, so let's talk about them now. A bot is a set of commands in a text file that you add to your client or IRC software program. They are usually a set of /on commands that generate responses when one of those /on commands are used in a channel or message to them.

Bots are like an extension of yourself; you can use them to help you control a channel, send out help or other information, or handle automated commands for you. There are many different kinds of bots programmed to do many different kinds of commands or responses for you. These range from very simple bots to complicated war bots. You can find a variety of bots at this location: http://www.eye-candy.com/bot.html.

If you go to that address, you can find a bot or several bots that interest you. Download the one or ones you like and add them to your IRC program. The readme or help files should help you with that. Then you are ready to add the bot to your channel (see Figure 8-27). Figure 8-28 shows you what the bot I downloaded does when you type certain commands. This is a bot that you use to help you control the channel. It distributes ops, kicks and bans people, and performs other such responses to your commands.

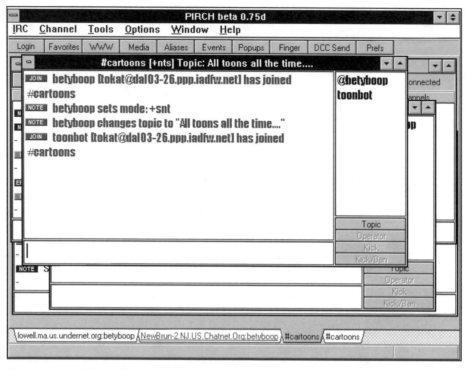

Figure 8-27   Adding a bot

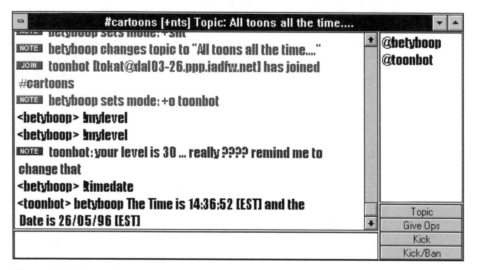

Figure 8-28   Bot actions

When you get really proficient with IRC or if you are a computer programmer, you are able to program or design your own custom bot. But that is for another book.

At some point you may want to create your own channel and possibly even register it on one of the nets that allows you to do that. The UnderNet, for example, lets you register channels. It also issues you a bot to protect the channel and keep it open around the clock. The bot it gives you belongs to the UnderNet and resides on its server/system. Notice that the bot is on many channels at a time.

To register a channel, fill out a registration form and mail it to the appropriate address for the net you want to register your channel. Usually they ask for your nickname, e-mail address, name of the channel, purpose of the channel, and anywhere from five to ten supporters with their nicks and e-mail addresses.

Once they approve your application, they send you an e-mail confirming the approval and giving you instructions about the bot—how to use it, how to get it on your channel, etc. Generally, the commands for a channel bot are issued through private message commands. However, when the bot responds back to you, you do not get a private message window. The message appears either in your status window or in your active chat window.

I have a registered channel on the UnderNet called #writers. The bot I have for that channel is called W. Whenever I want W to do something I simply type **/msg W <command>**. He responds by either doing the command or by replying to me in my windows with his response. For example, if I want to issue ops to someone I type **/msg W op <nickname>** (see Figure 8-29).

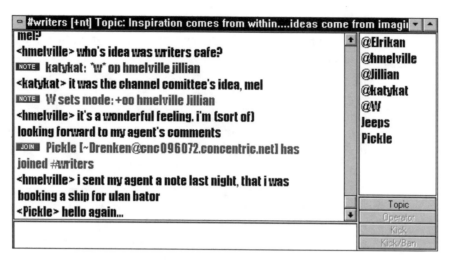

Figure 8-29   Example of granting ops status

With a channel bot you can add users to the bot's users list and instruct it to auto op and protect them when they join your channel. You can also give them access levels and passwords so that they can have limited or full access to program the bot to add or delete users from its users list or add and delete bans from its database. The channel bot is a nice way to control your channel and remain fairly neutral. Also, with a channel bot it is harder for others to try to take over your channel or flood everyone off.

As you get more comfortable with your software and learn the commands I told you about in Chapter 3, you may want to take the time to learn how to set up some remotes in mIRC or events in Pirch. Refer back to those chapters for instructions on how to set these functions up and how to make them work for you.

Here is a chart for you to reference at a glance the advanced features we just discussed.

More than one net	With Pirch, simply log in for each net you want to be on, selecting the server for that net. For mIRC, make two copies of the program and log into each program, selecting the servers for each net.
Bots	Download the bot you like from the web site, load it into your IRC software, and use it to control your channel or entertain your visitors.
Registered channels	Send your application to the appropriate net address. When you are approved, learn how to use your bot and utilize it to help you control your channel.

Summary

Using the steps in this chapter, combined with what you learned in the previous chapters, you can connect to IRC, select a server, and join a channel. You are able to change your fonts, start and carry on private conversations, change your nick, and perform action statements. (Use the charts to help you through these steps.)

As you get more comfortable with IRC, you may want to try some of the more intermediate challenges of it. You are able to use emoticons and acronyms with confidence when you review the chapter on netiquette and apply those characters to your messages. You may even want to try joining more than one channel at a time and see if you can keep up with the messages. You may want to exchange photos of your family or pets with other members of your channel or friends you meet in IRC. (Use the chart in this section to help you do all these intermediate functions.)

As you get more advanced in your adventures on IRC, you may want to join more than one net and channels there. Pirch offers you the easiest way to do that, and I hear that mIRC has a version coming out that emulates Pirch in letting you join more than one net and server at a time. Personal bots are programs that let you control your channel and perform automatic commands for you. You may want to add one of these to your channel to keep it open and protect it or greet newcomers as they join it.

Eventually, you may even want to create your own channel and register it with one of the nets that lets you do that. Use this chapter to learn how to do that and how to program the channel bot the net service issues you. As you get more proficient with your software, you may want to try programming your own remotes or events and controls to automate even more of those pesky IRC commands that you use most frequently. (Use the chart in this section to help you learn how to perform some of these advanced functions in IRC.)

Apply all that you have learned in the previous chapters to the charts and instructions in this channel and become an expert at IRC and your software in no time flat.

## Chapter 9

IRC Uses

Now that you have learned all these wonderful things, you are probably wondering, What do I do with it? There are many things you can do with IRC.

In this chapter you learn:

☑ How you can use IRC to socialize and get to know people from all over the country, the continent, other continents, and the world

☑ How you can use it to meet business associates, potential employees, or employers, and even set up target or test groups for your product

☑ How to use it to get valuable expert assistance with software or hardware problems or questions

☑ How you can even use it to keep in touch with your office, your traveling sales force, or out-of-town clients

☑ How to use it to set up classes or as a teaching aid for students

☑ How to use it for limitless possibilities of interaction

Why am I Here?

As just an average person sitting in your home staring at your computer you may ask why you would even consider using IRC. There are many reasons to use this wonderful communication tool. Do you have children in college? Brothers and sisters who live in another town or state? Relatives who are stationed overseas? Are you single and dissatisfied with the people you meet in bars, through personal ads, or through those personal agencies? Would you like to expand your horizons? Do you enjoy meeting and talking to people and want to meet more people? Are you a little on the shy side and tend to balk at face-to-face conversations but think you might do better talking to people if you don't have to look them in the eye?

IRC is the answer to all these questions. Let's take them one at a time. If you have children old enough to be attending college, you probably gasped in shock at your first long-distance phone bill after you shipped them off. Chances are extremely good that they have a free connection to the Internet through the university they attend. If they do not already have their own connection, they can get it simply by contacting the computer science department and requesting it. Then all you need to do is get connected yourself. Save some of that money you spend on long-distance phone calls back and forth. Set up times and a place to meet online and talk to your heart's content. No need to worry about how long you talk or how much it is going to cost you. With your child's free access and your monthly access fee, the cost is only pennies compared to the dollars you spend on phone charges. I know many parents who keep in touch with their college student children this way.

I have met several families that keep in touch with each other using IRC. One family has a brother who lives in Detroit, a sister who lives in Florida, and another brother in California. They meet online on IRC to catch up on family matters or to just cut up and carry on as they did when they were in the same house and same room with each other. Sometimes they get together as often as once a night, sometimes as seldom as once a month. But it is a good way for them to remain close to each other without having the expense of all those long-distance charges. This is not to say that IRC chatting replaces those wonderful voice-to-voice telephone calls; it just lets them talk to each other more often. And the nice thing about it is that all the family can get online and talk at the same time.

If you have relatives in the armed services who are stationed overseas, you already know the expense involved in making phone calls to each other. You also know how long it takes to get written communication back and forth to each other across the ocean. Wouldn't it be nice if there was a better way for you to stay in touch? There is—it is called IRC. Those years they have to spend over there flash by at lightning speed when you can talk to each other more often and for longer using IRC.

Warning: Many countries in Europe and Asia charge an hourly fee for any use of the telephone. But IRC is still much less expensive and much more reliable than long-distance phone calls.

Being single in the '90s is not like it was in, say, the '60s or '70s. The pitfalls of dating or finding that special someone are many and at times frightening. The bar scene, while fun, can be dangerous. The personal ads offer a plethora of lonely and sometimes stranger-than-fiction characters. The personal agencies do not fare much better, not to mention the expensive fees they charge. But IRC has so much more to offer. It gives you a chance to watch the people that come to the channels—see the personalities in action. You get a chance to get to know the person inside before you meet the outward persona.

This is not to say that you do not meet your share of jerks and femme fatales on IRC. You do. The people who frequent IRC are everyday people. There is nothing spectacular about them. They do not leave their problems hidden behind masks of normality. Often it is easier to get to know the real people here. There are no masks to hide behind on IRC. What you project is your personality. Granted there are some who see IRC as a fantasy and those people pretend to be someone other than they are. They take on false personas and act out those fantasies here. But, with time, you learn to recognize them here just as you do when you meet them face to face in the real world.

I have met many couples that found each other in one or another of the IRC chat channels. They found an attraction to each other's personalities and began talking to each other in private chats or created a personal channel and spent hours getting to know each other using this medium. Then they evolved their communication to the telephone. As they grew more comfortable and more attracted to each other, they arranged to meet face to face. Now, many of those couples are happily married or engaged to be married. Some of them found after the face-to-face meetings and with time that it just was not going to work out and they went their separate ways. But the important thing is they got to know each other's personalities first, then discovered after time together that they really were not meant for each other.

Any one of the thousands of IRC chat channels offers you the opportunity to meet people from all over the world. You might meet someone who lives in your same town—someone you might never have met otherwise. You might meet someone from another town or another state. You probably will meet people from other countries and learn about their culture and their way of life. Many lifelong friendships have been formed in this medium.

Over the past few years many of these people have grown so attached to each other and formed such a close bond that they have found a need to take the relationships a step further. Parties are planned—IRC parties. People fly in from all parts of the country and even from other countries to attend these parties. Sometimes they are held at one person's house and sometimes they are held at hotels. But no matter where they are held, fun and camaraderie is had by all. Several of these channels also have newsletters they produce to promote the sense of family and unity. They use these newsletters to keep the group informed of the happenings and goings-on of the members of the channel and the parties planned to unite all the members.

I have talked to many people online who tell me they are afraid to attend a gathering that had as many people at it that some of these channels have in them. They say they are too shy or too afraid of large groups to ever be comfortable meeting and talking to that many people at one time. But, with IRC, they can open up and join in the fun without the pressures of face-to-face encounters. After all, it is just them, their keyboard, and their monitor all alone in a room, yet talking to people everywhere. It is a nice way for them to relieve the loneliness without the threatening, overwhelming crowds.

So, jump right in. Get out there and explore what IRC has to offer. Try out some of the IRC channels until you find one that feels like home. You might find that special channel in one try or it might take you visiting several channels before you find just the right one. But it is out there. With the thousands of channels available on the two larger nets, the one that is just right for you is sure to be there.

What About Me, the Business Person? What's In It for Me?

The possibilities and opportunities for businesses and business people on IRC are limitless. You are limited only by your imagination and creativity. You can set up a channel to have professional discussions with associates about your industry. You can find target market groups here and conduct market research. You can set up test subjects and use IRC to let them discuss your test product. You can search for, screen, and interview potential employees on IRC. You can conduct classes or set up special training sessions here. You can even find experts to give you advice about your business, industry, or product. Keep in touch with your office or traveling salespeople using this powerful medium.

Many businesses have come online in the past few years. Most of them have found out the advantages of the World Wide Web, e-mail, and newsgroups. Several of them are learning about the endless possibilities of IRC. You find other professionals using this tool to help build their business. You might run across them by just visiting some of the channels or you could set up your own channel, give it a name that attracts others in your profession, and sit back and wait patiently for others to join you. If you keep it friendly, greet them when they come into your channel, and make them feel at home, within a few months you have a following that continues to grow as more and more people come online and discover IRC.

Out of the thousands and thousands of channels out there on IRC, you can find almost any target group you are looking for. Many of the channels are set up to attract people in the same age groups. Some are set up to talk about and share information about hobbies or special interests. A few are set up as professional discussion groups. Several are even set up for people from the same city, state, or country. All you need to do is generate a list of the channels, select the target groups from the channel names, and visit them. I suggest that you get to know the group before you jump in and try to get the group involved in a market survey. They are more likely to agree to help you once they get to know you and feel like you are part of the "family."

As you get to know people on these IRC channels, you can select those you want to help you out with a test product. Set up a special channel for them to meet on, decide how often you want to meet, and then arrange to have the discussion logged by you or one of your employees. Let them talk about your product after they have a chance to test it out. If the discussion is not going in the direction you want, redirect it by asking questions that get the group focused in the direction you want it to go.

With both the target market groups and the test groups, you have the advantage of logging all online conversations. This lets you keep a hard copy record of all these conversations. If you want them to answer specific questions and have a record of their answers, IRC lets you do that easily with the logging function. Then rather than produce and mail out copies of a questionnaire to each person in the group, you can type the question once and let each one respond on channel. With the log, you can print out a copy and have the answers all together.

The potential for finding employees online is boundless. There are people from all walks of life with every kind of experience conceivable on IRC. If you pay attention to the conversations and take notes, you are able to find dozens of qualified candidates for any position you have open. You can watch how these people handle problems and see how good they are at negotiations, problem solving, mediation, communication, etc., all by observing. I know of one publisher who finds all his freelance editors, proofers, and writers online. He recruits them off my #writers channel. As far as I know he has not been disappointed. He stays within his budget and gets the jobs done professionally and within his deadlines. The writers are able to supplement their incomes and everyone is happy. It has proven to be a very fruitful relationship for him and the writers.

Some teachers have found IRC very useful in conducting online classes. You, as a business person, could use it to conduct online training sessions. It gives you the opportunity to gather a group of people together and teach them almost anything. Even if you are trying to teach them hands-on applications, you can do it by using IRC and let them ask you questions after they try your instructions. With the new innovations being made for the Internet and that can be used with IRC, it is conceivable that you could have sight and sound interaction also.

Along these same lines, you can often find experts in many different fields in IRC. Many of these people are involved in computers and computer applications—hardware and software. But whatever their field of expertise, they are out there somewhere. And if they are out there, they are willing to help you out with any problem you have. If it is some problem that you need a warm body present to fix, they are able to direct you to the right source or even offer their services for a fee.

While you are out of town on business or if you need to keep in touch with traveling salespeople or personnel, IRC could very well be your best tool. You can conduct online sales meetings either weekly or monthly. Wouldn't it be nice to set up a time to meet on a channel to talk to your assistant and relay instructions to him or her? All this can be done and is being done by several businesses.

You can conduct these meetings using chat alone or you can add some of the newer technology enhancements to make these communications more personal. If you want to talk one on one to an employee while you are out of town, you can do that using IRC and one of these technological tools. One such tool is called I-phone. It is a piece of software you add to your computer along with a sound card, speakers, and microphone to let you use IRC for voice-to-voice conversations. You can read all about I-phone and download a trial copy at: http://www.vocaltech.com:80/.

If you want to talk to more than one person at a time, there are ways to do that, too. One tool you can add to IRC is called PowWow. It is a software program that lets you talk to up to nine people at one time using it and IRC. You can read all about the product and download a copy at: http://www.tribal.com/.

Now, if you want to see the people you are talking to, you can do that also. There is a tool that lets you have voice-to-voice and sight-to-sight communications. It is called CUSeeMe and it works in conjunction with IRC. To find out more about CUSeeMe, go to this site on the Web: http://cu-seeme.cornell.edu. It is a desktop video conferencing program and is available for both the Mac and the PC. It was designed to provide useful video conferencing at a minimal cost. In addition to this program you need cameras and digitizers on all ends of the communication.

There are several new innovations available for IRC and new software coming out all the time. If you want to see what is being offered, check out these two sites: http://www.tucows.com and http://cws.wilmington.net/inx.html. Both of these sites contain lots of different Internet software, covering almost any application you might need. They are a good source for software. Some of the software they offer is freeware and some of it is shareware. Whatever your need might be for Internet software, one or both of these sites have it.

By the time this book makes it to print and your bookstore, there likely will be even more innovations made for the Internet and IRC. The Internet is growing so fast, it is sometimes hard to keep up with all the new products being released. But IRC only changes as the software changes. If you keep up with the latest releases, you should be fine. Along with this book, they help you use this communication tool to the best of its capabilities and help you enjoy yourself while you are there.

Get out there and explore. See what you find. And most important of all, have fun!

Summary

Use this powerful communications tool to keep in touch with your out-of-town, out-of-state, or even out-of-country relatives and friends. Don't take out a second mortgage on your home just to pay those long-distance phone bills to talk to your child in college. Meet people in other countries and share cultures and customs as you find out how the rest of the world lives. Make new friends and even go to some of the parties these groups of people hold around the country.

Business people find all sorts of opportunities exist on this medium. They find potential employees, customers, business associates, and expert advice. As a business person you can use this tool to conduct market research, set up test groups, and conduct sales meetings and even training classes. The possibilities are endless.

Download some of the voice-to-voice or sight-to-sight software and use IRC for teleconferencing and save your company money. Use your imagination and this communication tool to its fullest potential.

Chapter 10

Troubleshooting

During the course of your adventures on IRC you might run into a few obstacles. I'd say it is almost inevitable. This chapter covers some of the obstacles you might encounter and how you can overcome or get around them.

Problem:

Disconnect after a /list command. Reason: Entire output of list commands are queued in a buffer on a server which gets overrun, which in turn disconnects you.

Solution:

Filter your list commands. Use the -max and -min parameters to limit the size of lists or use keywords. This will lower the size of lists returned to you and thus prevent you from being disconnected from the server.

Problem:

Receive Connection timed out error message when trying to connect to a server. Reason: Server could be down or broken or no longer in service.

Solution:

Try another server. From time to time system administrators have to take their servers down for repairs. Sometimes servers are being routed to or through other servers and connections slow down. Sometimes hackers take servers down. In any of these cases and although you will never know exactly why you can't connect to that server, your only solution is to try to connect through another server.

Problem:

Receive Unknown host error message when you try to connect to servers. Reason: If you get this on one particular server, it could be that you have an incorrect server name or the server's DNS is down. If you get this on every server you try, your provider's DNS could be down.

Solution:

If it's only one server you get this message on, locate the numeric number address for the server and try to connect using that. If it still gives you the Unknown host message, try another server. If you get this on repeated servers, call your provider and ask if their DNS server is having problems. You may have to wait for them to repair their problem before you can try to connect again.

Problem:

Not enough user parameters error. Reason: Local host name not filled in or filled in incorrectly.

Solution:

Check the entries in your setup menu for the client you're using to make sure the values are entered properly. Sometimes mIRC has trouble getting your IP address. You can enter this value manually and mIRC assumes that it's correct when it tries to log onto a server. However, if the value is wrong you can still log onto IRC, but you will not be able to initiate DCC sends or chats.

Problem:

You get a "haven't registered" error message when you try to connect to a server. Reason: Your local host name or IP address may be entered wrong or not filled in at all. It could also mean you are trying to connect to a non-public server.

Solution:

Check your client's setup dialog box and make sure the information is filled in correctly. Also make sure On Connect Always Get IP Address is checked and Local Host is On. Then restart the program. If you still get this error message and you are sure your address is correct, then you're trying to connect to a non-public server. You need a password to connect to these types of servers and need to contact the system administrator to get permission to connect to the server and a password.

Problem:

Disconnection at startup with any of these messages: **Ghosts aren't allowed on IRC, You are not welcome on this server, Closing link (K-lined)**, or **closing link (K-lined) no clone bots allowed**. Reason: All these messages mean you or your site have been banned from that server. This could be as the result of someone else's actions or actions on your part. Banning takes place for one of three reasons and has three forms:

➤ You are banned specifically due to something you did while you were online—harassing another user, flooding a user or channel, or some other reason.

➤ Your machine is banned for reasons that may have nothing to do with you.

➤ Your whole site is banned, and the site could include school, company, country, or provider. This is almost never your fault and the chance of getting this type of ban lifted is very slim.

Solution:

If you are the reason you are banned from a server—because of something you did while online—you can try to contact the server administrators to resolve the problem. However, be aware that you may have to eat some crow or your efforts could result in no satisfactory resolution for you. If your machine is banned, you just have to try another server. You can try to contact the system administrator and resolve the problem, but keep in mind these people are very busy, so be understanding. If your site is banned, there is little you can do to resolve the situation. You could try to have your provider contact the system administrator to resolve the problem, but these people are usually very busy trying to keep their systems running and have little time for this sort of thing. Your only true recourse in any of these situations is to try another server and to be aware of your activities online and act without causing harm to others.

Problem:

You connect to the Internet through Netcom or Pipeline service providers and cannot connect to IRC. Reason: Their winsocks are not compliant to Winsock 1.1.

Solution:

Contact your provider and have them help you configure Trumpet or Win95 Dialup Networking for your system.

Problem:

Unable to initiate or receive DCC sends or chats. Reason: Your IP address is incorrect.

Solution:

Check your IP address in your setup menu to make sure it's correct. You can check this by doing a /whois on yourself and comparing the numbers there with the numbers that show up in the IP address in the setup dialog box. If they are incorrect, enter the correct address manually. Be sure to check Always get IP address and Local Host on in this setup box.

Problem:

DCCs stall midway through transfers. Reason: The Internet could be sluggish or either one or both of your providers could be lagged.

Solution:

Change the packet size to a lower number. 1024 is a good one to try when you're experiencing this problem. You can also try to resend and resume the transfer. With large files and a sluggish Internet or IRC, it may take you several tries to send and receive these DCCs.

Problem:

Entries not showing up in Pirch's notify window. Reason: You did not specify a Network ID for the server when you added it to your server list. Pirch arranges notifications using this Network ID.

Solution:

Go to your server list and add Network IDs to all your servers. The Network ID is the name of the network the server belongs to. Then you will need to relog in to servers and your notifies should show up in the notify window.

Problem:

Long pauses between posts to the channel you're on. Reason: The server you are on is lagging.

Solution:

Ride out the storm, which is advisable during times when most of the servers are lagging on IRC. You will know this is the case when almost everyone in your channel is complaining about the lag. If the problem seems to be isolated to you, try changing servers to one that the majority of the users on your channel are using. This should eliminate most of the lag between your posts and theirs.

Problem:

Everyone leaves your channel at the same time. Reason: netsplit—when one or more servers split off from the other servers.

Solution:

If you seem to be the only one staying with a channel and everyone else is leaving, chances are your server is the one splitting off. Try another server, preferably one that most of the users on the channel are connected to. If several people stay and several others all leave at the same time, then several servers are splitting off. I suggest you ride out the storm. When several servers split off it is hard to find a server that's not splitting. This is usually an indication that the net you're on is having serious problems at that time. You can, of course, try to connect to the server that the majority of the users in your channel are connected to. However, when a net is having this much trouble, you may find it near to impossible to get connected to that server or any server. Sometimes patience is the best option. If you're short on patience then I suggest you quit for awhile and wait until the net repairs itself. This could take a few hours or it could take days.

These are the major problems you can run into while you're on IRC. Use these to help you determine a problem and find a solution to it. If you run across problems not covered here, ask someone you know has been using IRC for a long time to help you with it. Don't be afraid to ask questions. Most people on IRC will be more than happy to help you.

Chapter 11

Summary

When you make it to this point in this book, you have most if not all the ammunition you need to tackle IRC with confidence and appear to others as though you are one of the old hands. You know what all the commands are and how and when to use them. You know the ins and outs of two of the best chat software programs on the market. And you know the proper conduct that is expected of you before you ever join a channel.

In Chapter 1 you learned all about the nets. You learned how IRC got its start and how it has grown. EfNet was the first net and remains the largest net in this chat universe. It is where you go if you are interested in finding the most people on at any given time. If you are a marketer, this is the net where you can find the highest concentration of people to help you complete market research surveys or customer satisfaction questionnaires.

The UnderNet is the second oldest and largest of the nets. It was formed in rebellion to what some users perceived as lack of bandwidth and excessive lag and netsplits. This is another great net for you to meet a greater number of people and for businesses to concentrate their efforts. It is more organized than the EfNet and offers you the chance to register a channel and get a channel bot to help you control the channel and keep it open around the clock.

SuperChat formed shortly after the UnderNet split off from EfNet. It is still a rather small net but offers you virtually no lag and no splits. It too lets you register channels and promises that its administrators, or IRCops, are there for you if you need them.

DALnet started off as a game net, a place where users could come to play MUDDs and other games. It has evolved into a nice little net with a net bot that lets you register your nickname and channel. It is the third largest of the nets and promises to offer support and help to its users.

There are dozens of other nets and more are added monthly. Each one is small but has hopes of growing as more users find access to the Internet and learn about IRC. Some of these nets are set up as specialty nets like LinuxNet and Kidlink. Some are regular chat nets offering their users many of the same things the other larger nets offer without the lag, netsplits, or lengthy waits for available space on servers to get connected.

Each net has its own set of servers that connect you to that particular net. Most of them let you connect using the default port of 6667. However, if you find you are having a hard time getting connected or that you have a slow connection, you can try another port from 6660 and 6670.

Explore the possibilities each net has to offer and find the one that fits best with your personality and needs. Use the server charts in that chapter to find a server to connect you to the net of your choice.

In Chapter 2 you learned everything you wanted or needed to know about channels. You may have even learned a little more than you really wanted to know. But now you are armed and ready to tackle the myriad of channels that are offered to you on each net.

Use the examples of channels lists to guide you on your path to finding the right channel for you. Or generate your own list and search for the channel that appeals to you. Beware, though, of all the sex channels that come up on your list. Use the filters with your IRC software to screen out those unwanted channels from your list if you do not want to see them or even know they exist.

Take what you have learned about what kind of activity goes on in the various kinds of channels to ferret out the kinds of channels from that list that you want to explore. Then when you get more proficient in your IRC travels, try joining two or more channels at the same time. Be careful that you do not join too many channels or you might knock yourself off IRC or the Internet entirely and may even lock your computer up. But do not fret if this happens to you; just reset your computer and log back on. You might miss a few minutes of the conversations, but it does not harm you or your computer.

Chapter 3 explains the difference between user commands and mode commands. It gave you all the commands that are used with IRC and what those commands do. You also learned how and when to use them. This chapter helped you to understand what it is all those people in those channels are doing and how they can affect you or others or even the channel itself. Those commands are the basics you need in order to perform many of the tasks in IRC and are very important to you when you start using your chat software to its fullest potential.

Chat software has come a long way since the beginnings of IRC when there was no software at all. At first, the most you could hope for was the occasional IRC script or command program to automate some of the commands you used frequently. Then, some very industrious computer whizzes designed chat software that made life on IRC so much better and easier for the user. Today there are dozens of IRC software programs available for you to choose from, and by the time this book comes out in print there will be more. Check out the web sites at: http://www.tucows.com or http://cws.wilmington.net/inx.html to find either mIRC, Pirch, or any of the other IRC software programs available. mIRC is also available on this book's companion CD.

mIRC is one of the best and easiest to use of the IRC clients available at this time. It offers you many great features to make your life on IRC go much smoother by automating many of those common IRC commands. Once you custom configure it to meet your preferences, it lets you perform many of those commands with a click of your mouse button.

Use the aliases to set up hot buttons or abbreviated key functions to issue those IRC commands you use the most. Let the popups perform many of those CTCP and other general use commands that you normally type out. Learn how to create your own popup commands to function with your channel names list.

Then as you get more proficient in your command of this client, try your hand at programming some remotes to automate a users list and add friends to an auto-ops list or protect list, or even customize ping replies for those friends you get pinged by most often. Learn how to use this software to the fullest capabilities that it was designed for.

Pirch is another excellent chat software program. It offers many of the same features as mIRC and has some added enhancements. With this program you are able to be on more than one server at a time, allowing you to connect to more than one net while keeping everything in one application window. You can join as many channels and nets as you can keep up with and use the handy tabs at the bottom of the application window to tab or toggle between your channel or status windows.

Set up a bio on yourself and when someone asks, simply DCC Send it to them. You can even include a bitmap picture of yourself so they can see the person behind the nick.

Use the handy Operator Control Panel in each channel window to perform most of the operator's status commands when you get ops in a channel. Use the extended Popups here to add users to your users' list or to add them to your auto-ops or protect list or even to ignore them or put them on notify.

In Chapter 7 you learned what netiquette is and how you could avoid making social faux pas while you explore the channels of the nets. If you remember that there are humans behind those monitors and keyboards, you go further in meeting more people and making new friends. Treat others as you want to be treated—with respect and courtesy—and you get the same in return. If you are rude or offensive, you can bet you will be kicked and possibly even banned from channels.

Remember these channels are like small communities of people. Strong relationships and bonds are formed here. When these bonds are formed, the members of the group become very protective of their channel and the other members of their group or channel. Join channels, become acquainted with the groups there, and eventually you become part of the "family," too.

Use emoticons and acronyms to help you get your meaning across. Do not let this black on white, sterile medium keep you from expressing yourself. Use the special keys of your keyboard to emphasize certain words or to set them apart from others. Use ASCII art to show happiness or sadness. Instead of typing long phrases, learn how to use abbreviations and acronyms to convey the same thing.

Take what you learned in all the previous chapters and apply it to the step-by-step guide in Chapter 8. Try logging onto a net, joining a channel, and chatting with the people there. Try out a few of the commands you learned in Chapter 3 to see how they work and what they do. Test out the action command and the message command and get to know the people on the channels you join.

As you get to know these people, offer to exchange photos or a bio about yourselves. Use the DCC Send option to exchange those photos or files that you want to share.

Then try setting up your own channel and invite others to join you. If you have an idea for a new channel, register it with the net services that you want that channel to reside on and learn how to use your channel bot when it is issued to you. You may even want to try your hand at a personal bot until your channel bot is issued.

Test the waters in remotes and events in mIRC and Pirch. Use the instructions given for each and set up your own custom users' lists and ping replies. Use these two program functions to set up commands to work to your specifications and leave you free to spend more time chatting and less time answering requests for ops or information.

IRC is truly the communication revolution of the future. Although it is a text-only format, the possibilities are endless. You can add other programs to it to let you have voice-to-voice or even sight-to-sight and voice-to-voice conversations with one or more people.

Use it to keep in touch with family and friends in other cities, other states, or even other countries. Find and make friends with people from all over the world. Let IRC help you to find that extended family of friends you never knew was out there.

If you're in business, IRC can offer you endless possibilities to increase your business contacts, promote your product, or even get expert help when you need it. Use it to set up target groups and let them meet on a regular basis in a channel to talk about your test product. Let your market research people use the thousands of channels available on the nets to conduct surveys or customer satisfaction surveys.

Use the channels you visit to find employees and even set up a private conversation or channel to screen potential employees much as you do in a telephone interview. Use the logging functions of your client to keep a record of your conversations.

Set up training sessions or sales meetings online and use this tool to bring people together in one place that no other tool offers. Set up a channel and let these people talk to you and each other or conduct your class without interruption using the moderated channel mode. Give voice to those you want to speak when you are ready to hear what they have to say (or type).

Learn all you can about IRC, the commands, the software, and the proper conduct and behavior. Explore what each net has to offer and what channels there are on each net. Above all else, just have fun!

Index

A

acronyms, 217-218
actions, 58, 230
addresses, 10
alias identifiers, 122-123
aliases, 119-127, 184-186

B

bandwidth, 4
BBS (Bulletin Board Systems), 2
bots, 24, 43-45, 243-247
business uses, 253-256

C

channel
    bot, 246
    creating, 43-45, 245-246
    joining, 43, 224
    operators, 45-46, 50, 66
    registering, 43-45
channels, 27-48
    joining multiple, 46, 235-236
    lists, 33-40
chat software, 77-87
city channels, 36
clients, xiv, 80, 84-86
clone bots, 24
commands, 49-76, 134-141
    event, 136-141, 186-189
    mode, 50, 66-75
    user, 50-65
commercial online services, xii
configuring mIRC, 92-119
connecting to IRC, 222-223
copy and paste, 151

creating a channel, 43-45, 245-246
CTCP, 65
    commands, 65
    options, 197

D

DALnet, 6-7, 13
DCC, 62, 142-148
    chat, 142-148, 208-209
    commands, 63-65
    file server, 141, 146, 182-183
    get, 144-145
    send, 142-144
DNS (Domain Name Server), 93
Dreamer script, 78

E

Efnet, 3, 12
emoticons, 216-217
events, 136-141, 186-189

F

firewalls, 98-99
flames, 212
floods, 31, 78
fonts, 225-227
forward slash, 50

G

ghosts, 25

H

hacking, 3
harassment, 213
hot chats, 36

I

installing software, 80-82
Internet connection, xi
IRC, ix
 commands, 49-76
 connecting to, 222-223
 uses, 249-256
IRCops, 161

J

joining a channel, 43, 224
joining more than one net, 47, 241-242
joining multiple channels, 46, 235-236

K

k-lined, 24

L

lag, 25-26
list examples, 33-40
local providers, xii
logging, 45, 115
lurking, 29

M

mIRC, 78-82, 89-155
 address book, 154
 aliases, 119-127
 Catcher, 111-112
 channel tabs, 237
 Clicks, 107
 colored text, 124-127
 commands, 154
 configuring, 92-119
 Control, 105-106
 DCC chat, 142-148
 DCC file server, 141, 146
 DCC get, 144-145
 DCC send, 142-144
 Drag-Drop, 108-110
 Event Beeps, 107-108
 event commands, 136-141

 Extras, 117-119
 file server, 141-152
 finger server, 116
 Flood, 114-115
 general options, 99-119
 ident server, 98
 IRC Switches, 100-119
 Logging, 115
 Notify List, 104-105
 Perform, 112-114
 popups, 128-130
 Raw, 142
 remotes, 130-141
 Servers, 116-117
 setup, 92-99
 Sounds, 110-111
mode commands, 50, 66-75
MOTD (Message of the Day), 165

N

national providers, xi-xii
netiquette, 211-219
netiquette rules, 214-215
netizens, 4
nets, xvi, 3-10
 joining, 47, 241-242
netsplits, 25
newbie, 29
nick changes, 230
nick collision, 3
nicknames, 3, 42, 52, 54-58, 62-65
notify, 104-105, 152
numbered channels, 36-37

O

operator's status, 46, 66, 225

P

parameter string, 121
Phoenix script, 78
photos, 238
ping response, 57

Pirch, 79-82, 157-210
    aliases, 184-186
    Bio Viewer, 180-181
    channel menu, 166, 174-175
    channel windows, 167-171
    CTCP, 197
    DCC chat, 208-209
    DCC file server, 182-183
    events, 186-189
    favorite channels, 174
    finger client, 180
    ident server, 180
    Login menu, 171
    Media Player, 179-80
    menu bar items, 171-173
    Options menu, 192-209
    popups, 190
    remotes, 188
    server connection, 158-164
    Server menu, 173-175
    server/status window, 164
    Tools menu, 175-191
    window tabs, 237-238
    WWW links, 175-177
POPs (points of presence), xi
ports, 23-24
popups, 128-130, 190
private conversation, 228-229
private message, 36
professional channels, 38-39
protocol, 51
providers, xi-xii

Q
quitting, 239

R
reference chart, 247
regional providers, xii
registering a channel, 43-45
remotes, 130-141, 188
routing, 5

S
scripts, 78
scroll, 28
server routers, 13
server terminology, 24-26
servers, 2, 10-24, 50
servers list, 10-24
sex channels, 35-36
shareware, 78
showing emphasis, 235
showing expression, 236
site ban, 24
smart tools, 150-151
software
    chat, 77-87
    mIRC, 78-82, 89-155
    Pirch, 79-82, 157-210
special key combinations, 152
state channels, 36
status window, 222-223
step-by-step, 222-229
    charts, 232-233, 240, 247
SuperChat, 7, 14
surf, 40

T
technical channels, 40
teen channels, 37-38
troubleshooting, 257-262

U
Undernet, 4-6, 12-13
UNIX commands, 77
UNIX systems, 77
URL catcher, 111-112, 153
user commands, 51-65
uses, IRC, 249-256

V
variables, 134

About the CD

The CD-ROM included with this book holds the shareware version of mIRC software. As this is shareware, you are requested to submit the appropriate funds to the developer of this software. The fee, nominal as it is, enables the developer to continue bringing you excellent software and upgrades.

If you choose to use this mIRC software, please remit $20 to the following:

Khaled Mardam-Bey
23 St. Mary Abbots Court,
Warwick Gardens,
London W14 8RA,
Great Britain

This chat client is in executable format. To install it on your computer, simply place the CD-ROM in your CD drive. Double-click on the My Computer icon on your desktop. Then double-click on the CD drive. Select mIRC and double-click on it. Because this is an executable file, it automatically installs itself on your computer and gives you icons or shortcuts, as well as items in your Start menu.

Once the program is installed on your computer, you're ready to configure it to your preferences. Then you're ready to start using it and trying out the projects covered in this book. Have fun!